The Gilt-Edged Market

Studies in Financial Institutions and Markets

Edited by J. R. S. Revell
Emeritus Professor Economics
University College of North Wales
Bangor

The Gilt-Edged Market

Jeremy Wormell

London
GEORGE ALLEN & UNWIN
Boston   Sydney

George Allen & Unwin (Publishers) Ltd,
40 Museum Street, London WC1A 1LU, UK

George Allen & Unwin (Publishers) Ltd,
Park Lane, Hemel Hempstead, Herts HP2 4TE, UK

Allen & Unwin, Inc.,
8 Winchester Place, Winchester, Mass 01890, USA

George Allen & Unwin Australia Pty Ltd,
8 Napier Street, North Sydney, NSW 2060, Australia

First published in 1985

British Library Cataloguing in Publication Data

Wormell, Jeremy
    The gilt-edged market. – (Studies in financial institutions and markets)
1. Government securities – Great Britain
I. Title II. Series
332.64'2   HG5438
ISBN 0-04-332103-8

Library of Congress Cataloging in Publication Data

Wormell, Jeremy
    The gilt-edged market.
Bibliography: p.
Includes index.
1. Securities. I. Title.
HG4461.W67 1985   332.63'2044   85-7527
ISBN 0-04-332103-8 (alk. paper)

Set in 10 on 11 point Plantin by Fotographics (Bedford) Ltd
and printed in Great Britain by
Billing and Sons Ltd, London and Worcester

Contents

Editor's Preface

The Series combines both theoretical and practical approaches to cover the institutional aspects of the financial system. Various volumes will deal with the working of the many different kinds of financial institutions and markets, their regulation and supervision, competition between them, and the changes in their functions and operations that have come about in recent years and that can be foreseen in the near future. The focus will be on UK institutions and markets, but many of the studies will have an international slant, comparing conditions in several countries.

The volumes are designed to fulfil the needs of a broad range of readers. The main readership is seen as those actively engaged in the various institutions and markets, their professional advisers, members of their staffs who are studying for professional examinations, and those who use the services of particular institutions and markets. Since the studies will have a sound theoretical approach, they will appeal equally to academics and to students in higher education. They will provide a comprehensive introduction for non-experts, taking them beyond the stage reached by most popular introductions; they will be valuable to those whose expertise lies in adjacent fields; and the expert will find the views expressed and the approach adopted of considerable interest.

The authors will all be experts in their particular spheres of the financial system, including those with professional knowledge of the subject and academics. At a time of especially rapid change for financial institutions and markets, the main need is for authors who can speak with authority, based on long experience or on intensive research, of the recent changes and assess the likely direction and extent of future change. The authors have been chosen with this paramount need in mind.

Each volume will be completely up-to-date when it is published, and it will foreshadow the changes of the next few years. At a time of such rapid transformation it is vital to take a fresh look at the subject every few years; for this reason plans have been made to issue revised editions whenever circumstances warrant it.

Jack Revell

List of Figures and Tables

Figures

Tables

Acknowledgements

Anyone who works in the gilt-edged market is the recipient of ideas and perceptions from innumerable investment managers, officials, journalists, academics and brokers. Their contributions have enabled this book to be written.

Specifically I would like to thank those who have supplied material or commented on early drafts of parts of the text: Mr R. Davison of the Colonial Mutual Life Assurance Society Limited; Mr Ralph Egarr; Mr R. Farr of the Zurich Insurance Company; Dr D. Fitzgerald of The City University Business School; Mr G. E. Gilchrist of the Union Discount Company of London plc; Dr S. K. Howson of the University of Toronto; Mr G. G. Luffrum of the Life Offices' Association; those responsible for official operations in the gilt-edged market; the officers of the National Investment and Loans Office; Mr M. L. Pearce and Mr R. K. Hargrave of the Central Trustee Savings Bank. In addition I am grateful for help from others who have asked to remain anonymous. None of these are responsible for the views and analyses, which are entirely my own.

For permission to cite documents or publications I would like to thank the following: the British Bankers' Association; the Controller of Her Majesty's Stationery Office; The Life Offices' Association; LIFFE Ltd; Jones Lang Wootton; the *Financial Times*; Messrs Pember & Boyle; The Stock Exchange.

I would like to thank Messrs Pember & Boyle for the use of their records and office equipment and for giving me permission to reproduce parts of their daily yield list and switching charts. They are in no way responsible for the views expressed, which are entirely my own.

I have received help from my colleagues. In particular, Robin Bevan, who showed his usual healthy curiosity; Bill Allen; John Goddard; Bob Pearce; and Muhammed Tariq.

Roger Brown has been painstaking in compiling tables and gathering material. The book could not have been completed in its present form without his help.

Virginia Wormell drew the charts.

Jane Platten typed innumerable drafts of the manuscript, retaining humour under considerable pressure; her husband was uncomplaining about long evenings of absence which resulted.

Introduction

The size and burden of the national debt has shown a remarkable stability in its relationship to the economy as a whole during the last ten years, despite erratic and often high levels of public borrowing and inflation. Yet the importance and role of the gilt-edged market has undergone great change. The volume and timing of official debt sales has become a matter of public concern as monetary growth has come to be seen as a central aspect of economic management. Understanding of the influence of financial markets and of the importance of monetary growth has changed out of all recognition. As the gilt-edged market has been pushed towards the centre of the stage so the authorities' techniques of market management have evolved.

It is, however, misleading to emphasise this single aspect of change. Although it deals in debt, some of which will not mature for many years, the market exists in an environment that is in constant flux. This is in part because the gilt-edged market is where practice and commercial greed meet theory and the academic. The market has been dominated for many years by the actuaries with their high academic and ethical standards. More recently they have been joined by economists and those versed in mathematical and computer techniques. Latterly, trading in financial futures contracts and options has begun and the theorists are playing an important part in developing understanding of their use. Monetary theory, much of whose renewed influence is owed to work in the US, became increasingly powerful from the late 1960s and was considered an important aid in interpreting interest rate trends by the middle of the following decade. Monetary targets appeared in the UK in 1976. The International Monetary Fund (IMF) has been given the opportunity to impose limits on domestic credit expansion on two separate occasions.

It is in part because the long-term outlook for the real value of stock largely depends on political and social developments. In a narrow sense this means the levels of public spending, revenue and borrowing that emerge from the myriad of pressures that governments feel and translate into policy. In a wider sense it means the attitude to the priorities of growth, unemployment and price stability.

The structure of the gilt-edged market is itself undergoing change. Single capacity, the separation of the role of the agent and principal, is about to end. This has made the writing of this book more difficult, also more interesting. There will, however, be less of an upheaval in the markets in government debt than is generally feared so that most of the discussion in this book will remain valid in the new market. A change in the structure of the secondary market, provided liquidity continues, will not directly affect the structure, composition and life of the debt: the changing pattern of ownership; the continuous need to tailor instruments to investors' needs; the investment constraints of the institutions; the government's methods of borrowing and refinancing debt; the machinery with which the authorities work and make policy; the theory and working of the futures market; taxation; analysis of the term structure; or the mathematics that underlies the valuation of stocks.

Author's note

The term 'gilt-edged stock' has been used in the text as shorthand for British Government and government-guaranteed stocks listed on The Stock Exchange.

'Coupon' has several meanings, which are detailed in the Glossary. 'Coupon' and 'interest payment' are used in the same sense in the text.

References to 'money supply' and to the 'money stock' are to sterling M3. This does not imply that it is the most important aggregate. It is chosen since the connection between changes in the components, one of which is purchases of gilt-edged stocks by the non-bank private sector, and changes in the aggregate is an accounting identity. This makes explicit how the authorities' activities in the debt markets affect monetary growth. The change in sterling M3 is equal to:

The central government borrowing requirement (surplus –)

plus

The borrowing requirement of the rest of the public sector

less

The acquisition of public sector debt by the UK non-bank private sector

plus

Lending in sterling to the UK private sector by the monetary sector

plus

Bank of England Issue Department purchases of commercial bills

plus

Sterling deposits from banks abroad net of market loans
to such banks (increase –)

plus

Other overseas sterling deposits (increase –)

plus

Other sterling lending to the overseas sector

plus

Monetary sector foreign currency deposit liabilities net of
foreign currency assets (increase –)

plus

External finance of the public sector (increase –)

plus

Net non-deposit liabilities of the monetary sector (increase –)

1 The Context

The national debt, strictly defined, comprises the liabilities of the National Loans Fund (NLF)*. These include gilt-edged stocks, Treasury bills, national savings and tax instruments, as well as the foreign currency debt of the central government. It thus excludes market borrowings by local authorities and public corporations. However, this definition is misleading when the importance of the debt in the economy or its place in government finances is discussed. First, there are nationalised industry stocks which bear a government guarantee, which are listed on The Stock Exchange and which are traded in the gilt-edged market as if they were regular issues. Second, official bodies are themselves considerable holders of debt. The largest are the Issue Department of the Bank of England and the National Debt Commissioners (NDCs) (see Chapter 2). These holdings are excluded from the discussion where this is possible. The focus is on debt in market hands, although lack of data for official holdings means that all debt, or all gilt-edged stocks, has been employed in some places.

This chapter considers recent developments in the importance, structure and ownership of the debt. A dramatic growth in the nominal debt over fifteen years has been accompanied by inflation which has eroded its real value; it has declined as a proportion of national output since 1968; it has retained a broadly stable relationship since 1978. Within the total debt, the importance of stocks has risen and their issue has pushed other public sector borrowers and private companies out of the fixed-interest market. The importance of Treasury bills has declined whilst that of national savings has recovered from the low levels reached in the late 1970s. The need to control the money supply has shifted the ownership of marketable debt into non-bank hands. The importance of the non-bank financial institutions has increased as that of the personal sector has declined; however, the exposure of institutions has risen little since the mid-1970s because of improvements in the prices of their other assets. Finally, the average maturity of stocks in market hands has fallen.

The size of the debt

Nominal value
The nominal value of the national debt in market hands grew five times during the period 1968–84, while the nominal value of gilt-edged stocks outstanding grew six times (see Table 1.1).

* Technical terms used in the text are explained in the Glossary.

Table 1.1   *Nominal value[1] of the sterling national debt in market hands, 1968–84 (as at end-March)*

	Total sterling debt		British Government and government-guaranteed stocks	
	£m.	as a % of GNP[2]	£m.	as a % of GNP[2]
1968	24,435	67·7	15,876	44·0
1969	24,052	62·1	14,922	38·5
1970	23,382	57·0	16,209	39·5
1971	23,640	51·9	17,149	37·6
1972	26,619	51·3	19,558	37·7
1973	26,343	44·8	19,393	33·0
1974	27,716	41·1	21,268	31·5
1975	31,710	39·0	23,854	29·3
1976	40,407	43·6	29,148	29·0
1977	49,186	45·6	36,813	31·4
1978	56,995	46·4	43,496	32·7
1979	65,650	46·1	51,525	34·0
1980	73,458	43·7	60,297	34·0
1981[3]	91,900	46·9	75,536	37·3
1982	101,748	47·8	81,534	37·5
1983	111,451	47·2	87,675	36·3
1984	128,347	48·7	100,594	38·2

Notes: [1] Includes index-related capital uplift on index-linked stocks; excludes capital uplift on index-linked national savings certificates and SAYE contracts.
[2] GNP at factor cost, unadjusted, expenditure based, for financial years.
[3] £1,708m. nominal of gilt-edged stocks and £41m. Treasury bills belonging to the National Savings Bank Investment Fund moved from 'market holdings' to 'official holdings' on 1 January 1981 (*BEQB*, December 1981, p. 526).

Sources: cols 1 and 3 – articles in the annual series on the national debt in the *BEQB*.

However, the influence and burden of the national debt is not a matter of its absolute size. It needs to be compared with some measure of national output. The period saw some real economic growth and much inflation. Gross National Product (GNP) in money terms expanded six and a half times between 1968 and 1983. As a result the nominal value of the debt in relation to GNP actually declined. This decline reached a low point in 1975 as inflation accelerated. The ratio has since risen steadily, with a temporary reversal in 1979 and 1980 as inflation again increased nominal GNP.

Market value
Part of the national debt, national savings, is in theory repayable at par at any time. Part is in the form of marketable paper: gilt-edged stocks and Treasury bills. The government's liability for marketable paper is the

interest payments and the repayment of the principal at some specified date or, in the case of irredeemables, when it suits them.

Until redemption, the prices of gilt-edged stocks and bills fluctuate in the secondary market. The current value of the national debt to investors should therefore be considered using market prices. The market price of a Treasury bill, issued for three months, changes relatively little. The larger movements in market value are almost entirely the result of changes in the prices of stocks.

The changes in market value seen in Table 1.2 are a result of the revaluation of the existing debt to market prices together with the issue of new debt. The value of the debt in market hands rose six times between 1968 and 1984, broadly the same as the rise in nominal value, although at times their growth has been very different. This was particularly marked in the middle 1970s and in 1979/80 when market prices were falling whilst the nominal value continued to grow as the government borrowed; between March 1979 and March 1980 the market value of the sterling debt rose by only £2,000m., although the Central Government Borrowing Requirement (CGBR) was over £8,000m.

Table 1.2 *Market value of the sterling national debt in market hands, 1968–84 (as at end-March)*

	Total		British Government and government guaranteed stocks	
	£m.	as a % of GNP	£m.	as a % of GNP
1968	21,512	59·6	12,953	35·9
1969	20,432	52·8	11,302	29·2
1970	20,191	49·2	13,023	31·7
1971	20,789	45·6	14,258	31·3
1972	24,407	47·0	17,346	33·4
1973	22,431	38·2	15,481	26·3
1974	20,789	30·8	14,194	21·0
1975	25,415	31·2	17,559	21·6
1976	33,793	33·6	22,534	22·4
1977	43,416	37·0	31,043	26·4
1978	52,134	39·2	38,641	29·1
1979	60,297	39·7	46,172	30·4
1980	62,289	35·2	49,128	27·7
1981	81,937	40·5	65,573	32·4
1982	92,125	42·3	71,911	33·0
1983	111,440	46·1	87,665	36·2
1984	129,703	49·2	101,951	38·7

Note: See notes 2 and 3 in Table 1.1.

Sources: cols 1 and 3 – articles in the annual series on the national debt in the *BEQB* and Bank of England estimates.

The market value of both the total sterling debt and gilt-edged stocks as a proportion of GNP fell to a low point in 1974. It has since risen irregularly. Between 1974 and 1980 this was the result of an unhealthy brew of large additions from government borrowing, erratic annual changes in nominal GNP and violent fluctuations in market prices. The pattern then changed as gilt-edged prices rose and later steadied, whilst the growth in nominal GNP slowed and government borrowing stabilised.

The debt in constant prices

Until 1981 the national debt was almost entirely in the form of securities whose principal and interest were fixed in money terms. National savings with their redemption value related to movements in the Retail Price Index (RPI) were introduced in 1975, but were restricted to old age pensioners. The first index-linked gilt-edged stock was introduced in March 1981, restricted to pension funds. The restrictions on holders of national savings lasted until September 1981 and those on stocks until March 1982. Table 1.3 shows that index-linked debt as a proportion of the total in market hands grew from 2 per cent in 1979 to 8 per cent in 1984.

Table 1.3   *Nominal value*[1] *of index-linked debt in market hands, 1979–84 (as at end-March)*

	Stocks		National savings		Total	
	£m.	as a %	£m.	as a %	£m.	as a %
1979	–		1,079	2	1,079	2
1980	–		1,762	2	1,762	2
1981	1,000	1	2,895	3	3,895	4
1982	2,567	3	4,757	5	7,324	7
1983	5,679	5	4,541	4	10,220	9
1984	7,033	5	4,043	3	11,076	8

Note: [1]Excludes index-related capital uplift on index-linked national savings certificates and SAYE contracts. If they were included, the proportion in 1983 would have been 10 per cent. Includes index-related capital uplift on stocks.

Sources: 1979 and 1980 – *Financial Statistics*. 1981, 1982 and 1983 – articles in the annual series on the national debt in the *BEQB*, December 1982, December 1983 and December 1984.

The absence of index-linking meant that the real value of the government's liabilities and the real value of the investors' assets were vulnerable to the high inflation of the 1970s. Indeed, inflation was so high that in many years it reduced the real value of the debt by more than the debt was increased by new government borrowing. Between 1968 and 1975 the real value almost halved; it has since returned to the levels seen in the late 1960s (see Figure 1.1).

Since inflation was the dominant contributor to the growth in the money value of output, the value of the debt in constant prices moved broadly in line with its value as a proportion of nominal GNP.

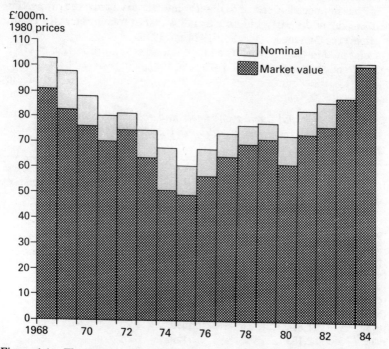

Figure 1.1   *The sterling national debt in market hands in constant 1980 prices, 1968–84 (as at end-March, adjusted using GDP deflator)*

Source: articles in the annual series on the national debt in the *BEQB*.

The annual burden

The cost of servicing the marketable stock component of the national debt falls into two parts – the nominal interest payments and the redemptions (see Table 1.4). The cost of the two parts can be calculated separately, but this provides a distorted picture when it is remembered that high nominal interest rates contain an element of early redemption payment.

The annual interest cost of servicing listed gilt-edged stocks rose tenfold between 1968 and 1984 – from about £1,000m. to about £10,160m. When viewed in relation to GNP the rise was less startling, but still substantial: it remained broadly stable until 1977 and then rose strongly, without faltering in the early 1980s despite high rates of inflation. Reduced borrowing and lower nominal interest rates on new issues produced falls in both 1983 and 1984 for the first time since 1975.

The nominal value of redemptions reached a peak in 1982 and 1983, with the annual value nearly doubling in 1982. The trend as a proportion of GNP has not been as defined as that for interest payments; the proportion was smaller in the early and middle 1980s than it was in the early 1970s, albeit higher than the low levels of 1974 and 1975.

Combined interest payments and redemptions as a proportion of GNP rose strongly between the mid-1970s and 1982, and then fell back in 1983 and 1984.

Table 1.4   *Nominal interest payments and redemptions on listed British Government and government-guaranteed stocks 1968–84 (years to end-March)*

| | Nominal interest payments | | Redemptions[1] | | Interest payments plus redemptions |
	£m.	as a % of GNP[2]	£m.	as a % of GNP[2]	as a % of GNP[2]
1968	995	2·8	1,573	4·4	7·1
1969	992	2·6	918	2·4	4·9
1970	973	2·4	1,325	3·2	5·6
1971	1,153	2·5	1,370	3·0	5·5
1972	1,280	2·5	1,722	3·3	5·8
1973	1,435	2·4	1,869	3·2	5·6
1974	1,676	2·5	1,054	1·6	4·0
1975	1,814	2·2	1,530	1·9	4·1
1976	2,192	2·2	2,150	2·1	4·3
1977	2,944	2·5	2,770	2·4	4·9
1978	4,055	3·1	3,206	2·4	5·5
1979	4,948	3·3	2,139	1·4	4·7
1980	6,170	3·5	3,388	1·9	5·4
1981	7,586	3·7	3,657	1·8	5·5
1982	9,222	4·2	6,133	2·8	7·0
1983	9,612	4·0	6,160	2·5	6·5
1984	10,156	3·9	4,597	1·8	5·6

Notes: [1] Including redemptions by sinking fund or cancellation. See Chapter 2, Table 2.9.
[2] GNP at factor cost, unadjusted, expenditure based for financial years.

The government and other borrowers

Government borrowing has dominated the fixed-interest market since 1974. Companies have been unwilling to lock themselves into paying high nominal rates and uncertain, but possibly high, real rates for long periods. Local authorities have been given incentives to borrow direct from the central government, rather than in the market in their own names; this borrowing has increased since 1982 to help counter the effects of over-funding in the money market (see Chapter 2).

As a result, gilt-edged stocks in market hands have risen as a proportion of all listed debt in every year since 1975. Figure 1.2 shows the outstanding nominal value of British Government and government-guaranteed stocks in market hands, the listed debt of local authorities and public boards and the listed debt of UK and Irish registered companies, including debentures, loan stocks, convertible loan stocks and preference shares. It can be seen that gilt-edged stocks now amount to nearly 90 per cent of all the sterling debt listed on The Stock Exchange. In the same period, the debt of local authorities and public boards has fallen from 8 per cent to 3 per cent of the total and that of private companies from about 25 per cent to 8 per cent.

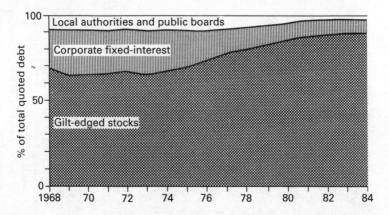

Figure 1.2   *The growth in listed British Government and government-guaranteed stocks and the decline in the listed debt of local authorities and public companies, 1968–84 (nominal values as at end-March)*

Sources: articles in the annual series on the national debt in the *BEQB;* The Stock Exchange.

Composition

There have been considerable changes in the composition of the national debt over the period 1968–84 (see Table 1.5). These changes have been particularly marked since 1976 when the debt became more important as an instrument of monetary policy.

The most conspicuous change has been the increase in gilt-edged stocks and the reduction in Treasury bills. This reflects the need to sell debt to

Table 1.5 Components of the nominal value of the national debt in market hands, 1968–84 (as at end-March)

| | Sterling debt | | | | | | | | | | Foreign currency debt | | Total |
| | Stocks | | Treasury bills | | National savings | | Other[1] | | Total | | | | |
	£m.	as % of total debt	£m.	as % of total debt	£m.	as % of total debt	£m.	as % of total debt	£m.	as % of total debt	£m.	as % of total debt	£m.
1968	15,876	59	3,077	12	3,683	14	1,799	7	24,435	91	2,302	9	26,737
1969	14,922	57	3,218	12	3,676	14	2,236	9	24,052	91	2,253	9	26,305
1970	16,209	63	1,448	6	3,559	14	2,166	8	23,382	91	2,234	9	25,616
1971	17,149	66	955	4	3,574	14	1,962	8	23,640	92	2,149	8	25,789
1972	19,558	69	1,321	5	3,967	14	1,773	6	26,619	93	1,879	7	28,498
1973	19,393	69	1,414	5	4,178[2]	15	1,358	5	26,343	94	1,616[3]	6	27,959
1974	21,268	73	1,065	4	4,075[2]	14	1,308	4	27,716	95	1,543[3]	5	29,259
1975	23,854	70	2,663	8	4,014[2]	12	1,179	3	31,710	93	2,323[3]	7	34,033
1976	29,148	67	4,828	11	4,334	10	2,097	5	40,407	92	3,451	8	43,858
1977	36,813	69	3,637	7	5,285	10	3,451	6	49,186	92	4,372	8	53,558
1978	43,497	71	3,065	5	5,832	10	4,601	7	56,995	92	4,629	8	61,624
1979	51,525	74	2,225	3	7,149	10	4,751	7	65,650	94	4,288	6	69,938
1980	60,297	78	2,281	3	7,902	10	2,978	4	73,458	95	3,949	5	77,407
1981[4]	75,536	80	1,209	1	11,556	12	3,599	4	91,900	97	3,083	3	94,983
1982	81,534	78	1,104	1	15,295	15	3,815	4	101,748	98	2,360	2	104,108
1983	87,675	77	1,300	1	17,760	16	4,716	4	111,451	98	2,601	2	114,052
1984	100,595	77	1,426	1	20,219	15	6,108	5	128,347	98	2,555	2	130,902

Notes: Percentages may not sum to 100 because of rounding.
See Table 1.1 for treatment of capital uplift on index-linked debt.
[1] Includes certificates of tax deposit, tax reserve certificates, tax deposit accounts, Ways and Means Advances, terminable annuities, life annuities, NILOs (see Chapter 2) and interest-free notes due to the IMF.
[2] Includes official holdings.
[3] Differ from data given in *Consolidated Fund and National Loans Fund Accounts: supplementary statements*, since an 'equivalent of parity' of £1 = $2∙89524 was used to find sterling value (*BEQB*, December 1982, p. 542n).
[4] On 1 January 1981 investment account deposits with the National Savings Bank Investment Fund were moved from the non-bank private sector to national savings. This added about 2 per cent to the proportion of the national debt represented by national savings. See also note 3, Table 1.1.

Source: articles in the annual series on the national debt published in the *BEQB*.

the domestic non-bank private sector to control the money supply. Borrowing from the non-bank sector has at times exceeded central government borrowing and Exchange Equalisation Account (EEA) sales of sterling (see Chapter 2). This has meant that the government has repaid debt to the banking system, which is the residual source of the finance normally provided on Treasury bills. Thus there has been both a proportional and absolute reduction in Treasury bills outstanding.

The importance of national savings fell until 1976 and then steadied. This reflected the unwillingness of successive governments to compete aggressively with building societies for small personal sector savings. The reversal of this policy in 1980 led to improvements in marketing, the range of instruments available and the speed with which rates were adjusted to reflect returns on competing private sector products. Sales of national savings reacted strongly to these changes and they now represent a larger proportion of the outstanding debt than in the late 1960s, although the proportion is still lower than in the twenty years following 1945.

The importance of foreign currency debt has declined, reflecting the increase in both the sterling-denominated debt and repayments. The government raised a $2·5b. eurocurrency bank loan in 1974, followed by another of $1·5b. in 1977, in order to finance balance of payments deficits. They also borrowed $400m. on the New York bond market in 1978 and issued the equivalent of £400m. of bonds to official overseas holders of sterling in 1977, in exchange for part of their sterling assets. The eurocurrency credits were repaid in 1980 and 1981.

Ownership

There are five market holders of the national debt: UK non-bank financial institutions; UK industrial and commercial companies; the UK personal sector, which includes holders that cannot be identified and allocated elsewhere; the UK monetary, or banking, sector; and the overseas sector. The money stock is reduced only when the government, the overseas and monetary sectors sell debt to the other holders, who comprise the non-bank private sector. Since industrial and commercial companies are rarely important buyers, the emphasis on money supply control since 1976 has required increased investment by the personal sector and non-bank financial institutions.

National savings are owned by the personal sector; their expansion since 1980 has thus also meant an expansion in the importance of the non-bank private sector. Table 1.5 has shown how the volume of outstanding Treasury bills, held mainly by the monetary and overseas sectors, has been reduced. There is a corresponding change in the ownership of gilt-edged stocks (see Figure 1.3).

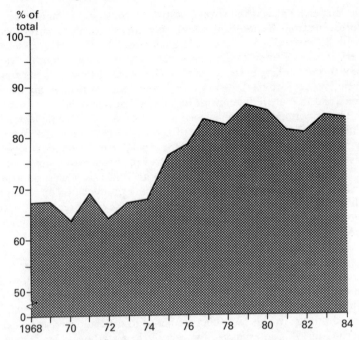

Figure 1.3   *Market value of non-bank private sector holdings of British Govern-ment and government-guaranteed stocks as a percentage of total market holdings, 1968–84 (as at end-March)*

Note: See note 3 in Table 1.1.
Source: Bank of England estimates for market value.

The trend in the market value of non-bank holdings in comparison with GNP is similar to that of total market holdings (see Table 1.6). There is a steep fall to 1974 and a recovery, although the recent increase in the proportion of market holdings owned in the non-bank sector means that the rise has been steeper: holdings as a percentage of GNP are now well above the highest level seen in the last fifteen years.

The increased importance of non-bank holders has been accompanied by a spectacular increase in the holdings of non-bank financial institutions, while the relative position of the personal sector has declined (see Figure 1.4). Between 1970 and 1984 the share of non-bank private sector holdings owned by insurance companies rose from 28 per cent to 37 per cent, the share of pension funds from 11 per cent to 26 per cent and the share of building societies from 8 per cent to 13 per cent. This expansion has slowed since 1982, in part because of the greater emphasis since 1980 on financing the Public Sector Borrowing Requirement (PSBR) by sales of national savings. Holdings of the group comprising the Public Trustee, industrial and commercial companies, private individuals and the 'residual' have to be treated as broad indications of magnitudes because of problems of identification. The trend to institutionalising personal sector savings is unmistakable, however. The group's share of market holdings has declined since 1974 from 48 per cent to 23 per cent. Part of this may reflect the switch to borrowing from individuals on national savings, although this does not explain the change since the late 1960s when the group's share of non-bank holdings has declined from a little over a half to under a quarter, while the share of national savings in the nominal national debt showed little change.

Table 1.6 *Market value of British Government and government-guaranteed stocks as a percentage of GNP, 1968–84 (as at end-March)*

	Total in market hands	Total in non-bank private sector hands
1968	35·9	24·1
1969	29·2	19·8
1970	31·7	20·4
1971	31·3	21·6
1972	33·4	21·6
1973	26·3	17·7
1974	21·0	14·2
1975	21·6	16·5
1976	22·4	17·6
1977	26·4	21·9
1978	29·1	23·9
1979	30·4	26·1
1980	27·7	23·6
1981	32·3	26·1
1982	32·8	26·5
1983	36·0	30·2
1984	38·7	32·2

Note: See notes 2 and 3 in Table 1.1.

Source: Bank of England estimates for market value.

Although the proportion of gilt-edged stocks owned by insurance companies and pension funds increased until 1977, the importance of gilt-edged stocks in their portfolios has shown little change recently (see Figure 1.5(a) and Chapter 3). The distribution of assets depends on the way in which new money is invested and changes in the market value of the different parts of the portfolios, including company securities and property, as well as the gilt-edged stocks themselves. The insurance companies and pension funds began buying gilt-edged stocks heavily in 1975 and continued to place 40–50 per cent of their new money in the market until 1979, when the proportion began to drop back (see Figure 1.6). However, the prices of both property and ordinary shares have risen strongly since 1974 (see Figure 1.5(b)). As a result, the importance of gilt-edged stocks in portfolios has remained static, despite the fall in yields – and hence rise in prices – that has taken place in gilt-edged stocks since 1981 (see Chapter 3).

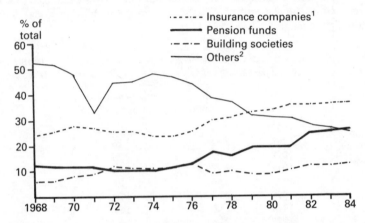

Figure 1.4   *Holdings of British Government and government-guaranteed stocks by the non-bank private sector as a percentage of total non-bank holdings, 1968–84 (as at end-March)*

Notes: [1] Long-term and general insurance. Long-term funds include some pensions business.
[2] Public Trustee and various non-corporate bodies, individuals, industrial and commercial companies, Friendly Societies and Other (residual).

Source: articles in the annual series on the national debt in the *BEQB*.

Purchases

Emphasis on marketable stocks

A mixture of financial and political pressures has pushed the gilt-edged market, and the volume of institutional buying, towards the centre of economic policy since 1975. A high level of public borrowing has meant increased supplies of government paper. The need, initially, to limit domestic credit expansion (DCE) in pursuit of IMF performance criteria and later to meet money supply targets meant that this paper had to be sold to the domestic non-bank sector. The reluctance until 1980 to compete

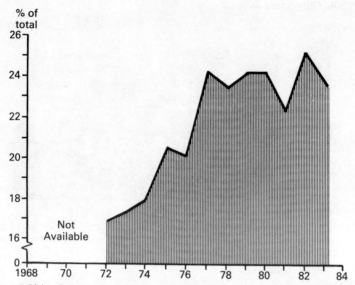

Figure 1.5(a) *Insurance company[1] and pension fund holdings of British Govern-ment and government-guaranteed stocks as a percentage of total assets, 1972–83 (as at end-December)*

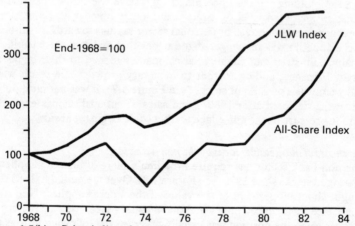

Figure 1.5(b) *Price indices for ordinary shares (FT All-Share Index) and property (Jones Lang Wootton), 1968–84*

Note: [1] Until 1973 excludes non-members of the British Insurance Association and Commonwealth life companies. From 1973 includes Commonwealth life companies that are members of the British Insurance Association and an estimate for non-members. Insurance company holdings at book values until 1975.

Sources: M5 Business Monitor; MQ5 Business Monitor; Annual Abstract of Statistics; Financial Times; Jones Lang Wootton for the JLW Index.

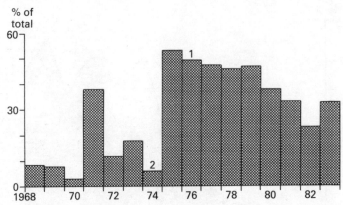

Figure 1.6   *Purchases of British Government and government-guaranteed stocks as a percentage of total insurance company[1] and pension fund acquisitions of assets, 1968–83 (years to end-March)*

Notes: [1] See note to Figure 1.5.
[2] Change in series.

Sources: M5 Business Monitor; MQ5 Business Monitor.

with the building societies precluded aggressive use of national savings, whilst an increased level of direct taxation combined with fiscal bias to direct a higher proportion of personal sector savings towards institutions, whose appetite was for longer-dated paper that matched their liabilities. Finally, industrial and commercial companies turned to their banks for external finance, adding further to monetary growth. The result was a heavy emphasis on sales of stocks (see Figure 1.7). It was not until public borrowing declined after 1980/1 and sales of national savings expanded that the pressure on the gilt-edged market could begin to subside.

Purchases of marketable stocks by the non-bank sector

The non-bank sector has acquired the lion's share of official supplies of gilt-edged stocks since 1970 (see Figure 1.8). Over the period to 1983 they bought about 90 per cent of the value of the stocks supplied. Non-bank dominance was reduced only when the monetary sector was a large buyer. In those cases the position was usually reversed the following year as the banks sold on to the non-bank sector the stock they had earlier bought from the authorities.

The behaviour of the overseas sector (see Chapter 4) has been strikingly different from that of the monetary sector. It might have been expected that the sector would hold for relatively short periods, and sell as soon as sterling was perceived to be expensive or the UK entered one of its recurring crises of the 1970s. This is certainly the myth of market

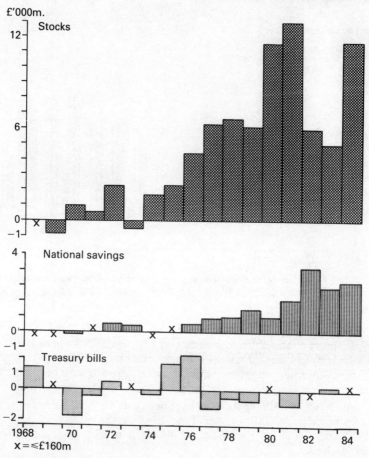

Figure 1.7 *The financing of central government borrowing: the use of stocks, national savings, and Treasury bills, 1968–84 (years to end-March)*
Source: BEQB.

practitioners. In fact, in aggregate, the overseas sector has displayed suspicion, not by selling, but by no longer buying. There are years of considerable purchases, but none of appreciable sales.

Within the non-bank private sector, the importance of the National Savings Bank Investment Fund, whose holdings were included in those of the non-bank sector until 1 January 1981, declined through the 1970s (see Table 1.7). There was a similar decline in the Trustee Savings Banks, which now form part of the monetary sector. Unit trusts were discouraged

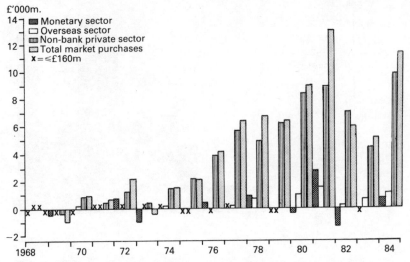

Figure 1.8   *Purchases of British Government and government-guaranteed stocks by the monetary, overseas and non-bank private sectors, 1968–84 (years to end-March)*

Source: BEQB.

by their tax treatment from investing in gilt-edged stocks until 1980 (see Chapter 4) and are still relatively unimportant holders. The major buyers as the authorities sought to control monetary growth have been building societies, insurance companies, pension funds and the personal sector.

Purchases by building societies have been volatile (see Chapter 4). They contributed importantly to overall non-bank purchases between 1970 and 1972, and again between 1981 and 1984 when insurance company buying was declining.

Maturity

Maturity of outstanding stocks

The average life of gilt-edged stocks outstanding has shortened since the mid-1970s (see Table 1.8). This process accelerated in 1983 and 1984, the authorities believing that borrowing at high nominal interest rates for long periods was not justified in view of the government's commitment to reduce inflation.

The most important official holders of gilt-edged stocks are the National Debt Commissioners and the Issue Department of the Bank of England (see Chapter 2). Both own a wide range of maturities, but the Issue Department will normally have a large portfolio of maturing stocks. This is

Table 1.7 *Purchases of British Government and government-guaranteed stocks by the non-bank private sector,*[1] *1968–84 (years to end–March)*

| | National Savings Bank investment account[2] | | Trustee Savings Banks[3] | | Investment and unit trusts | | Building societies | | Insurance companies[4] | | Pension funds | | Other | | Total |
	£m.	as % of total	£m.	as % of total	£m.	as % of total	£m.	as % of total	£m.	as % of total	£m.	as % of total	£m.	as % of total	£m.
1968	39	244	31	194	−64	−400	50	313	216	1,350	12	75	−268	−1,675	16
1969	30	7	6	1	−14	−3	−11	−3	67	16	−9	−2	−494	−116	−425
1970	29	3	4	0	67	7	181	20	157	17	52	6	410	46	900
1971	36	8	47	10	5	1	227	49	225	49	98	21	−176	−38	462
1972	64	5	132	11	0	0	324	26	434	35	151	12	124	10	1,229
1973	86	17	99	19	−18	−3	−123	−24	228	44	−12	−2	255	50	515
1974	26	2	37	2	31	2	60	4	272	18	224	15	837	57	1,487
1975	1	0	−3	0	82	4	293	13	554	24	439	19	924	40	2,290
1976	12	0	66	2	31	1	677	18	1,501	39	817	21	755	20	3,859
1977	73	1	227	4	43	1	−65	−1	2,078	36	1,422	25	2,019	35	5,797
1978	367	7	223	5	112	2	918	19	2,249	46	903	18	142	3	4,914
1979	202	3	445	7	−25	0	299	5	2,618	42	1,782	29	858	14	6,179
1980	193	2	166	2	13	0	847	10	3,013	36	2,334	28	1,762	21	8,328
1981	14	0	95	1	53	1	1,281	14	3,093	35	2,079	23	2,276	26	8,891
1982	–		184	3	−16	0	1,189	17	2,437	34	1,687	24	1,617	23	7,098
1983	–		–		149	3	894	20	1,680	38	1,361	31	371	8	4,455
1984	–		–		213	2	2,051	21	2,438	25	2,720	28	2,429	25	9,851

Notes: Percentages may not sum to 100 because of rounding.
[1] Mainly at cash values.
[2] Included in national savings from 1 January 1981.
[3] Included in the monetary sector from 1 January 1982.
[4] Long-term and general funds.

Source: BEQB.

the major reason why Table 1.8 shows 'Stocks held in market hands' as having a longer average life than 'All stocks outstanding'.

Table 1.8   *Average life of dated British Government and government-guaranteed stocks, 1968–84 (as at end-March)*

	All stocks outstanding[1]	Stocks in market hands[2]	Duration – all stocks outstanding[3]
1968	13·2	12·6	12·6
1969	12·8	13·3	12·5
1970	13·4	13·1	12·1
1971	13·5	13·3	11·6
1972	14·4	13·7	12·7
1973	14·1	14·5	11·9
1974	13·1	13·3	11·4
1975	11·9	12·0	10·6
1976	11·8	12·4	9·9
1977	12·0	12·5	9·4
1978	11·5	12·2	8·8
1979	11·6	12·5	9·2
1980	12·1	12·9	9·6
1981	11·6 (11·6)[4]	12·4	8·9(8·9)[4]
1982	12·4 (11·3)[4]	11·9 (11·6)[4]	8·7(8·6)[4]
1983	12·7 (10·5)[4]	11·1 (10·6)[4]	8·0(7·6)[4]
1984	12·4 (9·5)[4]	10·3 (9·6)[4]	7·8 (7·1)[4]

Notes: [1] Assumes that stocks with optional maturity dates standing above par at 31 March will be redeemed at the earliest date. A constant 5 per cent inflation rate is applied to index-linked stocks. Convertible stocks are assumed to have been converted if prices on 31 March were such that conversion would have taken place if the option were available on that day.

[2] *Source:* Bank of England and articles in the annual series on the national debt published in the *BEQB*. For 1981, 1982, 1983 and 1984 it is assumed that stocks with optional maturity dates standing 'above par on 31 March will be redeemed at the earliest possible maturity date'. For 1982, 1983 and 1984 the calculations give 'index-linked stocks a weight reflecting capital uplift accrued so far' (*BEQB*, December 1983, p. 515n). Before 1981 it is assumed that stocks will be redeemed on the latest possible date.

[3] Assumptions as in note 1. The calculation is the same as that made in the article by Downton (1977), except that it includes 'All stocks' instead of 'All stocks in market hands'. This is because the Bank of England does not make available data for official holdings of individual issues until five years have elapsed. 'The duration statistic measures the average life of a stock taking into account not only the time remaining before the principal is repaid (the life to maturity) but also the timing of interest payments. Interest payments occur at regular intervals (normally every six months), and their average life can therefore be considered to be at a point half way to the date at which the stock is finally redeemed. Thus the duration of an individual stock derives, in principle, from an average of:

a   the time to maturity;
b   the timing of the periodic payments of interest;

weighted by the sum of the principal outstanding and the total remaining interest payments' (Appendix, p. 324).

[4] Average life excluding index-linked stocks. See *BEQB*, December 1983, p. 515n.

Part of the coupons on fixed-interest stocks can be regarded as compensation to the holders for the reduction in the real value of the principal by inflation. The borrower, therefore, should regard some part of the coupon as the early repayment of his loan. The average of the period to maturity and the timing of the coupon payments, weighted by the amount of principal and the sum of the interest payments, gives the duration of a stock. The duration for any single stock will always be shorter than its life.

The issue of high coupon stocks in the 1970s and early 1980s had two effects. First, the difference between the average life of stocks outstanding and their duration widened: in 1970 the difference was 1·3 years whilst in 1984 it was 4·6 years. Second, the length of the market measured by its duration fell more sharply than its length measured by its average life: if index-linked stocks are included and a 5 per cent rate of inflation assumed, duration fell from 12·1 years in 1970 to 7·8 years in 1984, whilst average life fell from 13·4 years to 12·4 years; if index-linked stocks are excluded, duration fell from 12·1 years to 7·1 years and average life from 13·4 years to 9·5 years.

Measurement of the maturity of dated gilt-edged stock is only an indication of the length of the whole sterling denominated debt. The length of the whole cannot be identified precisely because national savings are technically repayable on demand, albeit at some cost to the holder, and there are no data for the maturity of Treasury bills in market hands. Treasury bills provide the government with its residual finance and private sector holdings vary widely from year to year. Inclusion of bills in the measurement of maturity would both shorten the life of the debt and add to the variability of its life. It would also alter the trend in the average maturity. The importance of bills has decreased quite sharply (see Table 1.5) so that the reduction seen in the average life of stocks gives something of a false picture. If dated stocks and bills are combined the average life in the early 1970s would have been reduced by between six and twelve months.

Maturity of new issues
New issues during a year represent only a proportion of outstanding stocks. Thus fluctuations in the average life and duration of new issues are greater than those on existing issues (see Table 1.9).

Until recently the average life of new issues in a financial year has been ten–fifteen years. The exceptions were either when the total volume of new issues was small, so that single issues could seriously affect the average (1968/9, 1971/2 and 1973/4), or when the authorities avoided issuing long-dated stocks to facilitate a drop in yields (1974/5). More recently the authorities have been reluctant to issue long-dated stocks on high nominal yields. Instead they have issued shorter stocks, anticipating that they would be able to refinance them at lower nominal yields once their policies had lowered investors' inflationary expectations. Thus they have sacrificed the certain future debt costs and greater private sector illiquidity provided by a longer-dated debt to the possibility of lower interest payments. Length has been provided by the lower initial cost, and possibly lower real costs, of index-linked stocks.

The high coupon issues of the 1970s and early 1980s had a similar effect on the duration of new issues as on outstanding issues. Duration dropped by more than life and the difference between life and duration widened.

Table 1.9   *Average life of new issues of dated British Government and government-guaranteed stocks, 1968–84 (years to end-March)*

	Average life[1]	Average duration[1]	Number of new issues[2]
1968	11·5	11·4	6
1969	2·1	1·3	3
1970	17·1	11·1	5
1971	13·8	10·1	6
1972	18·7	16·0	8
1973	10·7	8·8	6
1974	5·0	3·7	3
1975	6·7	7·2	9
1976	12·0	8·8	13
1977	13·1	8·9	14
1978	10·5	7·8	19
1979	16·5	12·7	18
1980	14·6	10·4	19
1981	12·4 (12·0)[3]	8·6 (8·6)[3]	32
1982	17·1 (10·1)[3]	9·2 (7·5)[3]	30
1983	15·2 (5·6)[3]	8·5 (4·0)[3]	25
1984	14·4 (6·8)[3]	8·4 (5·1)[3]	33

Notes: [1] See notes 1 and 3 to Table 1.8.
[2] Includes additional tranches of existing issues and conversions of maturing issues. Excludes stocks created by conversion of convertible issues.
[3] Excluding index-linked issues.

2 The Authorities

The volume of gilt-edged stock sold by the authorities is one of the principal determinants of monetary growth. It is also the most flexible instrument over the short term. The size of the revenue and expenditure that determine public borrowing cannot be altered without legal, political and administrative delay. Private sector borrowing from the banking system is dependent on economic activity and the balance between different parts of the economy; it bears a notoriously unpredictable relationship to movements in interest rates. The flows from the Exchange Equalisation Account (EEA) depend on wider policies on the exchange rate; those between resident and non-resident bank accounts result from private sector decisions often only loosely connected to official policies. Non-deposit liabilities depend on the banking system's profitability and retentions.

The gilt-edged market is itself a potential source of monetary expansion since there is a continuous stream of maturing issues to be redeemed by the government for cash. These need to be refinanced by selling other stocks. The authorities have developed techniques to improve their control over the timing of sales and to protect the money stock from the effects of redemptions. The introduction of money supply targets and concern over the burden of interest payments have quickened the pace of innovation since the 1970s. These changes are described in Chapter 7.

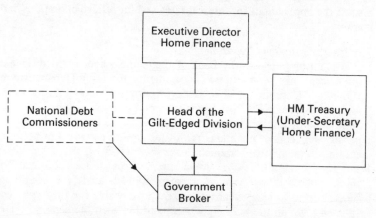

Figure 2.1   *Management of the gilt-edged market*

Machinery

Market management (Figure 2.1)

Official operations in the market are under the day-to-day control of the Head of the Gilt-Edged Division in the Bank of England. He reports to the Executive Director, Home Finance, who also has responsibility for the Money Markets Division. The Government Broker reports market developments to the Head of the Gilt-Edged Division and agrees with him official operations in the market. The Head of the Division is also responsible for liaison with the National Debt Commissioners and ensuring that their investment activities do not clash with the needs of market management.

The legal authority to make issues is given to the Treasury by the National Loans Act 1968, s. 12. At the same time the creation and sale of stock is an integral part of monetary policy, whose importance is partly a matter of political decision. There is therefore the need for constant communication with the Treasury. These contacts are in two parts. First, the Bank is close to the market, conducts official operations and needs room for manoeuvre. The legal and practical position requires that it works within a framework agreed with the Treasury, aiming to provide the monetary conditions desired by political decision. There is informal and frequent contact between the Head of the Gilt-Edged Division and the Treasury Under-Secretary in charge of the Home Finance Division by telephone, in writing and in meetings. Since the end of 1968 a daily report on the market has been prepared for the Chancellor by Treasury officials. Second, there is a regular cycle of discussion and consultation when the money stock data become available each month. The new information is considered independently by the Bank and the Treasury, who then meet to discuss the implications for interest rates and for official operations in the market.

The Issue and Banking Departments

For accounting purposes the Bank of England has been divided since the Bank Charter Act 1844 into two departments: the Issue Department and the Banking Department. The Issue Department's accounts record the Bank's liability for notes issued and the assets held against them.

The Bank of England acts as the main banker to the government. The Banking Department maintains the major central government accounts, including those of the National Loans Fund (NLF), the Consolidated Fund, the Paymaster General (including the EEA) and the National Debt Commissioners. The Banking Department also holds the operational balances of the London clearing banks, across which the final daily cash settlements within the banking system and between the banking system and the Bank of England take place. In addition the Banking Department holds the cash ratio deposits of the UK monetary sector, together with special deposits if they are called.

'Public deposits' in Table 2.1 comprise liabilities resulting from the Bank's role as the government's banker. They include the deposits of the National Loans Fund. This is a Treasury account into which the proceeds of government borrowing are paid; from it flow payments associated with the service of the national debt, loans to other parts of the public sector (including the sterling capital of the EEA), and the payments necessary to fund shortfalls on the other central government accounts. 'Other accounts' include the balances of overseas central banks, the Bank's few private customers and the Bank's own staff. On the assets side, 'Treasury and other bills' includes commercial bills.

Table 2.1   *Banking Department: balance sheet 29 February 1984*

	£m.		£m.
Capital	15	Notes and coin	13
Reserves	396	Cheques in course of collection	223
Public deposits	233	Treasury and other bills	1,114
Bankers' deposits	767	British Government securities	319
Other accounts	1,047	Other securities	23
Payable to the Treasury	22	Advances and other accounts	540
		Investments in subsidiaries	17
		Amounts owing	8
		Premises and equipment	222
	2,479		2,479

Source: Bank of England, *Report and Accounts.*

The Issue Department has only one liability – notes in issue. It may, with the agreement of the Treasury, hold 'securities and assets in currency of any country and in whatever form' (1932 Finance Act, s. 25). The assets held are normally gilt-edged stocks, Treasury bills and Ways and Means Advances, together with local authority and eligible bank bills purchased in the course of the Bank's money market operations.

The 'Government debt' in Table 2.2 of £11m. is a historical curiosity which does not change; it is 'an ancient debt' of £11,015,100 owed to the Bank and enshrined in the Bank Charter Act (Clapham, 1944, vol. II, pp. 180–4). It represents the original £1,200,000 debt to the Bank of 1694 together with later increases. It was transferred to the Issue Department under the terms of the 1844 Act. Commercial bills are the major component of 'other securities'.

The Issue Department makes large profits since its liabilities are non-interest-bearing notes whereas its assets are interest-bearing securities. All the profits of the Department are paid to the Treasury in accordance with the Currency and Bank Notes Act 1928 and the National Loans Act 1968, s. 9. These payments are in two parts. First, the income from investments less the cost of administering the note issue is paid into the NLF at regular intervals agreed with the Treasury. Second, surpluses thrown up by a quarterly revaluation of the securities are also paid into the NLF. For the purposes of distinguishing the two types of 'profit' the Department's accounting system treats all stocks as if they were short-dated gilt-edged stocks. The accrued interest is accounted for separately and is considered to be income when determining the profit payable to the NLF; the capital is then revalued each quarter. The 1968 Act provides that if the quarterly revaluation shows a deficit the Treasury will assume liability for the difference. The profits are then accumulated in the Department until the balance sheet is corrected.

Table 2.2   *Issue Department: balance sheet 29 February 1984*

	£m.		£m.
Notes issued:		Government debt	11
In circulation	11,457	Other securities of, or guaranteed by, the British Government	2,001
In Banking Department	13	Other securities	9,458
	11,470		11,470

Source: Bank of England, *Report and Accounts.*

The profits of the Issue Department are payable to the NLF as of right. The profits of the Banking Department, on the other hand, accrue to the only stockholder of the Bank – the government since nationalisation in 1946. The size of the twice-yearly payment and the profits to be retained in the Department are a matter of negotiation with the Treasury in a similar way to those of any other public corporation.

Settlement of market transactions
Transactions by the Bank in the gilt-edged market are ultimately reflected in movements of deposits and securities held by the Issue and Banking Departments.

The Issue Department's portfolio of gilt-edged stocks is available to the authorities for the purposes of market management. If the authorities buy one stock and sell another the Department's total gilt-edged portfolio will be unchanged but its composition will have altered. If a new issue is not fully subscribed by the public (thus becoming available to the market as a 'tap'), the Department will take up the balance, paying cash to the government. Other things being equal that would create a surplus on the NLF account with the Banking Department, which would be channelled back automatically to the Issue Department as a repayment of Ways and Means

Advances. The composition of the Issue Department's total portfolio would merely have changed, with an increased holding of gilt-edged stock matched by a lower level of Ways and Means Advances. When stock is subsequently sold to the market, the Department's holdings are reduced and offset either by an increase in eligible bills (purchased to relieve a market shortage created by the stock sales) or by an increase in Ways and Means Advances (if the stock sales offset a market surplus in respect of net central government transactions).

A sale of stock to the private sector first involves a cash payment to the Issue Department by the private banking system, which would otherwise lead to a reduction in bankers' operational balances with the Bank. Because the London clearing banks seek to maintain a target level of operational balances, the banks would withdraw call money with the discount market in order to replenish those balances. The discount market would then itself be 'short' and would offer eligible bills for sale to the Bank to relieve its shortage. Those bills would normally be purchased by the Issue Department, in whose portfolio they would replace the stock sold.

Although the daily transactions between the government, the Issue Department and the market normally more or less offset each other, the Issue Department's cash position will rarely exactly match the daily change in its note liabilities. When the Issue Department has a net cash surplus it uses those funds to buy bills from the Banking Department. Any Issue Department shortfall is eliminated by selling bills to the Banking Department. On occasions, the Issue Department may not buy sufficient bills from the market to enable the banks' operational balances to be restored. In that case the Banking Department may make advances direct to the market; the Banking Department would offset the increase in its assets in the form of advances by selling bills to the Issue Department, which would take the place of any stock sold to the market in the Issue Department's portfolio.

A complication arises if central government borrowing from the non-bank public in the form of stock or national savings is in excess of its borrowing requirement and sales of sterling by the EEA. At first the government repays debt to the banking system, buying back Treasury bills as it relieves market shortages. Once these loans have been repaid it begins buying commercial paper; in effect it lends back to the market the money it has borrowed that is in excess of the sums needed to repay borrowing from the banking system.

As stock is sold by the Issue Department and the proceeds are paid to the NLF, the government can repay Ways and Means Advances. This happened to such an extent in 1982 that Ways and Means Advances were likely to be fully repaid and cash balances to accumulate in the NLF. That would have led to conflict with the National Loans Act 1968, s. 12, which allowed the Treasury to borrow, paying the proceeds into the NLF, to provide 'the sums required to meet any excess of payments out of the National Loans Fund over receipts into the National Loans Fund' and to provide 'any necessary working balance' in the Fund. The section was amended in the 1982 Finance Act to allow the Treasury to borrow 'any money which the Treasury consider it expedient to raise for the purposes of promoting sound monetary conditions in the United Kingdom' even when borrowing is not required to balance the NLF. As a result, balances may now accumulate in the NLF account in the Banking Department. The Banking Department can buy commercial paper in the money market to relieve shortages – to provide cash to the banking system. Both sides of the Department's balance sheet are free to expand. The Issue Department can buy gilt-edged stocks and, instead of reducing its holdings of Treasury bills or Ways and Means as previously, supply commercial bills to the Banking Department. These in turn are held in that Department as the asset to match increased liabilities to the NLF. The amendment in effect enables the Banking Department to hold commercial bills in place of the Issue Department.

The Government Broker

The authorities' broker in their dealings in the gilt-edged market has been by tradition the senior partner of Mullens & Co. The Mullens partnership is divided into those who advise and deal for the authorities and those who operate a normal commercial broking house. The partners who service the authorities provide no information or assistance to the commercial partners. The advice the Government Broker is able to give to the authorities is aided by the firm's close involvement with the market as a commercial broker.

The Government Broker's role in the gilt-edged market has four aspects. First, he undertakes the day-to-day management of the Issue Department's portfolio under the direction of the Bank. The aim is the control of monetary growth, the funding of the borrowing requirement and minimising the cost of the debt. Second, he and his firm are responsible for the mechanics of dealing and settlement for their official clients. Third, he advises on the timing, amount and type of new issues. Fourth, he is broker to the National Debt Commissioners. Indeed, his formal title is Senior Broker to the Commissioners for the Reduction of the National Debt. They are responsible, at least in theory, for his appointment. This is a routine function since the Commissioners have relatively straightforward investment objectives. He advises on switches, the investment of new money and the reinvestment of the proceeds of maturing stocks. He liaises with the Bank to ensure that the Commissioners' moves are consistent with the needs of market management.

The arrangement gives the authorities several advantages: they have the use of a broker with ordinary commercial experience; they can tap the combined experience of a large commercial house via the normal daily contact of senior and junior partners, avoiding the need to ask questions around the market; they can ask specific questions through the Government Broker to which he can respond because of his commercial partners' normal contacts with other participants in the market; and the commercial partners can provide general information about institutional behaviour and attitudes, which enables their senior partner better to advise the authorities.

The relationship of the Government Broker to the authorities parallels that of any broker to his institutional clients. He is expected to provide information about market activity, the quality and volume of buying and selling, the maturities and coupons that are in particular demand. He also reports on the mood of the investors and advises on the appetite for stock, institutional cash positions and expectations. He sees the jobbers three times a day (at 10.30, before lunch and before the official close of business at 3.30) and reports to the Gilt-Edged Division in the Bank after each visit and at 5.30.

The influence of the Government Broker is dependent on the same mixture of personality, experience and record of good advice that determine any broker's relationship with his client. He must have a grasp of his client's needs, the realities determining the client's behaviour, the factors affecting other participants and skill in executing his client's business.

The two senior partners of Mullens & Co. responsible for official operations are due to become members of the staff of the Bank when dual capacity is introduced (see Chapter 5). They will join the Gilt-Edged Division of the Bank, where a dealing operation will be established to conduct official operations in the gilt-edged market.

The stock registers
The Chief Registrar of the Bank of England is required by The Government Stock Regulations 1965 to keep registers of stockholders, issue stock certificates and register transfers of the ownership of stock. The Registrar's Department also administers the issues of stock, conversions and the redemption of maturing stocks. It has similar responsibilities for the issues of some of the local authorities, quasi-public bodies, Commonwealth countries and EEC affiliates. The Department also provides same-day certification of transfers and settlement services for certain sections of the market over its 'jobbers' counter'.

The Registrar's Department is the Bank's largest single department, employing over 800 people in 1984. It provides these services as an agent, paid for by the Treasury, in the same way as the EEA. The extent of its activities is shown in Table 2.3.

Table 2.3   *Registrar's Department's activities, 1980–4 ('000s)*

	1980	1981	1982	1983	1984
Transfers registered	1,106	1,177	1,158	1,285	1,072
Number of accounts	2,225	2,274	2,340	2,297	2,245
Bearer bonds	102	83	77	69	54

Note: The figures exclude stocks on the registers of the Bank of Ireland and the Department for National Savings. 'Transfers registered' includes all stocks, rather than those for British Government and government-guaranteed stocks.

Source: Bank of England, *Reports and Accounts.*

The Banking Department in the gilt-edged market

At the end of February 1984 the Banking Department held 13 per cent of its assets in the form of gilt-edged stocks (see Table 2.4). The published accounts show that the Banking Department has raised its holdings of gilt-edged stocks roughly in line with the increase in its overall assets. This policy may have been pursued in order that, as far as possible, interest income will be maintained as rates fluctuate. Switching is limited by the accounting policy of taking profits and losses, on realisation, into the profit and loss account; Table 2.4 shows that large profits would be realised if sales were made.

Table 2.4   *Banking Department: holdings and income from bills and British Government securities, 1979–84 (£m.)*

	1979	1980	1981	1982	1983	1984
British Government securities,						
Book value	127	183	208	260	316	319
Market value	136	193	219	274	383	399
As a % of total assets	9	13	10	10	9	13
Total bills	567	417	654	719	1,340	1,114
As a % of total assets	40	30	30	27	38	45
Treasury bills	562	398	329	353	82	92
Other bills	4	19	326	366	1,258	1,022
Interest on Treasury and other bills	48	71	77	97	111	96
Interest on British Government securities	19	24	29	32	42	45

Source: Bank of England, *Report and Accounts.*

The Department used to deal directly with the Issue Department. It now deals in the market like any other institution. As a department of the Bank of England and banker to the government it subordinates its activities to the needs of market management, informing the Gilt-Edged Division of moves it is contemplating.

The National Debt Commissioners
The Commissioners for the Reduction of the National Debt, usually known as the National Debt Commissioners (NDCs), are a government body with the responsibility for administering various statutory funds. The Commissioners were originally appointed in accordance with the National Debt Reduction Act 1786. The functions are carried out by the National Debt Office, which enjoys considerable independence, is manned by civil servants and is responsible to Parliament. Since 1 April 1980 the staffs of the National Debt Office and the Public Works Loan Board have been amalgamated under the title of the National Investment and Loans Office (NILO); this merger did not affect the statutory functions and responsibilities of the two constituent offices.

The funds under administration are those whose spending is not a matter of direct government decision or where the source is not the regular system of Supply and Appropriation, with payments from the Consolidated Fund or National Loans Fund. The Commissioners were responsible for twenty funds at 31 March 1984 (see Table 2.5).

The Commissioners are conventional fund managers inasmuch as they are required to invest the assets they administer in the interests of the funds themselves. However, the funds are those of public or quasi-public bodies and the Commissioners regard speculation, including the withholding of funds from investment for more than a short period, as inappropriate. In any case the size of the largest funds would make market transactions of a trading nature impracticable.

Public ownership and the large size of the funds makes liaison with the Bank of England an important aspect of the Commissioners' investment function. The officers meet with the Bank officials responsible for gilt-edged market management once a week and are in telephone contact more often; they have a direct line to the Government Broker and consult him when considering switches or investing new funds. The Bank is thus privy to their needs and wishes.

The Commissioners have four methods of investing new money and the proceeds of maturities in the gilt-edged market.

First, they can use the Government Broker to buy stock from the jobbers in the market in the same way as any other investor. This is still the method used when investing for the smaller funds, but it has been largely discontinued when dealing with very big transactions. It is now unusual for the Commissioners to buy tap stocks in the market.

The authorities used to sell either tap stocks or unofficial lines from the Issue Department's portfolio when the Commissioners were buying in the market. This often had the advantage that it created the right climate for

Table 2.5 *Securities held by the National Debt Commissioners for funds under their administration*[1]

Fund	Year end	Total securities held £m.	Holdings of quoted British Government and government-guaranteed securities[2] £m.
Fund for the Banks for Savings[3]	20 November 1983	687	542
National Savings Bank: ordinary deposits[3]	31 December 1982	1,735	1,552
National Savings Bank: Investment Account Fund Residual Investments[3]	31 December 1983	81	–
National Insurance Fund: Investment Account	31 March 1983	3,939	3,176
Maternity Pay Fund: Investment Account	31 March 1983	21	21
Insolvency Services: Investment Account	31 March 1983	141	98
Funds in Court in England and Wales: Investment Account	28 February 1983	233	206
Redundancy Fund: Investment Account	31 March 1983	5	–
The Crown Estate	31 March 1983	21	5
National Heritage Memorial Fund	31 March 1983	23	13
Ironstone Restoration Fund: Investment Account	31 March 1983	–	–
Irish Land Purchase Fund	31 March 1982	–	–
Unclaimed Dividends Account[3,4]	31 March 1983	2	–
Unclaimed Redemption Moneys Account[4]	31 March 1983	10	10
3% Redemption Stock Sinking Fund Account	31 March 1983	17	17
Conversion Loan: Redemption Account[4]	31 March 1983	–	–
Cash Account[4]	31 March 1983	–	–
Donations and Bequests[4]	31 March 1983	–	–
Government Annuities Investment Fund[4]	31 March 1983	–	–
Life and other Annuities Warrant Account[4]	31 March 1983	–	–

the authorities to begin selling to private sector holders, but it had two drawbacks. It was found that stock did not necessarily pass straight through from the Issue Department to the Commissioners if the Commissioners were buying one stock and the Issue Department selling others. Thus it was not possible to ensure against there being an element of unfunding.

The Commissioners regard themselves as running gross funds and in practice buy stocks with high gross redemption yields; they also have requirements for certain maturities to match liabilities, for example in the Fund for the Banks for Savings. The Issue Department did not always own suitable stocks and there could be difficulties in buying on the required scale.

The second method of obtaining stock was introduced in 1977 as a response to these problems. Additional tranches of new issues began to be reserved for the Commissioners for the investment of the funds under their management. These tranches are identical with the rest of the issue to which they are attached and are saleable into the market in the normal way. This innovation had its own problems, however, since the stocks that the authorities might wish to issue might not be those that suited the Commissioners. The problem would have increased if public borrowing, and thus the number of new stocks issued, declined.

Thus in 1981 a third alternative for investing the Commissioners' funds was introduced at a time when the largest of the funds, the National Insurance Fund, was projected to move into substantial surplus. The Treasury arranged to create additional tranches of existing stocks that were suited to the Commissioners' investment needs. These tranches are distinguished by the name National Investment and Loans Office (NILO) (see Chapter 1, Table 1.5). The tranches are not listed on The Stock Exchange; they are not traded in the gilt-edged market; they are not transferable except to the Issue Department. Both creation and transfer to the Issue Department are at the middle market price at the close of official business on The Stock Exchange. There is provision for early redemption of stock by the Treasury, at the request of the Bank.

In 1984 a fourth method of issuing stock was introduced. Taplets were created and issued directly to the Commissioners. Since they are further tranches of existing issues (see Chapter 7) they rank *pari passu* with them and are fully marketable.

All four methods of investing new money or the proceeds of maturing stock are now in use.

The National Insurance Fund

The largest of the funds managed by the Commissioners is that for the National Insurance scheme (see Table 2.6). The social security schemes are administered by the Department of Health and Social Security, to whom the Commissioners are responsible for their investment activities in accordance with the Social Security Act 1975.

Table 2.6   *National Insurance Fund: securities held by the National Debt Commissioners, 1982 and 1983 (market values as at 31 March)*

	1982 £m.	1983 £m.
Ways and Means Advances	14	1
Treasury bills	–	100
British Government securities	3,461	3,176
Local authority stocks, bonds, mortgages and loans	329	662
Total	3,804	3,939

Note: Components may not sum because of rounding.
Source: National Insurance Fund, *Account 1982–83.*

Each year the Government Actuary provides a forecast for the surplus or deficit. The Commissioners use their experience, together with information on the timing of upratings of contributions and benefits, to estimate the seasonal pattern of flows in and out of the Fund. The intention of the Commissioners is to provide liquidity, maximise the yield and preserve capital. They have complete discretion within the statutory controls, but the size of the Fund, the need to maintain a balance of maturities and public ownership are powerful constraints. The bulk of the Fund is invested in gilt-edged stocks, with the balance in Treasury bills and local authority stocks, bills, bonds, mortgages and loans.

The accounts are published about a year after the close of the relevant period. A flavour of the Fund's investment activities may, however, be gained from earlier periods (see Table 2.6). In 1982/3 the Fund switched £240m. of gilt-edged stocks 'in order to improve the yield and maturity pattern. £212m. of the stocks purchased during the year were taken up under the arrangements whereby specific tranches were reserved for the public funds managed by the National Debt Commissioners' (*Account, 1982–83*, p. 7).

Fund for the Banks for Savings

The Trustee Savings Banks Act 1969 required that all deposits, except working balances, of the Ordinary Department of the Trustee Savings Banks (TSBs), be placed with the Commissioners. As part of the development of the TSBs into a commercial bank (see Chapter 4) these balances are being repaid according to a schedule laid down in the Trustee Savings Banks (Fund for the Banks for Savings) (No. 2) Order 1979. All funds may be withdrawn by November 1986 and the Fund closed.

The funds are withdrawable every six months at the TSBs' option. As a result there is a definite pattern of liabilities and as far as possible stocks have been bought with maturity dates to match.

Table 2.7   *Fund for the Banks for Savings: securities held by the National Debt Commissioners, 1982 and 1983 (nominal values as at 20 November)*

	1982 £m.	1983 £m.
Ways and Means Advances	21	1
Treasury bills	52	64
British Government and government-guaranteed securities	817	602
Other (including cash)	23	20
Total	914	687

Note: Components may not sum because of rounding.

Source: Fund for the Banks for Savings, *Accounts.*

Insolvency services

Trustees in bankruptcy and liquidators of companies must pay balances into the Insolvency Services Investment Account kept by the Department of Trade and Industry at the Bank of England. Sums in excess of current needs are invested by the Commissioners.

At end-March 1983 the Commissioners held securities on behalf of the Insolvency Services Investment Account with a market value of £141m. The account, although small, is active. In 1980/1 it purchased and sold securities with a market value of £832m., in 1981/2 it turned over £610m. and in 1982/3 £708m.

Activities

The authorities' operations in the market are aimed at funding the borrowing requirement and controlling monetary growth. Conceptually, these operations fall into two parts: the sale of stock for cash and the refinancing of maturing issues by selling other stocks.

Selling stock

The Issue Department is the repository of stock available for the purposes of market management. The replenishment of this portfolio, with the aim of having suitable stocks available for funding operations, is the normal reason for new issues shown in Table 2.8. This is referred to in both the Radcliffe Report (Committee on the Working of the Monetary System, 1959) and an article on the 'Gilt-edged market' in the *BEQB*, June 1979.

Table 2.8   *Number and nominal value of new issues, 1968–84 (years to end-March)*

	Number of new issues[1]	Nominal value of new issues £m.	Nominal value of net issues[2] £m.
1968	6	2,383	810
1969	3	59	−859
1970	5	1,861	536
1971	6	3,200	1,830
1972	8	4,000	2,279
1973	6	3,600	1,730
1974	3	1,650	596
1975	9	4,600	3,070
1976	13	7,000	4,850
1977	14	9,700	6,930
1978	19	12,824	9,618
1979	18	9,381	7,242
1980	19	15,058	11,670
1981	32	19,178	15,521
1982	30	10,607	4,474
1983	25	11,100	4,940
1984	33	16,500	11,903

Notes: [1] Includes additional tranches of existing issues and conversions of maturing issues. Excludes stocks created by conversion of convertible issues.
[2] Nominal value of new issues less nominal value of redemptions. See Table 2.9.

The authorities are a client of the Government Broker when they operate in the market, using the Issue Department's portfolio. As such the authorities are one operator among many; but they are the largest and often have superior or more timely information. They also differ in the way in which they operate. Since their operations are conducted primarily in pursuit of monetary objectives, they deal predominantly as a seller. They also differ in their approach to the market. They do not seek to sell aggressively, but react to market approaches. They do not aim to make short-term profits.

This dominance produces restrictions on their activities. First, they need to be aware that any move has market impact. There is a continuous game of cat and mouse as several hundred participants in the private sector seek scraps of information about official activities and hypothesise about their meaning. The most definite information, a statement of the authorities' judgement on the condition of the market at a certain point, is the announcement of a new issue. The size, type, maturity and timing of an issue will affect investors' views on the level of the market, the appetite for stock and the funding programme. Second, the authorities are large enough to ruin the market makers who are a vital part of the system for selling stock, handling redemptions and controlling monetary growth. The risks of making markets are inherently large. The authorities need to avoid adding to these by being heavy-handed or cavalier. Third, uncertainty has a cost to the borrower. Price volatility will be increased if the largest participant is a source of market disturbance. Investors will demand compensation in the form of higher yields; market makers will be unwilling to provide liquidity since disturbance may produce losses on their positions. It is in the government's own interest to avoid disruptive change, or when change is necessary, to introduce it with a careful eye to presentation and to the impact on the market.

These restrictions amount to principles of market management. They have several consequences at an operational level. The government nearly always issues a new stock on a yield basis that is comparable to those on existing issues of the same term. The authorities supply tap stocks at relatively predictable prices; the authorities do not supply at one price, withdraw, and reappear at an arbitrarily chosen higher or lower price. Non-tap stocks are supplied at market prices. The prices that are bid when the authorities are switching or buying maturing stock are market prices. The size, timing and terms of new issues have to be tailored to the state of investors' liquidity and the flow of new information; the authorities cannot simply churn out uniform issues as the needs of government finance or monetary policy dictate.

The need to operate within this framework and to deal at market prices has its dangers. Undue certainty of supply price can lead both investors and market makers to delay purchases if they could be certain that stock would be available if circumstances changed. Market makers may use investment buying to accumulate short positions. Buying can merely put the market maker in a position where he has an incentive to lower prices, rather than being met by government sales. Certainty and uncertainty in the handling of the market need delicate blending; inflexibility gives buyers reason to delay in safety whilst too much flexibility may ruin the market makers.

Both the principles governing market management, and the dangers inherent in them, are contained in the classic method of selling stock by tap. Sales take place within a fairly clear regime. The market makers and professional investors are aware of the price at which stock is likely to be available, are able to make judgements of the volume that will be sold at each price and can assess the amount remaining in official hands from the business they are seeing themselves. Each participant will have views on the value of the tap in relation to other stocks. These views rarely agree. As a result some investors will continue to buy the non-tap stocks as others are selling them to buy the tap. Thus taps are exhausted by a combination of straight buying and switching.

The authorities will attempt to produce a climate that will enable them to make tap sales. A common method is to leave investors uncertain about how much tap remains and how much has been bought straight for cash, since this will affect investors' judgements of the volume of stock to be supplied when the current tap has been exhausted.

One approach is for the authorities to buy existing stocks against sales of the tap. Investors find they can switch easily into the new stock and this implies that there are large buyers of the older stocks; investors may guess that the government is the buyer, but they cannot be sure. As a result uncertainty is created about the strength of the market. It is this element of uncertainty within a regime that is both the strength and the peculiarity of the tap system.

The authorities can combine this technique with that of only being prepared to supply more stock, in money value, than they are buying. This ensures that they are net sellers, whilst the market makers have an incentive to deal if they are profiting from the difference between the price they are paying the investor and the price they are being paid by the authorities. It also helps to keep the market makers long of stock and gives them an incentive to keep market prices firm – a state that is almost a precondition for official sales.

Switching

The authorities undertake switches to help liquidity and, as part of the policy of 'maintaining an orderly market', to increase the attractiveness of holding gilt-edged stock. Switching has now been reduced and profitability has become a criterion for undertaking it.

However, there are times when the authorities switch more freely to help develop the appetite for a new instrument; they facilitated switches between conventional stocks and variable coupon stocks in the late 1970s. The index-linked market was slow to develop in its first few years. As a result it was illiquid, with wide prices quoted by the market makers in relatively small amounts of stock. Prices moved sharply in response to small activity. Since it was in the government's longer-term interests to develop the market so that it could play an important part in its funding programme, the authorities were prepared to intervene to increase liquidity, using the Issue Department's portfolio to facilitate market switches between index-linked issues and between index-linked and conventional stock.

Maturities (see Table 2.9)

Until fifteen years ago the normal method of handling maturing issues was to offer investors the opportunity of converting their holdings into a longer stock; this stock could either be a completely new issue or an additional tranche of an existing issue. The two most famous conversions also aimed to reduce the interest cost of the debt. In 1888, Goschen successfully converted £591m. of three issues into £566m. of a stock with a lower coupon. This was 2¾% Consols 1923 or after; in 1903 the coupon was reduced under the terms of the conversion to 2½% (Clapham, 1944, vol. II, pp. 318–21). In 1932, £2,100m. 5% War Loan 1929/47, which represented a quarter of the national debt, was converted into £1,909m. 3½% War Loan 1952 or after (Sayers, 1976, vol. II, pp. 430–47). The last conversion was for a maturing stock, 3% Savings 1960/70, into 8½% Treasury 1980/82 in 1970.

Conversions have not been used recently for three reasons. First, the time required to communicate the terms of the offer to each holder and obtain their response means that it would have to remain open for two or three weeks. Thus conversions would entail a fixed-price offer with a lengthy option against the government. This did not matter when interest rates were stable for long periods, but could have proved expensive in the volatile markets of the 1970s and early 1980s. Second, the holders of maturing stocks could be different from those investors wanting the longer, conversion issue. Third, the government is now a continuous issuer (see Table 2.8) so that, in general, there are few periods when it does not have available a range of taps or taplets. It is thus in a position to supply longer stocks against purchases of maturities.

Until about 1980 the authorities had a continuous programme of lengthening the term of the debt held in market hands, normally being prepared to buy shorter stocks against longer on switches; this was the strict meaning of the term 'funding'. More recently the authorities have replaced this policy with one of buying in maturing stocks. Ideally, the Issue Department will own the bulk of a stock when it matures so that its redemption does not cause a sudden rise in money market liquidity or in the money supply. When the Department receives redemption monies for its holdings of maturing stocks, the cash is normally channelled back to the NLF in the form of increased Ways and Means Advances. The extent to which this is possible depends on the type of stock and the composition of its ownership. Stocks that are held by the banking system are treated as money market instruments as they approach maturity and the volume offered to the authorities responds sensitively to the level of their bidding. At the other extreme, low coupon stocks held mainly by the personal sector can be very slow to respond to official bids and there can be large market holdings at maturity. In the case of issues made in the 1940s and 1950s there were holdings of many millions still outstanding weeks after the redemption date.

Table 2.9   *Number and nominal value of redemptions, 1968–84 (years to end-March)*

	Number of issues redeemed	Nominal value of issues redeemed £m.	Redemption by sinking fund or cancellation £m.	Total £m.
1968	3	1,525	48	1,573
1969	2	867	51	918
1970	4	1,282	43	1,325
1971	2	1,326	44	1,370
1972	4	1,682	40	1,722
1973	3	1,794	75	1,869
1974	3	1,027	27	1,054
1975	4	1,499	31	1,530
1976	3	2,123	27	2,150
1977	4	2,750	20	2,770
1978	4	3,192	14	3,206
1979	3	2,100	39	2,139
1980	5	3,375	13	3,388
1981	6	3,645	12	3,657
1982	9	6,120	13	6,133
1983	6	6,150	10	6,160
1984[1]	6	4,588	9	4,597

Note: [1] Estimated.

Source: 1968–83 – *Consolidated Fund and National Loans Fund Accounts: supplementary statements.*

Between 1971 and 1981, stocks within one year of their maturity were eligible for inclusion in the banking system's minimum reserve asset ratios. These assets were required to be held by each bank in proportion to certain specified liabilities. Stocks within three months of maturity were bought at prices related to the yield on Treasury bills and those between three and twelve months at prices chosen by the authorities.

The minimum reserve asset ratio requirement was abolished in 1981 and the monetary significance of twelve-month stocks ceased. In consequence the authorities altered the basis on which they were prepared to buy maturing stocks. They always bid for penny stocks, those within three months of maturity, at prices that are consistent with their money market intervention rates. They will sometimes make a bid for three–twelve-month stocks, but at times the bids may be low, depending on the circumstances. It can be assumed, for example, that they bid better when they are selling longer-dated stocks.

The authorities' turnover

The authorities' market management, together with the investment activities of the other official bodies, make them responsible for around 10 per cent of gilt-edged market turnover. This proportion has dropped during the last six years (see Table 2.10), which probably reflects the reduction in the size of official switching.

Table 2.10   *Turnover of British Government and government-guaranteed stocks by official holders,*[1] *1978–84 (market values, years to end-March)*

| | Up to 5 years | | Over 5 years | | Total | |
	£m.	As a % of market turnover	£m.	As a % of market turnover	£m.	As a % of total market turnover
1978	9,073	11·8	5,199	10·1	14,272	11·1
1979	6,903	10·9	6,220	14·0	13,123	12·2
1980	7,814	12·7	6,712	10·3	14,526	11·5
1981	7,899	10·2	7,050	8·8	14,949	9·5
1982	7,560	9·6	6,747	9·6	14,307	9·6
1983	7,806	7·7	11,451	10·3	19,257	9·1
1984	9,097	7·2	9,482	8·9	18,579	8·0

Note: [1] Official holders include the Issue and Banking Departments, the National Debt Commissioners, the Northern Ireland Government and government departments (including the Paymaster General). The Ordinary Department of the National Savings Bank is included in the funds managed by the National Debt Commissioners. The National Savings Bank Investment Fund is included from 1 January 1981.

Source: Financial Statistics.

3   The Investor: Insurance Companies and Pension Funds

Investors in fixed-interest stocks are concerned with stability of income even if this involves fluctuations in capital values. Some investors are unconcerned about the possibility of price changes since they have arranged their liabilities so that they have no need for the capital until it becomes available on redemption; their assets and liabilities are matched. Others have an opposite concern: they deliberately mismatch by borrowing short, at a variable interest rate, and investing longer in the gilt-edged market. They judge they can make a capital gain as prices in the market vary. These speculators also find the gilt-edged market attractive because of its liquidity; it has many different participants, with different needs, so that it is usually possible to buy and sell large amounts of stock.

Some investors buy gilt-edged stocks because they judge the return will be greater than that on other assets – property and ordinary shares – at existing prices. They consider these returns in the context of their liabilities, spread of investments and objectives, as well as the investment background at the time. An important aspect is protection through diversity – the ownership of a range of assets with contrasting characteristics so that they will behave differently in different circumstances.

Investors may also buy gilt-edged stocks for supervisory reasons. Ordinary shares and property provide low initial yields and are bought for their potential capital gain. This gain is problematic, however, and supervisors may require that some fixed-interest assets be held as a safety net, to increase the certainty in the future of income levels and capital availability. For other investors, such as banks and discount houses, the liquidity of the gilt-edged market means that positions can be quickly changed, exposure to risk adjusted, if circumstances alter. As a result, the capital required by supervisors to support a given risk position is less than that required to support the same position in other markets.

The reasons for holding gilt-edged stocks differ for each of the categories of investor discussed in the next two chapters. The importance of each will be different for every participant within each category. A changing environment, commercial pressures and developing supervisory attitudes mean that their relative importance is constantly shifting.

This chapter discusses long-term insurance funds, pension funds and general insurance companies. The next chapter discusses building societies, trustee savings banks, investment and unit trusts, overseas residents, industrial and commercial companies, banks, discount houses and the personal sector.

Insurance companies – long-term funds

Liabilities

The liabilities of each long-term fund depend on the mixture of business it writes. The nature of these liabilities is the major constraint on a fund's investment policy and the major determinant of its demand for fixed-interest assets. Additional constraints are the method of valuing liabilities falling due many years in the future, the size of the fund's free estate, or surplus, the supervisory authorities and taxation. The last of these is discussed in Chapter 9.

Every contract or policy will contain one or more of:

- a liability to pay a definite sum of money at some maturity date;
- a liability to make a payment whose size is related to investment performance;
- a liability to pay in the event of death.

In addition there is business where there is no guarantee and the fund's role is that of investment manager.

Endowment policies are long-term savings plans that involve payment at the earlier of maturity or death. They can be of two types: a 'with profits' policy providing for a specified and guaranteed payment, together with participation in the investment profits of the fund; or a 'without profits' policy which pays out a larger guaranteed sum in return for the same premiums.

A whole life policy is a policy, with or without profits, where there is a liability to pay on death whenever it occurs.

Term assurance is a liability to pay a specified sum if death occurs during the period of the policy.

Immediate annuities are a liability to pay regular sums to the policy holder in return for a single premium. The payments are usually fixed in money terms or include a small annual rise as partial compensation for inflation. A deferred annuity is similar, but the premium, or series of premiums, is paid in advance of the first payment to the recipient. Annuities usually continue until the policy holder dies.

The value of unit-linked policies is determined by reference to a specific block of underlying assets. A charge is made for management and life cover, and the balance of the premiums is invested. With most unit-linked policies the premiums are paid into the main life fund; in return the fund earmarks specific securities to cover the liabilities. In other cases policies are issued by separate subsidiaries; the premiums are therefore used to buy assets that are held in a separate account. The element of life cover is usually small, and the fund's liability is limited to the value of the units or assets bought, or some multiple of the monthly premiums.

Managed pension funds are similar to unit-linked policies, with the premiums being used to buy units whose value is related to a specific block of assets. There may be several specialist funds, such as those for UK ordinary shares, overseas ordinary shares, fixed-interest securities and property. In these cases the policy holders or trustees are responsible for selecting the main area for investment, although this responsibility is returned to the company if the choice is a managed fund, where the distribution of the portfolio between the major markets is decided by the fund managers.

Insured pension schemes are policies where the fund agrees to receive pension premiums in return for payments to the policy holders. Insured schemes mainly cater for the small employer. The liabilities are usually stated in money terms, but otherwise the schemes vary widely: they may include liability for a payment for death in service, or to dependants, or for a lump sum on retirement; they may be with or without profits; performance superior to that assumed may mean lower premiums or higher benefits.

Salesmen's ingenuity has developed many variations on these basic products. The nature of each piece of business will determine the combination of assets that should be acquired to meet the liability.

Investment policy (see Table 3.1)
The core of a long-term fund's portfolio is conventionally regarded as long-dated fixed-interest stocks; this nowadays means gilt-edged stock. This is because a change in the general level of interest rates will change the present value of liabilities falling due for payment at some future date. An asset whose value will change exactly in line with the fund's liabilities as interest rates change is a risk-free investment for those parts of a fund's liabilities that have an identifiable money value and maturity or payment date. This asset will have four characteristics: it will be a good credit risk; it will be denominated in the same currency as the liability; it will provide a certain stream of income; and repayment will be of a definite amount on a specified day. A fund that buys such an asset is protected irrespective of movements in interest rates: 'matching implies the distribution of the term of the assets in relation to the term of the liabilities in such a way as to reduce the possibility of loss arising from a change in interest rates. This aspect of life assurances is of the greatest importance' (Redington, 1952, p. 287).

It is for this reason that funds carry out jobbing and tax switches, avoiding changes in the term of their holdings but improving the total return. Matching is of central importance in considering the explanations of the term structure and the substitutability of stocks discussed in Chapter 10.

Whilst matching protects a fund against loss, it also excludes it from profit. The extent to which a fund can move from a matched position in part depends on the size of its shareholders' funds. 'Shareholder' in this sense means ultimate risk-taker. In a public company this is the shareholder as generally understood. In a mutual fund it means the with profits policy holders, who are the owners of the assets remaining after the guaranteed liabilities have been met. The extent to which the risk of mismatching can be taken also depends on the size of the guaranteed liability business compared with the size of the with profits business. In practice the ability to accept risk is limited by the need to continue providing with profits policy holders with returns comparable to those provided by competing companies; a failure to provide this would mean the fund would fail to attract new business and run down over the longer term.

The pool of assets, the surplus or estate, that remains after guaranteed liabilities have been met and the with profits policy holders provided with a competitive return is needed for two other reasons. The costs of setting up a new policy absorb all of the premiums for the first year or two; the liability, however, exists from the start of the policy. An estate is needed to carry the fund over this period and the speed with which the fund can expand with new business is partly dependent on its size. The size of the estate is also important because it helps determine the risks the fund can tolerate in its investment policy. A small estate will point to the need for assets that closely match liabilities in term and certainty of yield; such a fund may well find itself at a disadvantage compared with competing funds that are more generously endowed and able to accept greater risks.

Supervision

Supervision of the long-term funds is carried out by the Department of Trade and Industry (DTI) in accordance with the Insurance Companies Act 1982. Each year the fund's actuary has to certify that the fund's assets exceed its liabilities and to provide an actuary's report on the fund's liabilities and assets, which includes a valuation of the former. The 1982 Act also requires that 'the reasonable expectations' of policy holders be fulfilled (s. 37(2) (a)). This is generally interpreted as meaning that investment should provide a combination of security and stability. It is also seen as a constraint on maturity value illustrations where future bonuses are expected to be lower than those earned in the past.

The valuation of liabilities, in accordance with the Insurance Companies Regulations 1981, is a major constraint on investment. These valuations

Table 3.1   *Long-term insurance funds: distribution of portfolios (as at end-December) and acquisitions (years to end-December), 1976–83 (at market values)*

	1976 £m.	1980 £m.	1981 £m.	1982 £m.	1983 £m.
Distribution of portfolios:					
British Government and government-guaranteed stocks					
Up to 5 years	389	513	602	1,106	1,634
Over 5 and up to 15 years	695	3,601	4,348	8,433	10,663
Over 15 years and undated	3,833	10,517	9,895	12,250	12,049
Index-linked Treasury stock	–	–	404	993	1,448
Total	4,917	14,632	15,249	22,782	25,794
As % of total assets	20	27	25	28	27
Total other assets	19,570	39,386	46,193	57,639	70,897
Total short-term[1]	930	1,887	2,524	3,102	3,535
As % of total assets	4	3	4	4	4
Ordinary shares,[2] property,[3] etc.	12,694	30,338	36,014	45,343	56,309
As % of total assets	52	56	59	56	58
Acquisitions:					
British Government and government-guaranteed stocks	1,512	2,176	2,207	1,841	2,092
As % of total acquisitions	73	44	37	29	32
Total other	572	2,716	3,777	4,405	4,466
All short-term[1]	–21	4	561	426	296
As % of total	–1	–	9	7	5
Ordinary shares,[2] property,[3] etc.	665	2,147	2,804	3,543	3,130
As % of total	32	44	47	57	48

Notes: [1] Cash, Treasury bills, UK local authority bills and temporary money, certificates of deposit, overseas short-term assets, etc., plus net amounts receivable from stockbrokers, amounts receivable from the Inland Revenue and other debtors.
[2] Listed, unlisted, overseas and authorised unit trust units.
[3] Land, property and ground rents.

Sources: Financial Statistics; MQ5 Business Monitor.

rely on conservative assumptions about expenses, mortality and investment income. They also require that a present value be placed on the
liabilities and be compared with assets. The higher is the yield assumed
when valuing the liabilities the lower will be their present value (see

Chapter 11). Solvency requires that this assumed yield be less than the existing yield on the fund's assets.

The assumed yield is derived from the 'reliable' yield on existing assets and the expected yield on future investments. The reliable yield on existing assets uses $92\frac{1}{2}$ per cent of the gross redemption yield (GRY) on fixed-interest stocks and the running yield on variable items such as property and equities; the yield on the latter two categories may not be higher than that on $2\frac{1}{2}$% Consols. It follows that a fund with a portfolio of high yielding gilt-edged stocks can place a lower present value on its liabilities than one with a high proportion of lower yielding ordinary shares or property.

In reality the ability of a fund to match itself is limited even if the structure of liabilities makes this desirable. Competition demands that funds create policies with few of the simplicities of straight non-profits endowment; many policies are attached to mortgage business where the actual length of the policy is less than the nominal length; there are insufficient stocks of a length to match pensions liabilities; many stocks have double-dates; high coupon stocks emphasise the problem of assuming investment rates for the flow of coupons that represent a high proportion of the calculated return over the life of the stock.

The shape of the industry's new business is changing. Single premium personal pensions, unit-linked assurance, and pensions managed funds are gaining in importance relative to term assurance and with and without profits endowment (see Table 3.2).

The result of the changing pattern of liabilities is that:

- Matching is becoming less important since the policy holder himself is taking more of the ultimate risk. The provision of life assurance is becoming less important and long-term funds are finding themselves providing professional fund management expertise for portfolios placed with them for tax reasons.
- Competition is intensified since valuation of a specific block of underlying assets can take place frequently, daily with unit-linked funds. There is less emphasis on products whose valuation is time consuming and periodic, involving actuarial valuations with often unstated and changing assumptions. The performance of with profits policies can be glimpsed only once a year when annual bonuses are declared.
- The life funds' appetite for long-dated fixed-interest stock is becoming more sensitive to returns on other assets.

Pension funds

Liabilities

The liabilities of pension funds are not specific like the traditional liabili-

Table 3.2 Selected life insurance in force by type of policy, UK, 1973–83 (£m.)

	1973	1974	1975	1976	1977	1978	1979	1980	1981	1982	1983
Ordinary individual non-linked life insurances:											
Yearly premiums	739	792	878	966	1,135	1,267	1,517	1,806	2,034	2,265	2,857
Single premiums	7	8	23	50	101	74	113	206	293	287	200
Ordinary individual linked life insurances:											
Yearly premiums	121	168	182	224	225	253	363	424	526	665	843
Single premiums	346	125	84	158	216	282	309	325	522	713	1,410
Industrial life insurances:											
Yearly premiums	377	409	450	500	554	621	843	938	992	1,070	1,150
Personal pensions:											
Yearly premiums	51	62	74	104	144	209	266	340	450	555	666
Single premiums	25	26	28	39	56	71	81	100	181	224	298
Pension and life insurance schemes:[1]											
Premiums receivable[2]	517	629	831	1,056	1,176	1,540	1,880	2,140	2,960	3,080	3,460

Notes: [1] Schemes set up by employers to provide benefits for employees. These benefits include pensions at retirement and lump-sum payments to dependants on death in service.
[2] Figures for years 1973–80 represent premiums in force at the end of the year and are not comparable with those for 1981 and 1982, which represent premiums receivable during the year.

Source: Life Offices' Association et al. (1978, 1983).

ties of the long-term insurance companies. This is for three reasons. First, most schemes are liable to provide pensions related to wages or salaries in the final year or years of employment. The liability is therefore open-ended inasmuch as it is linked to the unpredictable price inflation and earnings growth up to the year of retirement. Second, most schemes in the public sector, and some in the private sector, are wholly or partially inflation-protected.

Approaching two-thirds of the employees in the nationalised industries' and public corporations' pension schemes are in pension schemes the rules of which provide for inflation-proofed pensions. However, some of these schemes do provide that the full pensions increases may not be granted if the fund cannot afford them, unless the employer agrees to meet the extra costs ... nearly one-third of the employees in nationalised industries' and public corporations' pensions schemes are in schemes which, in practice, have provided inflation-proofing ... On the other hand, in the private sector ... Typically the most that is guaranteed is a fixed percentage increase, usually of the order of 3 to 5 per cent. (*Inquiry into the Value of Pensions*, 1981, p. 12)

Statutory inflation-proofing is also provided for local government employees: in their case the basic pension entitlement is funded and the indexing element is required to be met from the current revenues of the authority (Pensions (Increase) Act 1971, sch. 3, paras 1 and 2). Third, the rate of return assumed by the actuary is not a sufficient criterion by which to judge the adequacy of investment performance. Pension contributions are part of employers' wage costs and a reduction aids either competitiveness or profitability; it may also permit increased benefits to be paid. Performance producing superior returns to those assumed, allowing lower employer contributions, is therefore one of the aims of fund management. In this sense also the performance required is open-ended.

Supervision
Unlike long-term funds, pension funds are relatively unconstrained by the supervisory authorities in their aim of relieving their parent organisation of financial responsibility for pensions.

Pension funds are trust funds and the trustees are bound by their own trust deeds and common law: 'the trusts of pension funds are in general governed by the ordinary law of trusts, subject to any contrary provision in the rules or other provisions which govern the trust ... the trustees of a pension fund are subject to the overriding duty to do the best that they can for the beneficiaries' (Re Mineworkers' Pension Scheme Trusts: Cowan and others v Scargill and others, 1984).

In the same case, Sir Robert Megarry made six clarifying points about the duties of trustees and investment policy. First:

'[It] is the duty of trustees to exercise their powers in the best interests of the present and future beneficiaries of the trust ... they must put the interests of their beneficiaries first. When the purpose of the trust is to provide financial benefits for the beneficiaries, as is usually the case, the best interests of the beneficiaries are normally their best financial interests. In the case of a power of investment ... the power must be exercised so as to yield the best return for the beneficiaries, judged in relation to the risks of the investments in question; and the prospects of the yield of income and capital appreciation both have to be considered in judging the return from the investment.'

Second:

'In considering what investments to make trustees must put on one side their own personal interests and views ... Trustees may even have to act dishonourably (though not illegally) if the interests of their beneficiaries require it ... Powers must be exercised fairly and honestly for the purposes for which they are given and not so as to accomplish any ulterior purpose.'

Third: 'benefit' might not mean financial benefit where, for example, the beneficiaries hold strong moral views about some commercial activity. The judgement suggests, however, that such cases are likely to be rare,

'and in any case I think that under a trust for the provision of financial benefits the burden would rest, and rest heavy, on him who asserts that it is for the benefit of the beneficiaries as a whole to receive less by reason of the exclusion of some of the possibly more profitable forms of investment ... Subject to such matters, under a trust for the provision of financial benefits, the paramount duty of the trustees is to provide the greatest financial benefits for the present and future beneficiaries.'

Fourth:

'the standard required of a trustee in exercising his powers of investment is that he must 'take such care as an ordinary prudent man would take if he were minded to make an investment for the benefit of other people for whom he felt morally bound to provide' ... That duty includes the duty to seek advice on matters which the trustee does not understand, such as the making of investments, and on receiving that advice to act with the same degree of prudence.'

Fifth:

'trustees have a duty to consider the need for diversification of investments. By s. 6(1) of the Trustee Investments Act 1961, 'In the exercise of his powers of investment a trustee shall have regard – (a) to the need for diversification of investments of the trust, in so far as it is appropriate to the circumstances of the trust; (b) to the suitability to the trust of investments of the description of investment proposed and of the investment proposed as an investment of that description'. The reference to the 'circumstances of the trust' plainly includes matters such as the size of the trust funds: the degree of diversification that is practicable and desirable for a large fund may plainly be impracticable or undesirable (or both) in the case of a small fund.'

Sixth: the principles applied without modification to trusts of pension funds. The defendant had argued that the rules 'had been laid down for private and family trusts and wills a long time ago; that pension funds were very large and affected large numbers of people; that in the present case the well-being of all within the coal industry was affected.' Sir Robert could see

'no reason for holding that different principles apply to pension fund trusts from those which apply to other trusts. Of course, there are many provisions in pension schemes which are not to be found in private trusts, and to these the general law of trusts will be subordinated. But subject to that ... the trusts of pension funds are subject to the same rules as other trusts. The large size of pension funds emphasises the need for diversification, rather than lessening it.'

There are three other, relatively minor, controls. The Superannuation Funds Office of the Inland Revenue approves schemes before they are given tax-free status (see Chapter 9), although this is mainly to ensure that the schemes are genuine and the benefits in accordance with the tax laws. The Revenue's only control over investment is the power to withdraw tax exemption if the fund's activities are deemed to aim at trading profits rather than investment. This power has been rarely, if ever, used.

The Occupational Pensions Board set up under the Social Security Act 1973 supervises schemes; this supervision relates mainly to contracting out of the state's earnings-related scheme, equal opportunities and the rights of early leavers.

Local authority pension funds are subject to additional or more specific regulation. It is stipulated, for example, that in running a fund the authority shall 'have regard – (a) to the need for diversification of investments of fund moneys, (b) to the suitability of investments . . . [and] (c) to proper advice, obtained at reasonable intervals' (The Local Government Superannuation (Amendment) (No. 2) Regulations 1983, p. 2).

The local authority pension funds used to be restricted in the maximum proportions of their assets they could hold in certain classes of investment. They were, for example, required to hold at least 25 per cent of their assets in the 'narrow-range' of assets specified in Parts I or II of the First Schedule of the Trustee Investments Act 1961. This in effect meant gilt-edged stocks, local authority stocks and the stocks of public boards, the dominions and colonies. In addition, deposits with a range of banks and other institutions were included, together with the scheme administered by Local Authorities' Mutual Investment Trust (LAMIT).

The most important current controls, under regulations in force since 1983, are on the proportions of assets that local authority pension funds may hold in unquoted securities. There are four restrictions. First, a fund may not buy unquoted securities in the UK or overseas if they would represent more than 10 per cent of its total investments. Second, it may not buy a single holding that would represent more than 5 per cent of its total investments. The exceptions are, again, the narrow-range of assets specified in the Trustee Investments Act 1961, investment through LAMIT, and deposits with a bank or institution falling within section 2 of the Banking Act 1979. Third, it may not make such a deposit if it would bring deposits (or loans) with a single borrower to above 10 per cent of the fund's total assets. Fourth, it may not lend or deposit funds with a single local authority, including its own sponsoring authority, if it would bring the amount lent or deposited with that authority to more than 10 per cent of the fund's assets.

Investment policy

The impossibility of knowing pension liabilities in money terms and the open-ended performance required of investment managers lie behind the conventional view that pension funds should invest in assets that are inflation-linked and that will grow in real terms – ordinary shares and property – 'the primary objective being the accumulation of the largest sums possible' (Day and Jamieson, 1980, vol. I, p. 51).

Table 3.3 shows that pension funds have indeed accumulated ordinary shares, property and overseas assets. However, they also hold a substantial percentage of their assets in gilt-edged stocks, albeit on a scale that is both proportionately and absolutely smaller than the long-term insurance funds.

Table 3.3 *Pension funds: distribution of portfolios (as at end-December) and acquisitions (years to end-December), 1976–83 (at market values)*

	1976 £m.	1980 £m.	1981 £m.	1982 £m.	1983 £m.
Distribution of portfolios:					
British Government and government-guaranteed stocks					
Up to 5 years	456	270	222	340	788
Over 5 and up to 15 years	478	3,362	3,922	6,538	8,900
Over 15 years and undated	3,226	7,888	7,010	9,016	9,051
Index-linked Treasury stock	–	–	1,327	2,255	3,018
Total	4,160	11,520	12,481	18,249	21,757
As % of total assets	20	21	19	21	20
Total other assets	16,245	43,209	51,699	66,762	85,739
Total current[1]	1,505	2,485	2,571	3,055	4,740
As % of total assets	7	5	4	4	4
Ordinary shares,[2] property,[3] etc.	13,071	37,851	45,271	58,538	74,596
As % of total assets	64	69	71	69	69
Acquisitions:					
British Government and government-guaranteed stocks	1,176	2,083	1,873	1,283	2,565
As % of total acquisitions	40	32	27	19	35
Total other acquisitions	1,796	4,372	4,969	5,362	4,863
All net short-term[1]	–3	–313	299	353	1,329
As % of total	–	–5	4	5	18
Ordinary shares,[2] property,[3] etc.	1,696	4,554	4,232	4,280	3,352
As % of total	57	71	62	64	45

Notes: [1] Cash, Treasury bills, UK local authority bills and temporary money, certificates of deposit, etc., plus net amounts receivable from stockbrokers, income accrued on investments, amounts receivable from the Inland Revenue and other debtors.

[2] Listed, unlisted and overseas plus authorised unit trusts.

[3] Land, property, new buildings in the UK, ground rents in the UK and property unit trusts.

Sources: Financial Statistics; MQ5 Business Monitor.

In addition to the requirement under the Law of Trusts for diversification there are five reasons for a pension fund to hold gilt-edged stocks.

First, until index-linked stocks became available, high coupon, long-dated gilt-edged tended

> to be the yardstick against which other investment media [were] analysed . . . pension funds do look at the relative rates of return . . . and do try to calculate a discounted cash flow rate of return from these outlets . . . calculations made are basically very simple viz for gilts, the DCF rate of return is given by the gross redemption yield. For equities, the DCF calculation is a summation of gross dividend yield plus the estimated rate of growth in dividend. In the case of property, the DCF rate of return will be based upon the initial rental yield plus the expected rate of growth in rental income . . . If interest rates at the long end of the fixed interest market are particularly high then the likely return from equities and property must be high on a comparative basis before investments are made in them (Committee to Review the Functioning of Financial Institutions, 1977–8, vol. 3, p. 135)

When the authorities have needed to be heavy sellers of gilt-edged stock, yields have had to be pushed to levels where pension funds, as one of the largest sources of savings, have been attracted away from other markets. The high level of official sales to the non-bank sector in the years 1976–81 would not otherwise have been possible.

The yardstick has now become index-linked stocks. These provide an asset that is a risk-free match, except for the continued need to estimate the growth in real earnings. The demand for the new yardstick can be expected to depend in part on their yields relative to those on property and ordinary shares. This relationship has not yet had time to develop a history.

The demand by pension funds for conventional gilt-edged stocks, depending in part on the yield gap between ordinary shares and property on the one hand and gilt-edged stocks on the other, parallels that of the long-term insurance funds, although in their case there is the additional constraint that they cannot value their liabilities on an interest rate higher than the current yield on their investments.

Second, although pension funds are designed to relieve the employing organisation of the financial responsibility for pensions, the employers remain *de facto*, and, in many cases where pension arrangements are part of the contract of employment, *de jure*, the ultimate guarantors. If asset growth is over-assumed, or liability growth under-estimated, the parent organisation will have to top up the fund at the expense of its profits. Since the sponsoring organisation is the ultimate guarantor, its attitude towards the risk accepted by its pension fund in the pursuit of higher returns should be crucial. At the one extreme, the lowest risk investment, index-linked stocks, relieves it of most of the residual responsibility, but at the cost of higher contributions; at the other extreme, a portfolio of high-risk ordinary shares or property might, in normal times, provide returns that minimise contributions, but at considerable risk to the sponsor in other exceptional times. Logically, the portfolio will depend on the sponsor's geographical and industrial spread of business or other source of income, the strength of its balance sheet and its willingness to top up the fund. A reduction in economic growth or a squeeze on profitability will affect the ability of the ultimate guarantor to pay. At the same time the squeeze will be affecting the general outlook for dividends and rents, reducing asset values, and increasing the likelihood of such a call. Therefore by permitting its pension fund to invest in UK ordinary shares an industrial company is accepting a double risk. This vulnerability might be reduced by investing in overseas ordinary shares, but developments that affect one industrial economy often affect all simultaneously, with the result that profits and stock-market values move together. In addition many UK industrial companies have a worldwide spread of business and find themselves locked into the same developments in other economies as are the foreign-based competitors in whom their pension funds may be investing.

Third, the ratio of the active labour force to old age pensioners has fallen from 3·4:1 in 1951 to 2·8:1 by 1983, and is expected to fall further to 2·4–2·0:1 at the end of the century (Richardson, 1983, pp. 502–3). The resulting transfer of income from the working population to the elderly takes place irrespective of whether the method is taxation or profits, and is on a growing scale.

There may be circumstances where such a transfer is politically unacceptable, or where pressure groups acting selfishly, but perhaps without conscious intention, ensure that the resources are directed elsewhere. Thus pressure from organised labour for compensating rises in wages protected the real income of the workforce for two years after the rise in oil prices in 1973. As a result the brunt of the transfer of real incomes to the oil producers was felt by corporate profits and those on fixed incomes. The pension funds suffered as dividends were cut, ordinary share values fell and inflation damaged the real value of gilt-edged stocks and their coupons.

This economic shock where one part of the community was able to use its industrial power to shift the cost of adjustment on to others typifies the kind of problem that pension funds will experience in ensuring a smooth and socially acceptable transfer of real income from the workforce as the dependent population increases. A wide selection of investments is one protection, spreading the method and incidence of transfer: transfer via rents and dividends; transfers from overseas workforces via overseas ordinary shares and bonds; and transfer of tax revenues via holdings of gilt-edged and index-linked stocks.

Fourth, it might be argued that in circumstances where there is a deflation of demand and output, with a reduction in profits, dividends and rents, there will also be a reduction in the price level. Although a reduction in pension payments in money terms would be justified,

> This cannot be taken to too great an extreme . . . in that a fall in the value of such investment, even if combined with a fall in the cost of living, cannot be reflected too closely in individual pensions – most people have at least some fixed commitments. Therefore most pension funds will tend to hold a proportion of the assets in fixed interest. (Day and Jamieson, 1980, vol. I, p. 51)

Fifth, a fund that is mature or declining has negative cash flow. Since payments to pensioners cannot be met from cash flow when asset values or investment income are temporarily depressed the fund will need the guarantee of a fixed income, and definite maturity date and proceeds, provided by gilt-edged stocks.

Insurance – general business

Liabilities
General insurance covers risks such as fire, theft, motor accidents, industrial injuries and product liability.

These liabilities are normally short. Premiums are usually paid annually and the liability of the insurer ceases at the end of the relevant year. Claims relating to the insured period will continue to be settled after the end of the year of the insurer's liability, but most claims will have been settled within the following two years.

Some liabilities are considerably longer. It can take several years to settle claims where liability is contested or where the extent or existence of damage is slow to be known. Examples are product liability, personal injury, or employee accident insurance. The liabilities of reinsurance groups are longer than those of direct insurers.

Supervision
The Insurance Companies Act 1982 requires that the assets of an insurer exceed its liabilities, other than liabilities to shareholders, by a solvency margin that is in proportion to premium income. The valuation of assets for the calculation of this margin is governed by the Insurance Companies (Valuation of Assets) Regulations, 1981. These regulations accept market prices, where available, as the basis for the annual returns made to the Department of Trade and Industry.

Investment policy

The constraints on insurers' investment are based on commercial prudence and the need to meet these supervisory requirements. As with most investment, it is necessary to resolve conflicting needs (see Table 3.4).

Table 3.4 *General insurance funds: distribution of portfolios (as at end-December) and acquisitions (years to end-December), 1976–83 (at market values)*

	1976 £m.	1980 £m.	1981 £m.	1982 £m.	1983 £m.
Distribution of portfolios:					
British Government and government-guaranteed stocks					
Up to 5 years	620	1,101	1,179	1,428	1,617
Over 5 and up to 15 years	234	1,113	1,561	2,358	2,832
Over 15 years and undated	205	563	481	383	324
Index-linked Treasury stocks	–	–	–	88	124
Total	1,058	2,777	3,221	4,257	4,897
As % of total assets	19	24	25	26	26
Total other assets	4,404	8,911	10,095	12,101	14,095
Total current[1]	993	1,420	1,694	1,727	2,196
As % of total assets	18	12	13	11	12
Ordinary shares,[2] property,[3] etc.	1,597	3,930	4,461	5,254	6,160
As % of total assets	29	34	34	33	33
Acquisitions:					
British Government and government-guaranteed stocks	288	433	703	66	288
As % of total acquisitions	41	56	53	19	37
Total other acquisitions	416	340	619	278	487
All current[1]	175	–60	205	–39	408
As % of total	25	–8	16	–11	53
Ordinary shares,[2] property,[3] etc.	90	164	262	30	56
As % of total	13	21	20	9	7

Notes: [1] Cash, Treasury bills, UK local authority bills and temporary money, certificates of deposit, etc., plus net amounts due to stockbrokers and sums receivable from the Inland Revenue and other debtors.
[2] Listed, unlisted, overseas and authorised unit trust units.
[3] Land, property, new buildings and ground rents.

Sources: Financial Statistics; MQ5 Business Monitor.

The short-term nature of most liabilities points to an emphasis on money-certain assets with high liquidity such as bank deposits, Treasury bills and very short-dated gilt-edged stocks. However, it is often considered proper that investment be made on the assumption that the business will be a continuing concern. This means that the premium income can be treated as a method of paying claims, with the capital and reserves being held available to meet fluctuations in the balance between premiums and payments.

This approach is necessary since the real value of assets needs to be protected from inflation. This is for two reasons. First, if the business is to continue, its solvency margin must be maintained. Since premium income can be assumed to rise with inflation, assets must also rise, or additional resources be obtained from retained profits or the shareholders. Second, the delay between the receipt of premiums and the settlement of claims on some of the longer liability policies means that inflation will have affected the size of the final payment.

The need to protect income levels has emerged during the last few years as an additional constraint. The insurer has the use of the premiums until payment is made on claims and the policy holder expects that the level of premiums should reflect the benefit the insurer is deriving from these, just as the policy holder in a life fund expects his premiums to be returned with interest when his policy matures. Competition has forced down premiums so that many insurers lose money on their underwriting business. A sharp fall in interest rates would reduce income on this float of premiums if assets were held in bank deposits or short-dated paper. Competition therefore pushes insurers into holding longer-dated and more volatile stocks and away from low-income index-linked stocks.

The extent to which an insurer can buy inflation-protected assets such as equities and property, with their greater price uncertainty, depends on the generosity of its capitalisation. A large solvency margin enables an insurer to risk holding assets with high short-term volatility and thus protect its ability to continue insuring the same volume of business in the longer term. A smaller margin may mean conservative investment and contraction in the longer term, or perhaps being forced to protect its solvency margin, if market prices fall, by selling its portfolio at an unsuitable moment.

The part played by gilt-edged stocks in a general insurer's portfolio may be summarised as:

- a liquid and relatively price-certain asset enabling other investments to be made in less liquid assets such as equities and property;
- a range of maturities with differing volatilities which may be adjusted with changes in the value of other assets, the solvency margin and the ability or willingness to accept price risk;
- stability of income if interest rates fall.

4 The Investor: others

Building societies

Building societies are mutual organisations that take retail savings deposits and lend most of them to individuals buying their own homes.

Societies keep a proportion of their assets in liquid investments in case of a temporary excess of withdrawals over deposits and to supply working capital. Investments may also expand temporarily during periods of reduced mortgage demand. The Building Societies (Designation for Trustee Investment) Regulations 1972 require that a society qualifying for trustee status must hold a ratio of liquid assets to total assets of at least 7½ per cent. Membership of the Building Societies Association (BSA) has a similar requirement. Table 4.1 makes clear that this ratio is normally much higher.

The societies pay a special rate of corporation tax of 40 per cent on any profits, or surpluses, earned during a year; the balance is added to reserves. Commercial prudence, continued qualification for trustee status and membership of the BSA require that reserves grow in line with the societies' assets.

The societies thus have a twofold need: they require liquid assets in case withdrawals exceed new deposits, and they need to earn a high return on their investments so that they can add to their reserves and maintain their solvency margins. The latter aim must be consistent with prudence and the shape of a society's business; for example, there is a greater need for money-certain assets in a small society than there is in a large one which can expect a more even experience in the balance between withdrawals and deposits. The need for liquidity, the possibility of capital gains if yields fall and, usually, the existence of higher yields on longer-dated fixed-interest than on short-term deposits make the gilt-edged market attractive for societies' reserves and liquidity.

The extent to which societies can succumb to the temptation of higher yields in the longer maturities of the gilt-edged market is controlled by the authorities. The Building Societies (Authorised Investments) (No. 2) Order 1977 made under the Building Societies Act 1962 by the Chief Registrar of Friendly Societies permits only specified proportions of assets to be held in investments of varying price uncertainty. 'The purpose . . . is to ensure that building societies have sufficient liquidity which can be readily realised to meet short-term needs and to ensure that there should be no risk of significant capital loss on any of the securities held' (Committee to Review the Functioning of Financial Institutions, 1979, vol. III, p. 5).

Table 4.1   *Building societies: holdings of short-term assets (as at end-December) and acquisitions (years to end-December), 1976–83*

	1976 £m.	1980 £m.	1981 £m.	1982 £m.	1983 £m.
Holdings:[1]					
Total assets	28,132	54,317	62,147	74,485	87,190
Short-term assets and investments	5,160	10,557	11,833	15,894	17,595
As % of total assets	18	19	19	21	20
of which,					
British Government and government-guaranteed stocks					
Up to 5 years	1,936[2]	4,065	4,708	6,655	8,708
Over 5 and up to 15 years	339[2]	902	1,459	2,244	1,319
Over 15 and up to 25 years	13[2]	2	2	22	22
Total	2,288[2]	4,969	6,169	8,921	10,049
As % of total assets	8	9	10	12	12
Other short-term assets and investments	3,085[1]	5,588	5,664	6,973	7,546
Acquisitions:[3]					
British Government and government-guaranteed stocks					
Up to 5 years	67	383	702	777	370
Over 5 and up to 15 years	102	491	549	674	818
Over 15 and up to 25 years	3	−1	0	20	0
Total	172	873	1,251	1,471	1,188

Notes: [1] Book values.
[2] Nominal values. 'Total' holdings of gilt-edged stocks plus 'other short-term assets and investments' do not add up to 'short-term assets and investments' because the latter uses gilt-edged stocks at book value.
[3] Cash values.

Source: Financial Statistics.

The Order requires that the first $7\frac{1}{2}$ per cent of a society's assets be held as cash, as a current account deposit in a bank or in certificates of tax deposit, national savings paper, Treasury bills, local authority bills, short-term local authority deposits and various marketable public sector or quasi-public sector securities with a maturity of not more than five years. The second $7\frac{1}{2}$ per cent can be held in longer local authority deposits and the various marketable public sector and quasi-public sector securities included in the first 7½ per cent, but with a maturity of not more than fifteen years.

Thereafter a society can invest in yet longer local authority deposits and the same categories of public sector marketable securities with a maturity of not more than twenty-five years.

The Regulations are intended to control two risks: the possibility of a default by the borrower is minimised by the limitation of investments to public sector and quasi-public sector paper; the possibility of fluctuations in the value of marketable securities is limited by the proportion of a given maturity, and therefore volatility, that may be held. Within these constraints the societies are free to invest so as to produce their preferred mixture of liquidity, money-certainty and net return.

Trustee Savings Banks

The Trustee Savings Banks (TSBs) consist of sixteen regional unincorporated societies managed by local boards of trustees providing banking and savings services to the personal sector. Until 1976 they acted as savings banks with strict Treasury control over their investments, which were held mainly in a range of marketable and non-marketable public sector securities and as deposits with the National Debt Commissioners. The Trustee Savings Banks Act 1976 relaxed these controls and enabled the banks to begin transforming themselves into a competitive commercial organisation providing the full range of customer services. Until 1 January 1982, TSBs were included in the non-bank private sector; they then became part of the monetary sector. It is intended that the TSB Group will become a publicly quoted company in due course. It will then consist of the original sixteen banks grouped to provide a single new bank offering normal banking facilities.

The TSBs' holdings of gilt-edged stocks reflect these origins as savings institutions and the stage they have reached in their evolution into a regular bank (see Table 4.2).

The Treasury has powers under the Trustee Savings Banks Act 1981, s. 20, to direct the TSBs to hold minimum specified assets of two classes in proportion to their liabilities to depositors. The first class includes money and near-money instruments such as seven-day bank deposits, Treasury bills and gilt-edged stocks within one year of their final redemption date. The second class is the balance of assets needed to cover deposit liabilities. It includes the money and near-money instruments included in the first class plus, amongst other longer instruments, gilt-edged stocks of whatever maturity. At 31 December 1983 the Treasury required the TSBs to hold in the first class of asset the equivalent of 20 per cent of sums due to depositors.

The TSBs are also indirect holders of gilt-edged stock through an agreement to hold deposits with the Debt Commissioners. These deposits are included in both of the two classes of investment under the 1981 Act and are the remaining assets of the TSB Ordinary Department, abolished in 1979. Until then this department was required to hold all its assets, except working balances, with the Debt Commissioners; after 1979 the funds became part of the TSBs' overall assets. The deposits are repayable in cash, at the option of the TSBs, in six-monthly instalments; the final payment is due on 20 November 1986. The investment of the Fund for the Banks for Savings is discussed in Chapter 2.

Table 4.2   *Trustee Savings Banks: distribution of portfolios, 1981–3 (market values as at 20 November)*

	1981 £m.	1982 £m.	1983 £m.
Total assets	7,889	8,335	9,129
British Government and			
government-guaranteed stocks	2,005	1,959	1,884
As % of assets	25	24	21
Up to 1 year	492	578	266
As % of total assets	6	7	3
Deposits with the National Debt			
Commissioners	1,066	880	666
As % of total assets	14	11	7

Note: Excludes net assets of the life insurance fund.

Source: TSB *Group Reports.*

The Treasury's powers, and the agreement with the Debt Commissioners, have an additional purpose. The Ordinary Department had built up considerable deposits with the Debt Commissioners during its existence as a savings bank. At the same time the remaining department (the Special Investment Department or 'new department') had built up large directly owned holdings of stock. Moreover, these holdings were long dated by the standards of a conventional bank. This was an inheritance from the 1960s and early 1970s when the need to offer competitive interest rates on deposits had pushed investments longer. The arrangements are aimed at ensuring that the TSBs do not produce avoidable shocks in the financial system, and especially the gilt-edged market, as assets are rearranged in the process of transformation from savings institutions to a regular member of the banking system. At the same time the pull to maturity is curing the problem of an over-long portfolio bought at higher prices, whilst liability growth and a lengthy period for adjustment is reducing proportionate exposure to gilt-edged stocks.

Investment trusts (see Table 4.3)

Investment trusts are limited liability companies, incorporated under the Companies Act, which invest money subscribed by the public. Unlike unit trusts they are closed-ended. They are not subject to any special DTI regulation.

An investment trust normally seeks approval by the Inland Revenue; in this case it must meet the criteria in the Income and Corporation Taxes Act 1970 and the Finance Act 1972. These include a Stock Exchange quotation, income derived mainly from holdings of shares and securities, and rules on the spread of investments. It is also required that surpluses obtained from sales of investments be retained in the business and not distributed as dividends.

Table 4.3 *Investment trusts: distribution of portfolios (as at end-December) and acquisitions (years to end-December), 1976–83*

	1976 £m.	1980 £m.	1981 £m.	1982 £m.	1983 £m.
Distribution of portfolios:					
British Government and government-guaranteed stocks					
Up to 5 years		61	53	58	84
Over 5 and up to 15 years		87	58	95	125
Over 15 years and undated		188	72	46	101
Total	164	266	183	199	310
As % of total assets	3	3	2	2	2
Total other investments	5,902	8,086	8,721	9,852	13,061
As % of total investments	97	97	98	98	98
Acquisitions:					
Total	−8	82	−33	208	261
British Government and government-guaranteed stocks	6	−47	−54	−3	127

Source: Financial Statistics.

Investment trusts aim to provide their shareholders with a steady, secure and increasing income and capital value over the long term.

The role of gilt-edged holdings is therefore twofold: first, to increase the average yield on portfolios that are mainly in low-yielding ordinary shares; second, to enable steadily increasing dividends to be declared from income.

Unit trusts (see Table 4.4)

Unit trusts are open-ended funds in which the subscriber receives units in proportion to his contribution and acquires a fractional interest in the assets and income. In this way the subscriber obtains a share of a much larger and more diversified portfolio than would be possible if he invested as an individual.

Until 1980, unit trusts specialising in fixed-interest stocks were discouraged by their tax treatment. An authorised unit trust was subject to corporation tax, rather than income tax and capital gains tax (CGT). Dividends from UK companies were franked – that is, exempt from corporation tax in the hands of the trust – but corporation tax was payable on income from gilt-edged stocks and on other interest.

The Finance Act 1980, s. 60, reduced the tax payable by trusts receiving interest payments from the corporation rate to the basic rate. At the same time such trusts participated in the introduction of the general exemption of authorised unit trusts from CGT, which became payable only by the underlying holder on profits made on disposal of units.

Table 4.4   *Unit trusts: holdings of gilt-edged stocks, 1976–83 (market values as at end-December)*

	1976 £m.	1980 £m.	1981 £m.	1982 £m.	1983 £m.
Holdings of British Government and government-guaranteed stocks	32	72	175	322	415

Source: Financial Statistics.

These trusts are run by many of the major management groups, including insurance companies and merchant banks. Units are valued and published frequently, often daily, allowing performance to be monitored closely. Managers tend to be aggressive in their approach to the market and to use to the full the freedom provided by their exemption from CGT.

Overseas residents

Overseas residents' holdings of gilt-edged stocks are broken down in the official statistics into those of international organisations, central monetary institutions (CMIs), and 'others'. Acquisitions are divided into CMIs and 'others' (see Table 4.5). Details of the sectoral and geographical spread of holdings are few. Thus the holdings' behaviour and the reasons for investment cannot be identified in the manner of the domestic sectors.

Table 4.5 *Overseas residents: holdings (as at end-March) and acquisitions (years to end-March) of British Government and government-guaranteed stocks, 1977–84 (market values)*

	1977 £m.	1980 £m.	1981 £m.	1982 £m.	1983 £m.	1984 £m.
Holdings:						
International organisations	76	250	300	373	463	624
Central monetary institutions	937	1,032	1,905	2,439	2,452	2,635
Other	1,508	3,110	4,215	4,091	4,798	6,234
Total	2,521	4,392	6,420	6,903	7,713	9,493
As % of total market holdings	8	9	10	10	9	9
Acquisitions:						
Central monetary institutions	−141	422	825	147	−3	250
Other	467	665	688	64	662	936
Total	326	1,087	1,513	211	659	1,186

Source: articles in the annual series on the national debt in the *BEQB*.

Central monetary institutions

CMIs comprise overseas central banks and currency boards. They hold gilt-edged stocks as part of their official foreign currency reserves or as backing for note issues. The attractions include political and social stability, marketability, and yield. As Table 4.6 makes clear they mainly hold shorter stocks. Some governments, especially oil exporters, have long-term investment arms; these bodies purchase longer-dated stocks than the central banks; they tend not to buy stocks longer than fifteen years.

Overseas governments and other public borrowers also hold matching gilt-edged stocks with sinking fund money accumulated to pay off publicly issued debt or other sterling liabilities. This source of demand has steadily contracted during the last fifteen years as issues have matured and have not been replaced by new borrowings.

CMIs and their investment arms either administer their portfolios themselves, dealing direct with brokers on a discretionary basis, or have them managed in London by banks, brokers or the Crown Agents, who manage many of the holdings of the smaller ex-colonial territories.

Table 4.6   *Overseas residents: holdings of British Government and government-guaranteed stocks by maturity, 1977–84 (nominal values as at end-March)*

	Up to 5 years	Over 5 years and up to 15 years	Over 15 years and undated
1977:			
International organisations	19	60	–
Central monetary institutions	607	170	231
Other	415	248	1,128
Total	1,041	478	1,359
1980:			
International organisations	209	72	–
Central monetary institutions	627	268	323
Other	890	1,046	1,926
Total	1,726	1,386	2,249
1981:			
International organisations	211	155	–
Central monetary institutions	1,352	427	308
Other	265	2,601	2,132
Total	1,828	3,183	2,440
1982:			
International organisations	359	32	–
Central monetary institutions	1,495	947	229
Other	434	3,316	878
Total	2,288	4,295	1,107
1983:			
International organisations	366	105	–
Central monetary institutions	1,443	917	109
Other	466	3,368	866
Total	2,275	4,390	975
1984:			
International organisations	542	60	–
Central monetary institutions	1,475	1,011	113
Other	464	5,132	378
Total	2,481	6,203	491

Source: articles in the annual series on the national debt in the *BEQB*.

International organisations
International organisations include the EEC and its affiliated institutions, UN agencies and regional development banks. They own gilt-edged stocks for the same reasons as CMIs, but in shorter maturities; in many cases they are restricted in the terms they can buy. They tend to deal directly with brokers in London.

Others
General insurance and reinsurance companies are required by the DTI to hold sterling assets against their UK insurance liabilities. Gilt-edged stocks, usually in the shorter part of the market, are often bought and placed on deposit as a convenient, marketable, high-yielding asset acceptable to the Department.

Swiss banks have large holdings, assumed to have been bought on account of clients. It is assumed that the bulk of these are held on behalf of rich non-Swiss individuals taking advantage of the secrecy legally permitted to Swiss banks.

Other overseas holders include overseas pension funds, commercial and industrial companies, oil companies and banks using their own resources.

Personal sector

The personal sector includes unincorporated businesses (such as farmers, accountants and solicitors), jobbers, churches, charities, universities and trade unions, as well as individuals and trusts. There is also a residual category, which includes holders who cannot be identified and allocated to the other categories, usually because the ultimate beneficiary is shielded by a nominee name. The residual item will include some holders who should be allocated to the personal sector; the data in Table 4.7 should therefore be treated with caution.

The personal sector includes both those who pay no tax on income and those who pay 60 per cent. It also includes those who have a preference for a guaranteed income, even at the price of capital instability, and those who have a preference for capital stability. Holdings are therefore spread over the full range of coupons and maturities, with the centre of gravity in 1984 in five–fifteen-year stocks.

If a trust fund has no specific investment instructions in its deed, it is obliged to invest in accordance with the Trustee Investments Act 1961. This requires that the fund be split into two equal parts and invested in a 'narrower-range' of securities and a 'wider-range'. The narrower-range includes national savings, gilt-edged stocks and quasi-public sector debt, which may be either quoted or unquoted. Although a trust may invest all its assets in the narrower-range, it may not invest more than half its assets in the wider-range.

Table 4.7   *Personal sector: holdings of gilt-edged stocks, 1977–84 (market values as at end-March)*

	1977 £m.	1980 £m.	1981 £m.	1982 £m.	1983 £m.	1984 £m.
Public Trustee and various non-corporate bodies[1]	200	277	347	354	413	445
Individuals and private trusts[2]	5,926	8,045	10,302	10,896	12,681	13,002
Total	6,126	8,322	10,649	11,250	13,094	13,447
As % of total market holdings	20	17	16	16	15	13

Notes: [1] 'Comprises a few identified holders, in particular the Public Trustee, the Church Commissioners, and the Official Custodian for Charities' (*BEQB*, December 1983, p. 519).
[2] 'The accuracy of the analysis is impaired by the large number of nominee accounts, which conceal the identity of the beneficial owners. The figures ... also include an estimate of private holdings on the national savings stock register' (*BEQB*, December 1983, p. 519).

Source: articles in the annual series on the national debt in the *BEQB*.

Industrial and commercial companies

Industrial and commercial companies are unimportant holders of gilt-edged stocks (see Table 4.8). They own them for two main reasons: first, to maximise the return from liquid assets as part of the overall treasury function of liability and asset management; second, to hedge long fixed-interest liabilities, whether in bank borrowings or publicly quoted debt.

Table 4.8   *Industrial and commercial companies: holdings of gilt-edged stocks, 1977–84 (book values as at end-March)*

	1977 £m.	1980 £m.	1981 £m.	1982 £m.	1983 £m.	1984 £m.
Holdings[1] of British Government and government-guaranteed stocks	286[2]	556[2]	1,090	997	1,110	1,520
As % of total market holdings	1	1	1	1	1	2

Notes: [1] 'Holdings of gilt-edged stocks [since 1981] are based on quarterly returns to the Department of Industry by about 200 large companies, grossed up roughly to give a broad estimate for all industrial and commercial companies. The holdings are at book values (generally purchase values) and no attempt has been made to convert them to nominal or market values' (*BEQB*, December 1983, p. 519).
[2] Not comparable with later years. It covers 200 large companies making returns to the Department of Industry, with no grossing up to give an estimate for the whole sector.

Source: articles in the annual series on the national debt in the *BEQB*.

Monetary sector, excluding the discount market

The 'monetary sector' was introduced in 1981 and includes retail banks, accepting houses, other British banks, overseas and consortium banks, the National Girobank, the Trustee Savings Banks and the Banking Department of the Bank of England. Their holdings of gilt-edged stocks are shown in Table 4.9.

Table 4.9 *Monetary sector: holdings of gilt-edged stocks, 1976–84 (market values as at mid-December make-up day)*

	1976 £m.	1980 £m.	1981 £m.	1982 £m.	1983 £m.	1984 £m.
Holdings of British Government and government-guaranteed stocks						
0–1 year	517	782	505	–	–	–
1–5 years	1,422	2,088	2,355	–	–	–
Over 5 years and undated	381	1,152	1,287	–	–	–
Total	2,320	4,022	4,147	4,231	6,618	6,696

Note: Years are not comparable because there have been several breaks in the series.
Source: BEQB.

Banks hold gilt-edged stocks as part of their portfolios of short-term assets to meet supervisory requirements for diversity and marketability in their holdings of liquid assets and to protect against a fall in interest rates that would reduce the profitability of their current account liabilities. Commercial prudence and the Bank of England's supervisory requirements dictate that each bank hold liquid assets of varying maturities in relation to the size and maturity of their liabilities. The amount they need to hold depends on the assets' marketability and price certainty. A deep market, including many holders with differing needs, increases the amount of paper that can be sold for cash at a given price. Thus the Bank's paper on the measurement of liquidity for supervisory purposes says:

> The treatment of marketable assets takes account of the extent to which they can be sold for cash quickly (or used as security for borrowing), incurring little or no cost penalty; and of any credit or investment risks which may make their potential value less predictable. It is important that the market for the asset should be sufficiently deep to ensure a stable demand for it. An important factor in this is the willingness of the central bank to use the asset in its normal market operations. (*BEQB*, September 1982, p. 400)

The discounts the Bank applies to different assets and maturities when measuring a bank's liquidity take into account the quality of gilt-edged stocks as a credit risk and the depth of their market in comparison with other instruments. The discounts applied are:

Nil discount	Treasury, eligible local authority and eligible bank bills. This means such paper with a maximum maturity of three months. Government and government-guaranteed marketable securities with less than twelve months remaining term to maturity.
5% discount	Other bills and certificates of deposit with less than six months remaining term to maturity. Other government, government-guaranteed and local authority marketable securities with less than five years remaining term to maturity or at variable rates.
10% discount	Other bills, certificates of deposit and floating rate notes with less than five years remaining term to maturity. Other government, government-guaranteed and local authority marketable debt with more than five years remaining term to maturity.
Discount to be determined	All other marketable assets.

(*BEQB*, September 1982, p. 402)

This approach to supervision means that a bank's resources can buy a longer portfolio of acceptable liquid assets, or more such assets of a given maturity, in the form of gilt-edged stocks than in the form of other paper. Thus the resource cost of adopting an aggressive posture if interest rates are expected to fall is minimised.

The Bank of England also aims to ensure that 'banks' management policies apply a prudent mix of . . . forms of liquidity'. The mix includes cash, liquifiable paper of varying price-certainty, flows from maturing assets and a 'diversified deposit base in terms both of maturities and range of counterparties' (*BEQB*, September 1982, p. 399). This is interpreted to mean that some gilt-edged should always be held in the liquid asset portfolio, even if interest rates are expected to rise, and that they should include a range of maturities so there is a continuous flow into cash.

The deposit banks have large current account liabilities on which they pay no interest. Such interest-free resources are clearly most valuable when interest rates are high. Banks seek to reduce the effect of falling interest rates on this source of profit by buying longer-dated assets, locking in a high fixed income. The resource cost and the ease with which large positions can be adopted has made gilt-edged stocks the primary vehicle for such hedging.

Discount market

The ten discount houses that are members of the London Discount Market Association stand between the Bank of England and the banking system. They are the major conduit by which the authorities change the supply of cash to the banks; the authorities do this by dealing with the discount houses, buying and selling money market paper. The interest rate at which the authorities 'intervene' is an important signal of official intentions for monetary policy.

The mechanism that connects the Bank of England and the banking system via the discount market includes a requirement that each bank keep deposits with the discount market in accordance with the size of certain specified liabilities. The market finds additional resources by taking deposits from both the banking system and other sectors. The discount houses use these resources to buy assets such as Treasury, local authority and commercial bills and CDs.

They make part of their income from the difference between the cost of their liabilities and the yields on money market assets. This often involves mismatching – liabilities are shorter than assets. They also seek to maximise their return on capital by holding longer assets when interest rates are expected to fall. Since gilt-edged stocks are the only really marketable security with a maturity of over a year they are used as the vehicle for these speculations (see Table 4.10).

Table 4.10 *Discount market: holdings of gilt-edged stocks, 1976–84 (market values as at mid-December make-up day)*

	1976 £m.	1980 £m.	1981 £m.	1982 £m.	1983 £m.	1984 £m.
Holdings of British Government and government-guaranteed stocks						
0–1 year	5	61	174	236	–	–
1–5 years	217	838	533	265	–	–
Over 5 years and undated	39	57	35	54	–	–
Total	261	956	742	555	364	401
Change in year	+165	+202	–214	–187	–191	+37

Source: BEQB.

Prudent management and official supervision ensure that the holdings of longer and riskier assets are consistent with capital resources. The supervisory system takes into account an asset's length and marketability: price-uncertainty, and therefore the need for supporting risk capital, increases with length and the narrowness of the market. 'Experience suggests that investment risk increases with the term to maturity of the asset and that forced sale risk is less for holdings of gilt-edged stocks than for other assets of comparable maturity' (*BEQB*, June 1982, p. 209).

The risk classification of assets is detailed in 'Prudential arrangements for the discount market' (*BEQB*, June 1982, pp. 209–11). This shows that a discount house can take a longer position for a given amount of risk capital in gilt-edged stock than it can take in any other asset. For example, the rules equate the risk of holding three–six-month certificates of deposit with that of holding a three–eighteen-month gilt-edged stock or of holding a one–three-year certificate of deposit with holding an eighteen-month–five-year gilt-edged stock.

5   The Market Place

The structure of the market in which existing gilt-edged issues are traded and in which the authorities operate using the techniques described in Chapters 6 and 7 is to change radically in 1986.

The existing structure relies on members of The Stock Exchange acting in only one of two capacities. The jobber acts as a principal, buying and selling stock on his own account. He is rewarded by the 'turn' – the difference between his buying and selling price – and by correct judgement of market movements. The broker deals with the jobber, buying and selling stock as an agent on the instructions of investors – the individuals, banks, insurance companies and pension funds described in Chapters 3 and 4. Brokers also provide a range of other services – research, portfolio advice and market intelligence. With limited exceptions, Stock Exchange rules forbid jobbers from transacting business directly with investors and brokers from transacting business on their own account. Thus business is channelled to a jobber. To ensure that the broker has no reason to break the rules and carry out transactions on his own account, The Stock Exchange requires him to charge a fixed minimum commission on medium- and long-dated stocks. Competition ensures that this minimum is also the maximum, except on very small bargains. Commissions on short-dated stocks are at the discretion of the broker.

The system, commonly known as 'single capacity' since each participant may act in only one role, originated at the beginning of the century at a time when the number of brokers was growing faster than the volume of business. Competition was forcing down commissions and the large brokers were winning business from the smaller. Competition was also leading large brokers to earn two commissions by taking their business to outside commission-paying houses (mainly overseas banks) instead of channelling it to the jobbers; business was sometimes transacted with outside houses even when prices were worse for the investor. This diversion of business outside The Stock Exchange was in turn putting pressure on jobbers to transact business directly with the investor.

Rules enforcing single capacity came into effect in February 1909; jobbers were forbidden to deal directly with the investor and, as a *quid pro quo*, brokers had to show all their business to the jobbers. Specifically, members could not carry on business in the 'double capacity of Broker and Dealer' (Rule 75); a broker was forbidden to 'receive brokerage from more than one Principal on a transaction carried through directly between two Principals, and the contract note shall state that the bargain has been done between Non-members' (Rule 75b); and brokers could not transact business with a non-member unless he could 'deal for his Principal to greater advantage [a better price] than with a Member' (Rule 75c). Minimum commissions were introduced in 1912 when it was found that jobbers were circumventing the 1909 rules by dealing directly with investors and booking the bargains through 'dummy brokers'. These charged little or no commission, income being derived entirely from the profit on the jobber's transaction. Fixed commissions put genuine and dummy brokers in the same competitive position vis-à-vis the jobbers and thus made the latter redundant.

Although the rules were introduced as a restriction to protect members from price competition they have advantages for the investor. These were increasingly emphasised by The Stock Exchange as the legality of the rules came under pressure in the late 1970s and early 1980s from action taken under the restrictive practices legislation.

The system can be defended on two grounds. First, the potential for conflict between the interests of a member and an investor is minimised. The broker is an agent with no financial interest in the price at which a transaction is carried out and will therefore transact the bargain at the best price for the client. Since he does not run a book and has no interest in which direction a price moves he can give disinterested advice. The jobber, on the other hand, does run a book; he has an interest in ensuring the investor pays the highest price when buying and obtains the lowest price when selling. He also has a position – he is long or short of stock – and cannot give disinterested advice. The investor is protected, however, since the jobber is not allowed to carry out a transaction directly with him. Second, it is argued that the single capacity system is self-policing. Every transaction involves two independent parties – a jobber and a broker. There are two large jobbers in the gilt-edged market and others who will deal in half a million pounds of stock. This ensures competitive price making. A system where the investor deals with an entity that simultaneously gives advice, receives orders and carries out transactions would have neither of these two safeguards (Committee to Review the Functioning of Financial Institutions, 1980a, pp. 102–3).

The core of the new market structure will be about two dozen 'market makers' who will be members of The Stock Exchange. They will be able to transact business directly with the investment institutions, buying and selling stock on their own account. They will have dual capacity since they will include the function of jobber and broker within a single business. There will be several different kinds of market maker. Some will operate on the floor of The Stock Exchange, making prices to other members in the same manner as the pre-1986 jobber. It is probable that in the main these will transact the business of the small institutions and private individuals who may continue to use brokers as intermediaries. Some may deal on the telephone in a relatively limited range of stocks; they might confine themselves, for example, to the shorter-dated maturities. Others, who will see the major part of the business, will deal on the telephone in the full range of sterling debt instruments – conventional gilt-edged stocks, index-linked stocks, futures, bulldogs, loan stocks, debentures, gilt-edged options and Treasury, local authority and eligible bank bills.

The market makers will be linked by a system of visual display units (screens) run by inter-dealer brokers (IDBs). Market makers will be able to show bids and offers of stock on the screens. This will enable them to transact business with other market makers, but since the IDB stands as principal between the two market makers, they will remain anonymous to each other. In this way the new system will have an important attribute that is missing from the pre-1986 market where the two major jobbers rarely deal with each other since they would disclose the state of their books to a competitor. As a result the jobber has to quote a price that will compensate him for the entire price risk of a transaction with no possibility of passing the position on to others at his own initiative.

The market makers will have one fundamental obligation. They will have to quote realistic and continuous two-way prices, standing ready to buy and sell stock irrespective of the state of the market. In this way the investing public will be provided with liquidity at all times. A subsidiary obligation will be to make prices impartially to all member firms other than other market makers, money brokers or IDBs.

In return for providing this continuous liquidity market makers will be given five privileges.

First, and most important, they will have a direct dealing relationship with the Issue Department of the Bank of England – the largest and most powerful single participant in the market. They will be the conduit for open-market operations and will have better information on the Bank's activities than other participants. Specifically, the Issue Department will be prepared:

(i)   to receive directly from market makers – just before the official market opening or at any time during the normal day – outright bids for stock, including particularly tap stocks, which it may have in its portfolio: the Bank will respond to such bids entirely at its discretion;

(ii)   at its discretion to undertake switches of stock proposed to it by market makers on such terms as it may agree;

(iii)   to bid a price of its own choosing for stock with three months or less to maturity offered to it by market makers;

(iv)   to bid a price of its own choosing for index-linked stock offered to it by market makers;

(v)   at its discretion to purchase outright, at prices of its own choosing, other stock that may be offered to it by market makers. The Bank expects to exercise this discretion more liberally for stocks with between three and twelve months to maturity than for other stocks. (Bank of England, 1984, p. 2.)

Second, market makers will be able to borrow and lend stock through Stock Exchange money brokers in the same manner as the pre-1986 jobbers. A market maker needs this facility so that it can be long (borrowing money on the security of stock) or short (borrowing stock in return for a deposit of money). Without this facility a market maker would be unable to deal in a stock unless it already owned it and it possessed the capital to finance the entire position. The lenders of stock are the major investment institutions who would find their tax positions compromised (see Chapter 9) if a loan or recovery of stock were to be treated as a disposal or acquisition for tax purposes. However, the Inland Revenue will not treat the loan and recovery of stock as a disposal or acquisition provided the lender is approved, the loan is arranged through an approved Stock Exchange money broker and the borrower is approved. A market maker, in common with the pre-1986 jobber, will be an approved borrower.

Third, a market maker will have two tax arrangements similar to those available to jobbers. It will be exempt from the Income and Corporation Taxes Act 1970 (s. 472 (i)) and will be able to claim relief for the full dividend when it buys a stock cum-dividend and sells it ex-dividend, regardless of the interval between the two transactions. It will be able to offset for tax purposes dividends paid on the stock it has purchased against dividends it has had to pay out on stock it has sold.

Fourth, the market maker will have privileged borrowing facilities. The Bank will lend up to maximum amounts related to a market maker's capital and reserves. Loans by monetary sector institutions to market makers will be treated by the Bank as a high-quality risk with a low weighting when determining capital adequacy. Secured loans at call or overnight by monetary sector institutions to market makers or Stock Exchange money brokers will continue to count as an offset when calculating banks' eligible liabilities.

Fifth, market makers will be the only participants to have access to the screens and dealing facilities of the IDBs. They will thus be able to deal at the finest prices and have superior information on market activity. Other participants will have access to prices only at the discretion of the market makers, who will provide them on screens, over the telephone or on the floor of The Stock Exchange.

The new system is expected to have four advantages. First, a greater number of market makers will intensify competition and narrow price spreads – the difference between the quoted buying and selling prices for a stock. Second, there will be no commissions paid to market makers. This, with the narrower price spreads, will reduce the cost of dealing for the investor. Third, the new system is similar to that in other government bond markets, especially that in US Treasury paper; officials hope that this will enable UK houses to develop an expertise that will allow them to compete more effectively overseas. Fourth, competition and the end of fixed commissions will also produce a more exact relationship between the provision and pricing of services; individual services, such as portfolio advice and valuations, will bear specific charges instead of being provided as a non-price method of competing for commission-bearing business.

The investor will, however, be thrown more on his own resources. Whilst greater competition may improve the service available to large institutions, the smaller institutions and private individuals will no longer benefit from the research made possible by the income from fixed commissions paid by large institutional investors. They will pay separately for research whilst they will no longer have the benefit of disinterested and well-informed advice. The quality and timeliness of advice will also deteriorate for all investors since market makers will have an incentive to keep their ideas and information to themselves until they have positioned their books. The authorities are aware of the problems posed for the smaller investor and expect to introduce measures for their protection.

6 Selling Stock by Tap Issues–the Classic Game

The prospectus (see Appendix 2)

The Treasury has powers to borrow in accordance with the National Loans Act 1968, s. 12. This enables the Treasury to 'create and issue such securities, at such rates of interest and subject to such conditions as to repayment, redemption and other matters (including provision for a sinking fund) as they think fit'. The Bank of England acts as agent for the Treasury when issuing in the gilt-edged market, and publishes prospectuses for new stocks, which contain the terms and conditions under which tenders are received and the stock held. The terms of the prospectus are binding until the stock is redeemed. Resting on the law of contract, the prospectus is an invitation to treat; applications from the public make them the offerors and the offer is accepted when the allotment letters are dispatched. Prospectuses are also subject to The Stock Exchange's rules governing the listing of securities contained in *Admission of Securities to Listing*, pp. 2.09–2.12, 2.17–2.18, 3.43–3.44 and 5.53–5.54. Much of the more formal information in the prospectuses is required under these rules as the precondition for listing and the securities becoming eligible to be dealt in on The Stock Exchange. The prospectus is published in at least two leading London daily newspapers, together with an application form in those cases where the public is being invited to tender.

In the minority of cases where a stock is issued directly to the Issue Department of the Bank, a prospectus is produced and published, but it is headed by a notice that it does not constitute an offer for sale. The prospectuses have always included the price paid by the Department, except in the case of the variable rate issues. Such methods of issue are discussed in Chapter 7.

A prospectus does not accompany the issue of a taplet since it is an additional tranche of an existing stock 'ranking in all respects *pari passu* with that Stock and subject to the terms and conditions of the prospectus for that Stock, save as to the particulars therein relating to the amount of the issue, the price payable, the method of issue and the first interest payment' (Press Notice, Bank of England, 12 March 1982). The Bank does, however, issue and publish in the press a notice that announces that the additional stock has been created, details the amounts, and states how the price paid by the Bank was determined. It does not constitute an offer for sale.

The issue of NILO tranches to the National Debt Commissioners is accompanied by an internal prospectus, which is really just a statement that stock has been created. It is not published.

The issue of 'A' and 'B' tranches of existing stocks is accompanied by prospectuses; again, these are not an offer for sale if the stock has been issued direct to the Bank.

As well as stating the name of the stock and the nominal amount being issued, a prospectus specifies the rights of the holder over the life of the stock and, where this is relevant, the conditions under which the public may apply. The statement of the holder's rights includes:

- the interest; the interest payment date; the amount of the first interest payment; the redemption date;
- a statement that 'The Stock is an investment falling within Part II of the First Schedule to the Trustee Investments Act 1961';
- a statement that 'The principal and interest are a charge on the National Loans Fund, with recourse to the Consolidated Fund'. This is required by The Stock Exchange's listing rules and is in accordance with the National Loans Act 1968, s. 12;
- the places of registration of ownership; the method of transferring ownership; the minimum amount of stock that may be transferred; a statement that transfer is free of stamp duty;
- where relevant, a statement that 'the interest payable . . . will be exempt from all United Kingdom taxation, present or future, so long as it is shown that the stock or bonds are in the beneficial ownership of persons who are neither domiciled nor ordinarily resident' in the UK.

The conditions under which the public may apply include:

- the minimum tender price, if any; the reservation of specified tranches for the NDCs, if relevant;
- if the stock is partly paid (see Chapter 7), the amount of the initial deposit and the amount and date of the calls; the date of the final payment;
- the place and the latest time for lodging tenders; the multiple of the price at which each tender must be made; the minimum nominal amount of stock that can be applied for;
- statements that tenders lodged without a price will be assumed to have been made at the minimum tender price; that the Treasury reserves the right to reject any tender or allot less than the amount tendered for; that the balance of stock not allotted will be allotted to the Issue Department at the minimum tender price;

- a statement of the manner in which stock will be allotted if the issue is over-subscribed; how interest may be charged on late payment of calls; the Bank's right to cancel allotments if calls are not paid;
- details of how the balance of application monies will be repaid in the event of partial allotment or an unsuccessful tender;
- the timetable and method of surrendering allotment letters for registration.

In addition, the prospectuses for variable rate stocks include: the method of calculating the half-yearly interest payments; details of how the stocks would become conventional fixed-interest stocks if there was 'a change in the arrangements for or relating to the issue of Treasury bills which in the opinion of the Bank of England would or could be detrimental to the interests of stockholders'; and the right of stockholders to require the stock to be redeemed at par in such a contingency.

A certificate for 3½% War Loan 1952 or after

Security Code
0-93862-8

3½ PER CENT. WAR STOCK.

45

Principal and Interest charged on the National Loans Fund, with recourse to the Consolidated Fund of the United Kingdom.
Interest payable half-yearly on the 1st June and the 1st December.

ACCOUNT NUMBER
45-90-02578

£ 0.01***

CERTIFICATE NUMBER
230-734710

JEREMY JOHN HOWARD WORMELL care of Pembol Nominees Ltd. P.O.Box 435

30 Finsbury Circus London EC2P 2HP

THIS IS TO CERTIFY THAT THE ABOVE-NAMED IS/ARE THE REGISTERED HOLDER(S) OF
One penny 3½ per cent.War Stock.

2nd May 1984

BANK OF ENGLAND

REGISTRATION CLERK

CHIEF REGISTRAR

No transfer of the whole or any part of the holding represented by this Certificate will be registered until the Certificate has been delivered at the Bank of England.
The Stock is transferable in multiples of 1p.

'Stock will be transferable in any sums which are multiples of a penny'
(Prospectus, 5% War Loan 1929–1947, 12 January 1917).

The prospectuses for index-linked stocks also include: the method for calculating the interest payments and redemption proceeds; the method for calculating the interest payments and redemption proceeds if the retail price index (RPI) is rebased; the responsibility of the Bank to publish an estimate of the RPI if the regular index is not published; and the condition that the Treasury will offer to redeem the stock early if there is a change in the 'coverage or the basic calculation of the Index which, in the opinion of the Bank of England, constitutes a fundamental change in the Index which would be materially detrimental to the interests of stockholders'.

The prospectuses for convertible stocks also include the conversion terms and an outline of the machinery that will accomplish conversion.

History

The issue of a new stock and the invitation to the public to tender for it does not normally result in the full amount being sold. Instead, the balance is taken up by the Issue Department of the Bank of England and is available to meet demand as it develops in the secondary market.

The tap system for stocks originated in 1940 at the time of Dunkirk and the collapse of France. At that time an issue that opened and closed for subscription within a day or two could well coincide with adverse war news. The alternative of making a succession of monthly issues was dismissed as 'ludicrous', but the need was for continuous supply to gather in the steady flow of institutional, personal and corporate money awaiting postwar investment. By implication this flow was expected to be invested unevenly in response to developments in the war. In addition, the authorities wished to fight a low interest rate war, avoiding the high rates that were paid at times in the First World War. As part of this policy they aimed to match the supply of stock in each maturity with the demand. A tap system, enabling the authorities to have supplies of different maturities constantly available, met both requirements.

Initially the taps were open-ended: the nominal amount to be made available was not decided when the stock was first issued, but the taps were turned off when the authorities considered enough had been issued in that particular maturity. It followed that there was no need for the Issue Department to take up stock, although it did so for its own investment purposes (Sayers, 1956, pp. 197–210.) Taps became closed-ended issues after 2½% Treasury 1975 or after was turned off in January 1947. The Issue Department took up stock that was not subscribed by the public and peddled it out as demand was felt.

The reliance on this system of occasional issue and continuous availability of supply had reached such a stage of development by 1959 that the Radcliffe Report could state:

> though the authorities welcome cash subscriptions from the public to new issues, and endeavour so to manage the market as to give their issues the best chance of attracting public subscriptions, in recent years the main consideration in the minds of the authorities in determining the timing of new issues has become ... the need to keep an adequate supply of 'tap' stocks in the Issue Department. (Committee on the Working of the Monetary System, 1959, p. 37)

This emphasis was repeated in 1979: 'The Bank issues periodically new stocks which normally are intended to replenish the portfolio which is available for market operations, although recently some issues have been fully or nearly fully subscribed on application' (*BEQB*, June 1979, p. 137).

The tap system today

The weakness of the tap system is the poor control it can give the authorities over the timing and volume of their sales. The system can offer an option against the government and in favour of the investor. This option has three elements: the size of individual issues; usefully accurate market estimates of the amount of stock remaining in official hands; relatively small and predictable changes in the price at which the authorities sell.

The size of the issues that are the source of government taps have been around £1,000m. during the last five years (see Table 6.1). This has been the equivalent of 6–10 per cent of the annual investible cash flows of the pension funds and long-term insurance funds. Each issue represents a substantial investment, even if other financial institutions and the personal and overseas sectors are buyers.

The institutional sector investing in the longer part of the market has a small number of competing participants: at the end of 1978, forty-three long-term and general funds controlled 86 per cent of the industry's assets; in 1979, fifty-eight funds controlled 69 per cent of pension fund assets (Committee to Review the Functioning of Financial Institutions, 1980b, p. 458 and p. 466). Two jobbers dominate market making and access to the Issue Department, while perhaps ten brokers dominate in advising the institutions. The result is a close-knit market where the activities of each participant are the subject of scrutiny, gossip and well-informed speculation, usually from those who have known each other over long periods. In this community there is continuous discussion about the cash awaiting investment, the amount of an issue that has been taken on application, the prices tendered, and the volume of stock bought in the secondary market.

Thus the institutions are able to make judgements about the amount of a stock that has been applied for and the amount the Issue Department still owns; they have evidence that enables them to assess the safety with which purchases can be delayed. The frequency with which they misjudge the supply position depends on the circumstances of each issue; the network tends to break down, for example, when a large outside participant, such as an overseas resident, throws in his weight.

The combination of monetary targets (introduced in 1976), forecasts for public and private borrowing, and a floating exchange rate enables the investor to make estimates of the volume of stock to be sold in a given period once the existing tap has been absorbed. The authorities may have somewhat different assumptions or information that will enable them to accept a reduction in yields without selling stock. But in general there are forces pushing them to exploit a yield basis fully once it has been shown that it attracts buyers, with the result that price changes tend to be relatively small once a tap starts running.

First, the authorities clearly aim to sell stock at the lowest possible yield. There is therefore the presumption that the yield at which they are supplying is the lowest, given the circumstances, at which they think they can sell the required volume. Since they judge they cannot sell on a lower yield basis and they prefer not to have to sell on a higher, it can be assumed they will sell aggressively once a level has been established.

Second, the events that influence the demand for gilt-edged stock are numerous, and many of them are completely outside the government's control. Even in the unlikely event of the government always exactly reaching its borrowing forecasts and a certain level of private sector loan demand there is always the unpredictable Middle East. The basic uncertainty of affairs means there is a bias towards selling heavily once the authorities have identified a level where there is demand.

Third, on the other side of the hill the investor is aware of this. He has his own judgement of the realistic yield level; in aggregate he may have already bought some stock from the authorities, thus showing at least provisional agreement with their judgement. If circumstances are unchanged he will ask why the government believes stock can be sold at lower yields. The presumption would therefore be that a drop in yields following a relaxation in official supply will be temporary and prices will soon fall back. The only result will have been unnecessary uncertainty and a cessation of funding.

Fourth, a new and higher yield basis is usually a response to a change in circumstances that has altered either the demand for stock at the lower yield basis or the volume of stock that needs to be supplied. It is rare for an event to be absorbed immediately into participants' views and for the market to move smoothly to a new level. Perspectives have to develop and events take time to unfold. A major event may well dry up demand for a

Table 6.1 *Issue of new stocks, 1981–4, excluding taplets*

Stock	Amount issued (£m. nominal)	Date announced	Date issued	Minimum tender price or issue price	Gross redemption yield %	Price if cut[1]	Size of cut[2]	Gross redemption yield %	Date exhausted	Price when exhausted[1]
12¼% Exchequer 1999 'B'	1,100	2.1.81	7.1.81	89.75	13.79				11.3.81	90.75
12% Exchequer Convertible 1985	1,000	23.1.81	28.1.81	97.00	12.96 (to 1985)				2.2.81	97.75
12% Treasury 1986	1,150	6.2.81	11.2.81	96.00	13.08				24.2.81	*96.25*
3% Treasury 1986	500	27.2.81	4.3.81	69.50	10.80				withdrawn 24.7.81	*last supplied 69.4375 as a short*
2% Index-Linked Treasury 1996	1,000	10.3.81	27.3.81	100.00[3]	*2.15*[6]				27.3.81	sold out at tender
12½% Exchequer 1990	1,000	11.3.81	11.3.81	95.00[5]	13.49				23.3.81	*95.50*
11½% Treasury 1985	1,100	27.3.81	1.4.81	96.50	12.60	93.875	*2.6875*	*13.49*		
						91	*2.9375*	14.52		
						86.75	*4.25*	*16.33*	6.10.81	87.00
2% Index-Linked Treasury 2006	1,000	3.7.81	8.7.81	86.00[3]	*3.04*[6]				9.7.81	86.375
15% Exchequer 1997	1,000	9.10.81	14.10.81	95.50	15.77	93.25	2.25	*16.224*	9.11.81	94.00
14% Exchequer 1986	1,000	13.11.81	19.11.81	95.75	15.27	93	2.875	*16.137*	19.1.82	93.00
3% Treasury 1987	500	30.12.81	7.1.82	64.50	11.97				23.2.82	65.00
2½% Index-Linked Treasury 2011	750	22.1.82	28.1.82	90.00[3]	*3.14*[6]				4.8.82	*95.00*
13¼% Exchequer 1987 'A'	750	8.2.82	8.2.82	93.25[5]	15.22				22.2.82	94.25
2% Index-Linked Treasury 1988	750	9.3.82	19.3.82	97.50[3]	*2.79*[6]				*24.8.82*	*98.875*
12¼% Treasury Convertible 1986	750	4.6.82	9.6.82	97.75	12.99 (to 1986)				12.7.82	*98.50*
12% Treasury 1987 'A'	500	3.8.82	3.8.82	99.625[5]	12.10				13.8.82	*99.8125*
10½% Exchequer 1987	800	16.8.82	19.8.82	98.75	10.84				20.8.82	*99.50*
2½% Index-Linked Treasury 2001	250	20.8.82	26.8.82	94.00[3]	*3.04*[6]				14.10.82	*95.00*
10½% Exchequer 1988	1,250	24.9.82	29.9.82	97.00	11.24				29.9.82	sold out at tender
9½% Treasury 1988	750	11.10.82	11.10.82	96.25[5]	10.36				19.10.82	*97.375*
2½% Index-Linked Treasury 2009	400	19.10.82	19.10.82	98.50[5]	*2.63*[6]				21.10.82	*99.125*
2½% Index-Linked Treasury 2003	250	22.10.82	27.10.82	98.00[3]	*2.70*[6]				*6.1.83*	*98.75*
8¾% Treasury Convertible 1985	1,000	1.11.82	4.11.82	100.25	8.61 (to 1985)				4.11.82	sold out at tender

2½% Exchequer 1987	500	30.12.82	6.1.83	84.00	7.02	81		8.52	16.9.83	*81.50*
2½% Index-Linked Treasury 2016	750	14.1.83	19.1.83	99.00[3]	*2.51*[6]				*11.4.83*	*100.0*
10½% Exchequer 1987 'A'	750	11.2.83	17.2.83	98.50	10.96				18.2.83	*98.875*
10½% Exchequer Convertible 1986	1,100	14.3.83	14.3.83	98.75[5]	10.99 (to 1986)				15.3.83	*99.75*
10½% Treasury 1989	1,100	8.4.83	13.4.83	96.00	11.41				4.5.83	*96.375*
2½% Index-Linked Convertible 1999	1,000	28.4.83	5.5.83	97.50[3]	*2.64*[6]	91.875	*5.75*	*3.23*[6]	12.7.83	91.875
10¼% Treasury Convertible 1987	1,000	27.5.83	2.6.83	98.25	10.84 (to 1987)				9.6.83	*98.75*
9½% Treasury 1988 'A'	800	10.6.83	16.6.83	95.00	10.77	92.75	2.25	*11.48*	8.9.83	*93.125*
10% Treasury Convertible 1986	1,000	12.8.83	17.8.83	97.25	11.24 (to 1986)				17.8.83	sold out at tender
10% Treasury 1987	1,100	12.9.83	15.9.83	97.00	11.00				21.9.83	*97.50*
9¾% Treasury Convertible 1988	1,000	26.9.83	29.9.83	96.50	10.72 (to 1988)				9.11.83	*96.75*
2½% Index-Linked Treasury 2020	750	12.10.83	12.10.83	91.50[5]	*2.93*[6]	89 84.25	*3.125* *5.00*[6]	*3.10* *3.51*[6]	*14.8.84*	*85.75*
10% Exchequer 1989	1,150	11.11.83	16.11.83	97.00	10.72				5.1.84	*97.125*
2½% Exchequer 1986	500	21.12.83	24.12.83	84.50	8.46				21.12.83	*84.875*
2% Index-Linked 1990	300	29.12.83	5.1.84	91.00[3]	*3.64*[6]	*88.50*	*2.625*	4.40[6]	27.3.84	*88.50*
10% Treasury Convertible 1990	1,200	13.1.84	18.1.84	96.00	10.84 (to 1990)				18.1.84	sold out at tender
9¾% Exchequer 1998	1,000	3.2.84	8.2.84	94.50	10.51				5.3.84	*95*
10% Exchequer 1989 'A'	1,250	2.3.84	7.3.84	98.00	10.50				14.3.84	*97.25*
9½% Treasury Convertible 1989	1,100	27.4.84	2.5.84	95.50	10.70 (to 1989)	93.125 *91.625*	*2.375* *1.875*	11.37 *11.81*	*1.6.84*	*91.625*

Notes: [1] Price as if fully paid.
[2] The difference between the last identified supply price and the price when cut, in points.
[3] Price at which the stock was allotted at tender.
[4] Real yield calculated on the assumption that inflation will continue at the rate experienced in the six months to the most recently published figure (*BEQB*, June 1983, p. 180n).
[5] Price at which the stock was issued directly to the Issue Department.
[6] Real yield calculated on the assumption of a constant 5% inflation rate.

Source: BEQB, except the data in italics.

period and allow monetary growth to accelerate. Thus a backlog of stock sales is created and the volume to be sold, once the new basis has been established, is swollen.

These forces that push the authorities to sell aggressively once a suitable yield level has been identified, making small and relatively predictable changes in the prices at which they supply stock, need to be seen in the context of the demands that are being put on the market. A high level of public or private borrowing means that few risks can be taken with the yield basis since monetary growth will move rapidly above target if stock sales are not continuous. In principle, however, it can be assumed that the yield is the lowest deemed realistic and it will continue to be exploited as long as events do not intervene.

This principle needs to be modified in two ways. First, within the yield basis in general, there must be room for the market to be led higher; it is part of both market and official lore that the authorities can 'only fund on a rising market'. The technique is to persuade potential buyers that if they do not buy today they will need to pay a higher price tomorrow. This involves the authorities performing the feat of giving the impression that there is a shortage of supply at current prices, whilst actually selling.

Second, there have been several periods when monetary growth has been above target and the authorities judged to be keen sellers. The knowledge that the authorities have to sell is cause for buyers to delay in expectation that yields will need to rise. This feeds on itself: the longer the buyers delay the higher will be monetary growth; the higher is monetary growth the greater is the need for official sales. This is the pattern of the 'buyers' strikes' that have been much discussed since 1976.

The reverse is also true. Investors appreciate that once the authorities have sold and covered their immediate needs they have greater freedom to withhold stock from the market; buyers become markedly more enthusiastic when they know the government has the freedom to refrain from selling. Factors that were earlier regarded as merely potentially encouraging suddenly become immediate and real, grounds for chasing the market higher.

The classic game

Selling a tap

There are too many ways in which the market can develop during the sale of a conventional £1,000m. issue for a description to be anything but schematic. However, a simplified picture will indicate some of the weaknesses in the tap system and is necessary as the context for Chapter 7, which discusses how funding methods have been modified. The system is treated further in Chapter 2.

The announcement of a new issue can be greeted with relief. The authorities are the single largest participant and, at least in the longer maturities, are predominantly a seller. It is therefore important for the investor to know the yield at which they are prepared to supply. At the same time they are the best informed of the participants: they know their own intentions; they may have better or more timely information about relevant factors such as the trend of monetary growth, public borrowing or events in the foreign exchange market; they have information supplied by the market makers on turnover and the quality of the buying and selling; they can judge how well previous official sales have been absorbed from information provided by the market makers on their book positions. For these reasons the announcement of a new issue is seen as a statement of the authorities' judgement and, since it is well-informed, the decision is treated with respect. The result is that the announcement of an issue can have a steadying effect, especially if prices have recently moved sharply.

If it is assumed that the market accepts the minimum tender price as realistic and able to attract demand, the market makers will attempt to hold prices steady whilst selling stock; if buying builds up they will move prices gently higher. By selling stock they are taking out 'bear' positions (going 'short') in the knowledge that they have the option of tendering for the new issue. This option, covering the days between announcement and tender, means that they have the opportunity to judge the scale of investor response to the issue, see how events develop, before deciding either to tender for sufficient stock to cover their bear positions or to tender on a greater scale to turn themselves into 'bulls' (become 'long' of stock). The market makers will retain their bear positions only if they judge that enough stock will be left with the authorities to enable it to run as a tap. In this case they know that they can buy stock from the government in the secondary market if they decide to alter their position from short to long.

The option that can be built up between the announcement of a new stock and the tender has considerable risks. First, there is the inherent uncertainty of not knowing the scale of tenders and whether the stock will run as a tap. Second, if the market moves higher it can be expected that the new stock will be over-subscribed at the minimum tender price and be allotted at a premium. The size of this premium is rarely obvious in advance. Events or changed perceptions may push the market higher. With convertible issues the value of the option to convert is a matter of opinion and will have a different value for each institution with its differing liability structure. If there has been a radical change in the level of the market the new stock will have a size of coupon that will not have been supplied recently; this will mean that the relative supply position of stock with other coupons has changed and relative values will need to adjust. If the new stock is of a maturity that has not been sold recently, it may be regarded as particularly attractive because of its scarcity or particularly unattractive as a harbinger of a change in the terms of official supply. The stock may be of a maturity that is unexpected, so that the shape of the yield curve has to adjust to a new set of expectations about official thinking. It is only when the stock is comparable in coupon and maturity to the immediately preceding issues that its relative value is unmistakable.

The market makers may, however, have opened bears in existing stocks in the period between the announcement of the new issue and the tender at price levels that are comparable (in the sense discussed in Appendix I and in Chapter 10 on the term structure) with the new issue. However, the new issue has only a minimum tender price; the market makers may tender at very high prices to be certain of being allotted the stock they need at the minimum accepted price, but this may still imply higher prices for existing stocks than those at which they had earlier opened bears when they were assuming the new stock would not be allotted at a premium. Thus, although the market makers can normally be certain of being allotted the volume of stock they need, they can be vulnerable to investors' changing their attitude between announcement and tender and to the stock being allotted above the minimum tender price.

The result of a tender can be:

(i)   Little or no interest, in which case the stock is allotted to the Issue Department at the minimum tender price.

(ii) Tenders partly cover the issue and allotments are made to the public at the minimum tender price with the balance of the stock being allotted to the Issue Department at the same price.

(iii) Tenders at the minimum tender price do not fully cover the issue, but there is insufficient stock remaining for it to operate as a tap. In this case the rump of the issue is allotted to the Issue Department at the minimum tender price.

(iv) The issue is over-subscribed at the minimum tender price. In this case the Issue Department is allotted no stock; public tenders above the minimum accepted price are allotted in full and those at the minimum accepted price are scaled down. All stock is allotted at the minimum accepted price (see Chapter 7).

If there is full or nearly full subscription for the new stock (cases (iii) and (iv)) and the market makers have judged demand correctly, they will be long of stock after the tender; they will therefore seek to push the market higher and sell their positions at a premium to the allotment price. Their willingness and ability to raise prices will depend on the size of the speculative holdings that have been acquired in the new stock at the tender; the premium these speculators want before they sell; the size of unsatisfied demand from the long-term investment institutions; expectations about further official sales; and, of course, new developments. In general, market makers will reduce their long positions in stages as prices advance, unless they judge the background justifies a significant drop in the yield basis. In this case they will try to hold on to their positions by continuously raising prices to avoid selling.

If the stock is under-subscribed (cases (i) and (ii)) and the market makers have judged the demand correctly they will have failed to apply and will be short of stock after the tender. This is perhaps the best possible situation for a market maker – he is short of stock at tap levels (the price level at which it is assumed that the tap stock will be supplied). If demand unexpectedly develops he knows where he can buy stock and has a reasonable idea of both the volume that is available and the price. The larger the size of the conventional issues in relation to potential demand the lower the risk of the stock not being available or not being available in a sufficient volume. Whilst the market maker is short he earns the interest from the funds released by the bear positions and can hope to lower prices, with the expectation that bluff or events will encourage investors to sell, enabling him to close his position at a profit. If the ploy fails, or instead of sellers he finds buyers, he can push prices rapidly back up to levels where he believes he can buy the stock that is on tap.

If a market maker misjudges the demand at the tender and finds himself long at levels where there is now a tap running, he will try to hold prices up, bluffing investors into buying, and thus create the short positions in secondary market trading that he failed to create earlier. In this case investor buying does not enable the authorities to sell. Instead it merely creates a short position for the market maker who then has an incentive to move prices lower, reducing the authorities' chances of making sales.

Advantages of a tap for the market maker

The interests of the market maker and the government are opposed if the authorities' aim is to sell a new issue on tender or to have official control over the timing and volume of sales in the secondary market.

The market maker has three sources of profit if a stock is sold as a tap; none of these are available if the stock is sold out at tender. Moreover the risk attached to these profits is reduced by the protection the tap provides and the information available to the market makers whilst a tap is running.

First, the market maker makes a small turn (profit) from the difference between the price at which the government sells him stock and the price at which it is bought by brokers for their clients; this profit is usually 1/64 of a point (£156·25 per million) in the shorts and 1/32 (£312·50 per million) in the mediums and longs. The market maker may also have an opportunity to buy some stock from the government in excess of the immediate demand he is seeing when he judges the tap price (the government supply price) is about to change. If his judgement is correct he can then sell this stock at a higher price – this price being above the authorities' previous price but usually beneath the authorities' next, higher, price.

Second, the market maker benefits from the increased turnover that accompanies a tap running in the market. Traders buy from the market makers in the morning and hope to sell later in the day at a higher price after the authorities have moved their tap price higher. Investors switch into the tap from existing stocks and other investors buy those stocks. On each deal the market maker has the opportunity to make a profit representing the difference between his buying and selling price.

Third, a further potential source of profit comes from buying enough stock from the authorities as a tap runs out to become long and then to move the market higher. The jobbers' behaviour at this stage will be similar to that when they are long after full subscription at a tender. The jobbers are in a stronger position than any other participant to judge how much stock remains in official hands: the two major jobbers see over 80 per cent of the total turnover and a larger proportion of the government's tap sales. They can judge from their own experience how much stock is being supplied at each price; the volume supplied often tends to fall as a tap nears exhaustion.

These three sources of income, together with the potential for profit from opening bears at tap levels and closing them by buying stock from disenchanted investors at lower levels, are only possible if a new stock runs as a tap. For this reason the jobbers will try, in the period between the announcement of a new stock and the tender, to create the impression that there are no buyers, no enthusiasm, perhaps actual or potential sellers. Their freedom to do this is clearly limited by events and investor behaviour; they cannot lower their prices if there are determined buyers waiting for cheap stock. But they can exaggerate the effect on their bid prices of adverse news and imply they have seen no buyers even if this is not, strictly, true. The lowering of jobbers' bids in the half hour in the morning before tenders close is a much-loved ritual.

There is a final potential source of profit if the authorities are forced to cut their tap price. This happens when the yield at which the stock was issued does not attract investors either because it has been overtaken by events or because the authorities have misjudged the yield at which they can sell. These are both weaknesses inherent in the tap system. One of the reasons for a market maker to be short at tap levels is the possibility that the unpredictable will intervene and enable him to move the market lower; uncertainty means there is always the possibility of bad news, whilst the market maker is covered against the possibility of good news by the availability of the tap. The system relies on the authorities having exceptional judgement; in a world of constantly changing perspectives and information they have to choose the lowest yield at which to sell a given volume of stock. Their judgement is sometimes wrong.

The market makers, perhaps having opened bears at tap levels, may take the opportunity presented by adverse news to lower prices. The same news may have discouraged investors and the market makers may find few buyers, despite the higher yields. Over a period, realising that the authorities need to sell, the market makers take the opportunity of any bad news to lower prices further. If from time to time there is buying as yields rise they may add to their bear positions.

The authorities do not lower their tap price at once if small buyers appear, nor do they force the market makers to buy stock to close their positions. They are hunting bigger game. They need to know that there is substantial demand at a new yield basis, perhaps that there is enough to run out the remainder of their tap, before they cut their price. Buying by investors signals when that yield has been reached and this builds up the market makers' bear positions, making them profits if the market falls. At the lower level the authorities may test demand by supplying unofficial lines of stock. The sequence is one in which the interests of the jobbers and the government at last coincide in their mutual desire to lead the market lower and find buyers.

7 Variations in Funding Techniques

The greater emphasis on monetary discipline from the mid-1970s high-lighted the clumsiness of the conventional tap system and the coarse control it provided over the timing of official sales. Timing became more important as rates of monetary growth experienced over relatively short periods became significant in forming expectations. The need was for a method of making investors anticipate that delaying a decision to buy could be expensive. This led to discussion of various methods of auction or tender, which some thought would ensure that the yield was more quickly found where the authorities could sell the required volume of stock.

The need to borrow at high nominal yields was a further encouragement to innovation. The Conservative government elected in 1979 placed a high priority on the control of inflation, and was more aware than the investor of the strength of its own commitment to its reduction. It followed that the investor continued to demand high nominal yields, which the government increasingly felt to be expensive in real terms.

The authorities also feared that if high levels of public borrowing continued alongside the policy of controlling the money supply, official sales of fixed-interest gilt-edged would unbalance non-bank portfolios. On several occasions they believed they were paying a heavy premium to sell to institutions, such as pension funds, for whom fixed-interest stocks were an unsuitable investment. It has been seen in Chapter 1 that the concern was largely unjustifed, at least when viewed over a long period, but at times it was thought that demand was becoming less responsive to increases in yields, with implications for both debt costs and monetary control.

The official response was to make a series of small changes in the type of stocks created and in the methods of issue. Cumulatively, these changes amounted to something of a revolution. But the evolutionary manner of their introduction was consistent with the need for certainty in the authorities' handling of the market discussed in Chapter 2. This chapter describes these innovations: taplets; partly paid stocks; convertible, variable coupon and index-linked issues; changes in the timing and method of issue; and the introduction of minimum price tenders.

Taplets

Taplets are issues of additional small tranches of existing stocks to the

Issue Department. Individual tranches have been between £100m. and £300m.; two, and up to six, issues have been made on any one day and have totalled between £250m. and £750m. They do not require new prospectuses since they are similar in every way to the existing issues. The new tranches are created at the middle market prices of the existing issues at the official close of business on the day of the announcements. The announcement of the creation of the stocks and their issue to the Bank have always been on the same day. In some cases the stock has been available for sale in the market on the business day following the announcement, but in most cases it has been after one working day's delay (see Table 7.1 for examples).

Taplets were first issued at Christmas 1980 when a conventional tap would have meant applications from the public at a time of seasonal postal delays and money market shortages (*BEQB*, March 1981, pp. 27–8). It was made clear at the time that this method of issue was considered exceptional. This was emphasised when a conventional long tap was promptly issued at the beginning of January although the taplets were still untouched in the Issue Department's portfolio.

Taplets have since developed into a permanent and oft-employed technique of market management providing a greater flexibility than conventional taps: they can be issued quickly to meet surges in demand; they can be tailored to areas of the market where there is buying, without threatening to swamp it; they are not so large that the market makers can feel safe opening short positions under their cover, or for the institutions to think that there is sufficient stock to protect them from unexpected market movements; they are always created at the price of the existing stock, so the market can read little meaning into the issue level; they are not issued at a formal minimum price in a prospectus, although the prices are known, and the prices of official supplies are not as easily discovered as those of conventional taps.

In addition, market participants attach less importance to the price at which taplets are created than to the terms on which large conventional issues are made. They also attach less importance to the price at which they are supplied to the market. This is not to imply that the timing or yield on creation are thought to have no significance; on the contrary, taplets, in common with conventional tap issues, are considered to be statements that the authorities think they can sell stock at prevailing levels. But the smaller size of taplets means they can be absorbed by buying that may be difficult to detect and this makes participants nervous. The difference lies in the degree of certainty – the difference between knowing there is a large seller and knowing there is a small seller.

There is also less official embarrassment if the price of a taplet has to be cut. The press is often vague about the price at which the stocks were originally created and the uncertainty about the prices at which stock is

Table 7.1 Issue of taplets

Stock	Nominal amount of issue £m.	Date announced	Date issued	Date available in the market	Presumed issue price[1]	Yield at presumed issue price	Date exhausted	Price when exhausted[2]
10% Treasury 1987	200	26.3.84	26.3.84	28.3.84	99 5/16	10.528	27.4.84	98 9/16
10¼% Exchequer 1995	200	26.3.84	26.3.84	28.3.84	98 7/8	10.984	26.4.84	98
10¼% Conversion 1999	100	26.3.84	26.3.84	28.3.84	101 7/8	10.465	28.3.84	102 1/4

Notes: [1] Middle market closing price of the existing issue on 26 March 1984.
[2] Market information.

supplied makes criticism of official actions more tentative. The authorities do not enjoy cutting a price – taking a loss – but taplets help make the experience less painful.

Most importantly, the authorities are aware that any new issue has market impact; there is always nervousness whilst the market is learning to accept the presence of an issue. Taplets are considered to have less impact than conventional tap issues, even when these are partly paid. Thus conventional taps are still used when the direction of the market appears clear and one single factor dominant. Taplets are used when the market appears set to ebb and flow, without overall direction, and the authorities need to be equipped to take advantage of any sudden rallies.

Partly paid stocks

Partly paid stocks are issues where only a part of the price is payable on application, with the remainder payable in up to three further instalments. These later payments are timed to coincide with expected deficits in Exchequer transactions.

Partly paid stocks had been the normal method of central government issue since the early nineteenth century. The method was discontinued after the issue of 3% War Loan 1955/59 in 1940 (Sayers, 1956, pp. 198–9 and *BEQB*, June 1977, p. 164) and reintroduced in March 1977 with the issue of 12¼% Exchequer 1992. The first partly paid short-dated stock was issued in August 1979.

Example 7.1 *10½% Exchequer 1987 'A'*

£750m. issued 17 February 1983 at 98.50 to yield 10·96%
£30% payable on application, £68·50% on 28 March 1983

Partly paid issues have three advantages for buyers. First, they can lock in existing yields even when the cash is not yet available. Second, a speculator can take a larger position than his cash resources would otherwise allow, although this has become less important since he can now obtain gearing in the futures market. Third, institutional investors, such as life companies, can quote firm terms when selling liabilities although the money may not be paid to them immediately and yields may have changed before it can be invested.

Market management has been aided in several ways. First, the authorities can assure themselves of cash receipts for future banking periods. Second, the authorities can tap the yield level once identified, capturing

An example of a gilt-edged yield list

TUESDAY 31st JULY, 1984, for settlement tomorrow

Highest Closing prices Net 1933-1984	Lowest Closing prices at 1933-1984	Official closing Quotation 30/12/83	LIFE	Amount in mns. quoted	STOCK and issue details including gross redemption yield (£ %)
			Yrs. mths. days	£	
27 101^{7}_{16} 25/4/49	32^{27}_{32} 3/1/75	$81\frac{1}{4}$xd ($81\frac{1}{4}$ Net)	3.11.0	1302	**3% Brit. Transport 1 July,** **78/88** 1/1/48: Nationalisation Issue at 100 to acquire home railways securities. Part of the National Debt since 1/1/63. Issued to Bank of England † : £250mn. 26/6/84
28 $98\frac{1}{2}$ 5/3/83	$88\frac{1}{2}$ 23/7/84	$95\frac{3}{4}$ ($95\frac{3}{4}$ Net)	4.2.24	2050	**9½% Treasury 25 Oct.,** **1988** 11/10/82: £750mn. Issued at 96.25 (10.35) to Bank of England may be bought by public. Calls: – £20 on 11/10/82; £40% on 22/11/82; £36.25% on 10/1/83; £800mn. Issued at minimum tender price 95 (10.76). Calls: – £40% on application; £30% on 25/7/83; £25% on 22/8/83. First interest payment £2.6302% on 25/10/83. Issued to Bank of England†: £250mn. 24/1/84. £250mn. 20/7/84.
29 105^{27}_{32} 3.11.82	77^{13}_{32} 26/10/81	$106\frac{1}{4}$ (102^{5}_{32} Net)	4.6.21	2250	**11½% Treasury 22 Feb.,** **1989** 12/9/79: £600mn. at minimum tender price 95.50 (12.32). Calls:– £40% on application; £55.50% on 23/10/79. 26/11/80: £1,350mn. at minimum tender price 92 (13.10). Calls: – £30% on 16/1/81. Issued to Bank of England †: £300mn. 21/7/82.
30 $95\frac{1}{2}$ 2.5.84	$88\frac{1}{16}$ 23/7/84		4.8.17	1100	**9½% Treasury Convertible 18 Apr.,** **1989** 2/5/84: Issued at minimum tender price 95.50 (10.70). Calls:– £50% on application; £45.50% on 4/6/84; First interest payment £3.9895% on 18/10/84. Convertible at holder's option April and Oct. on 18/4/85 to 18/4/87 inc. into £99, £97, £95, £93, £91 nominal respectively of 9½% Conversion per 2005 £100 nominal.
31 100^{5}_{16} 14.3.84	$91\frac{1}{16}$ 23/7/84	99 (98^{17}_{32} Net)	4.10.13	1200	**10½% Treasury 14 June,** **1989** 13/4/83: Issued at minimum tender price 96 (11.41). Calls:– £25% on application; £35% on 16/5/83; £36% on 13/6/83. Issued to National Debt Commissioners £100mn. 20/7/84.
32 $97\frac{7}{8}$ 14.3.84	89^{3}_{16} 23.7.84	97 ($96\frac{1}{16}$ Net)	5.0.0	2400	**10% Exchequer 1 Aug.,** **1989** 16/11/83: £1,150mn. Issued at minimum tender price 97 (10.71). Calls: £20% on application; £40% on 14/12/83; £37% on 16/1/84. First interest payment £6.1421% on 1/8/84. 7/3/84: £1,250mn. Issued at minimum tender price 98 (10.50). Calls:– £40% on application; £30% on 9/4/84; £28% on 14/5/84. First interest payment £3.2184% on 1/8/84.
33 98 17.8.59	$38\frac{5}{8}$ 3.1.75	$82\frac{3}{4}$ (81^{23}_{32} Net)	5.2.14	601	**5% Treasury 15 Oct.,** **86/89** 10/8/59 to 26/8/59: £144mn. in exchange for 3% War 55/59, plus £2 cash payment. 12/8/59: £157mn. Issued at 98 (5.13). 9/5/62: £300mn. Issued at 84.50 (6.21).
34 117^{9}_{32} 30.9.77	84 27.10.76	$108\frac{1}{4}$ xd ($108\frac{13}{16}$ Net)	5.5.14	a 950	**13% Treasury 15 Jan.,** **1990** 15/1/76: £600mn. Issued at 9 (13.64). Issued to Bank of England †: £250m. 20/11/81; £100mn. 12/7/82.
35 110^{13}_{32} 3.11.82	80^{9}_{16} 26.10.81	$109\frac{1}{2}$ ($106\frac{1}{8}$ Net)	5.7.21	1000	**12½% Exchequer 22 Mar.,** **1990** 11/3/81: £1000mn. Issued at 95 (13.48) to Bank of England † Calls:– £15% on 11/3/81; £25% on 3/4/81; £55% on 15/5/81.
36 $104\frac{3}{4}$ 27.1.72	$15\frac{1}{16}$ 2.1.75	$90\frac{1}{2}$ (90^{5}_{32} Net)	5.10.14	a 600	**8¼% Treasury 15 June,** **87/90** 8/9/71: Issued at 96 (8.68).
37 98 14.3.84	87^{11}_{32} 27.7.84		6.2.24	1200	**10% Treasury Convertible 25 Oct.,** **1990** 18/1/84: minimum tender price 95.75. Issued at 96 (10.85): Calls:– £20% on 18/1/84; £45% on 13/2/84; 31% on 12/3/84. First interest payment £6.8888% on 25/10/84. Convertible at holder's options Oct. and Apr. on 25/10/84 to 25/10/86 inc. into £98, £96, £94, £92, £90 nominal respectively of 9½% Conversion 2004 per £100 nominal.
38 108^{3}_{16} 30.9.77	$76\frac{5}{8}$ 26.10.81	$102\frac{3}{4}$ xd (103^{5}_{32} Net)	6.5.9	2000	**11¾% Treasury 10 Jan.,** **1991** 2/6/77: £800mn. Issued at 94 (12.68). Calls:– £15% on application; 15% on 7/7/77; £64% £64% on 8/8/77. 23/7/80: £1200mn. Issued at minimum tender price 94 (12.80). Calls:– £20% on)% on application; £30% on 22/8/80; £44% on 26/9/80. .26/9/80
91 128^{5}_{16} 9/1/84	84^{23}_{32} 26/10/81	$130\frac{1}{4}$ ($126\frac{3}{4}$ Net)	19.7.25	1250	**13½% Treasury 26 Mar.,** **2004/08** 17/4/80: £100mn. Minimum tender price 95. Issued at 97.75 (14.11). Calls:– £20% on application; £30% on 16/5/80; £45.75% on 6/6/80. Issued to Bank of England †: £250mn. 20/11/8
92 100^{13}_{16} 14/8/63	31^{7}_{32} 3/1/75	$63\frac{3}{4}$ ($62\frac{1}{16}$ Net)	28.1.9	a 1000	**5½% Treasury 10 Sept.,** **2008/12** 5/10/60: £500mn. at 95 (5.81). 5/9/62: £500mn. at 95 (5.81).
93 96^{5}_{32} 28/1/72	43^{5}_{16} 3/1/75	$81\frac{3}{4}$ xd ($82\frac{1}{16}$ Net)	30.5.25	600	**7¾% Treasury 26 Jan.,** **2012/15** 26/1/72: Issued at 96 (8.06).
94 121^{1}_{32} 13/3/84	78 26/10/81	$120\frac{1}{2}$ (119^{29}_{32} Net)	29.4.11	1000	**12% Exchequer 12 Dec.,** **2013/17** 15/6/78: Issued at 96 (12.50). Calls:– £15% on application; £30% on 27/6/78; £51% on 14/7/7
95 118^{13}_{16} 9/1/35	$22\frac{3}{8}$ 13/12/74	$39\frac{3}{4}$ xd ($40\frac{1}{8}$ Net)		359	**4% Consols 1 Feb., 1 Aug.** 6/1/27: £81mn. at 85. £379mn. by various conversions 1927/32. Redeemable on any interest date on three months' notice.
96 $114\frac{7}{8}$ 4/11/46	20^{5}_{32} 15/11/74	44 ($43\frac{1}{8}$ Net)		169	**3½% Conversion 1 Apr., 1 Oct.** 1921/22/27: £805mn. by various conversions. 1925: £130mn. by tender. Sinking Fund (1% per half-year of amount outstanding when price is below 90) effective rate 5.95% for 1981/82. Redeemable on any interest date on three months' notice.
97 109^{9}_{16} 3/1/35	19^{25}_{32} 3/1/75	36 (35^{23}_{32} Net)		a 1909	**3½% War Loan 1 June, 1 Dec.** July 1932: In exchange for 5% War 1929/47 plus £1 cash bonus if offer accepted by July 31. Redeemable on three calendar months' notice.

| | | | GROSS | | | INTEREST AND REDEMPTION GAIN OR LOSS TAXED AT 40.0% | | | INTEREST TAXED AT 37.5% | | | | | |
| | | | Yield | | | | | | | Net Yield | | | | |
Price and next ex. div. date	Accrued interest + or − * (days) £	Price excluding accrued interest £	Interest £	Redemption # £	var. in price = in Red. Yield p	Net Redemption Yield £	Grossed-up Net Red. Yield £	var. in price = in Grossed-up Red. Yield £	Net price allowing for tax on accrued	Interest £	Redemption # £	var. in price = in Red. Yield p	Grossed-up Net Red. Yield £	5p var. in tax = in Net Red. Yield p
77⅜	+0.255 (31)	77.375	3.877	**10.139** (1988)	1.1	**6.334**	**10.557**	1.3	77.471	2.420	**8.798**	1.1	**14.076**	17.9
88¼	+2.551 (98)	88.250	10.765	**13.180**	1.1	**7.978**	**13.296**	1.1	89.207	6.656	**9.050**	1.0	**14.480**	55.1
94⅝ Clean	−0.662 (−21)	94.625	12.153	**13.103**	1.0	**7.946**	**13.243**	1.0	94.377	7.616	**8.705**	0.9	**13.929**	58.6
87⅝	+1.959 (91)	87.625	10.842	**13.087**	1.0	**7.947**	**13.245**	1.1	88.360	6.720	**9.019**	0.9	**14.430**	54.2
90⅝	+1.381 (48)	90.625	11.586	**13.148**	0.9	**7.965**	**13.274**	1.0	91.143	7.200	**8.832**	0.8	**14.132.5**	
	Accrued interest in price				⅛ Variation ø			⅛ Variation ø				⅛ Variation ø		
88⅞ xd	0.000	88.875	11.252	**13.102**	3.8 (1.7)	**8.002**	**13.337**	4.1	88.875	7.032	**9.066**	3.4 (1.6)	**14.506**	53.8
77⅝	1.479	76.146	6.566	**11.150** (1989)	3.8 (1.5)	**6.939**	**11.565**	4.2	76.700	4.074	**8.792**	3.6 (1.4)	**14.067**	31.4
100⅛	0.605	99.520	13.063	**13.104**	3.3 (1.7)	**7.852**	**13.087**	3.5	99.747	8.146	**8.173**	2.9 (1.5)	**13.077**	65.7
101¾ 6th Aug.	4.521	97.229	12.856	**13.189**	3.3 (1.7)	**7.808**	**13.014**	3.4	98.925	7.897	**8.046**	2.8 (1.5)	**12.874.6**	68.6
84⅝	1.062	83.563	9.873	**12.244** (1990)	3.4 (1.5)	**7.516**	**12.528**	3.7	83.961	6.141	**8.697**	3.1 (1.3)	**13.915**	47.3
91½	4.558	86.942	11.502	**13.096**	3.3 (1.5)	**7.872**	**13.120**	3.5	88.651	7.050	**8.630**	2.8 (1.3)	**13.808**	59.6
94¾	0.708	94.042	12.494	**13.129**	3.0 (1.5)	**7.927**	**13.212**	3.3	94.307	7.787	**8.500**	2.6 (1.3)	**13.600**	61.7
118⅛ 20th Aug.	4.734	113.391	11.906	**11.731** (2004)	1.5 (1.8)	**6.850**	**11.417**	1.5	115.166	7.326	**7.002**	1.1 (1.3)	**11.203**	63.0
56⅝ 6th Aug.	2.170	54.455	10.100	**10.604** (2012)	2.3 (1.3)	**6.589**	**10.982**	2.5	55.269	6.220	**7.149**	1.6 (0.9)	**11.438**	46.1
73⅜	0.127	73.248	10.580	**10.743** (2015)	1.8 (1.4)	**6.574**	**10.957**	2.0	73.294	6.609	**6.965**	1.3 (0.9)	**11.145**	50.4
109¼	1.644	107.606	11.152	**11.109**	1.4 (1.5)	**6.600**	**10.999**	1.4	108.223	6.930	**6.844**	0.9 (1.0)	**10.950**	56.9
					Interest Yield		Grossed-up Net Interest Yield	In Grossed-up Interest Yield				Interest Yield	Grossed-up Net Interest Yield	
36 xd	0.000	36.000	11.111		3.8 (1.4)	**6.667**	**11.111**	3.8	36.000	**6.944**		2.4 (0.9)	**11.111**	
40⅞	1.170	39.705	8.815		2.8 (1.1)	**5.227**	**8.712**	2.7	40.144	**5.449**		1.7 (0.7)	**8.719**	
32⅝	0.585	32.040	10.924		4.2 (1.4)	**6.507**	**10.845**	2.7	32.259	**6.781**		2.6 (0.9)	**10.850**	

Highest Closing prices Net 1933-1984	Lowest Closing prices at 1933-1984	Official closing Quotation 30/12/83	LIFE	Amount in mns quoted	STOCK and issue details including gross redemption yield (£ %)
			Yrs. mths. days	£	

INDEX-LINKED STOCKS

101 105$\frac{1}{8}$ 2/2/83	94$^{15}_{16}$ 6/4/82	104$\frac{1}{4}$ (104$\frac{1}{4}$ Net)	3.7.29	**1000**	**2% Index-Linked Treasury 30 Mar.,** **1988** 19/3/82: £750mn. Issued at 97.50 (2.45) by tender with no minimum price. Calls:– £50% on application; £47.50% on 29/4/82. Next interest payment £1.1531% on 30/9/84. Indexation as 2% Index-linked Treasury 1996. Base month (July 1981) = 297.1. RPI gain to date = 18.4%. Issued to Bank of England †: £120mn. 10/12/82.
102 91$\frac{1}{8}$ 5/1/84	85$^{15}_{32}$ 27/7/84		5.5.24	**300**	**2% Index-Linked Treasury 25 Jan.,** **1990** 5/1/84: Issued at 91 (3.08) by tender with no minimum price. Next initial payment £1.0512% on 25/1/85. Indexation as 2% Index-linked Treasury 1996. Base month (May 1983) = 333.9. RPI gain to date = 5.4%.
103 110$^{31}_{32}$ 11/1/83	89$^{29}_{32}$ 29/9/81	106 (105$\frac{3}{32}$ Net)	12.1.15	**1000**	**2% Index-Linked Treasury 16 Sept.,** **1996** 27/3/81: Issued at 100 (1.92) by tender with no minimum price. Calls:– £35% on application; £30% on 1/5/81; £35% on 26/5/81. Next interest payment. £1.27% on 16/9/84. Both principal and interest are related to the change in the General Index of Retail Prices, subject to a lage of 8 months. Base month (July 1980) = 267.9. RPI gain to date = 31.3%
110 99$^{23}_{32}$ 18/4/83	82$^{27}_{32}$ 27/7/84	92$\frac{7}{8}$ xd (92$^{1}_{16}$ Net)	31.11.25	**750**	**2$\frac{1}{2}$% Index-Linked Treasury 26 July,** **2016** 19/1/83: Issued at 99 (2.40) by tender with no minimum price. Calls:– £25% on application; £35% on 14/2/83; £39% on 14/3/83. Next interest payment £1.3625% on 26/1/85. Indexation as 2% Index-linked Treasury 1996. Base month (May 1982) = 322.0 PRI gain to date = 9.3%.
111 92 2/11/83	81 27/7/84	91$\frac{1}{4}$ (91$\frac{1}{8}$ Net)	35.8.15	**750**	**2$\frac{1}{2}$% Index-Linked Treasury 16 April,** **2020** 12/10/83: Issued at 91.50 (2.78) to Bank of England †. Call:– £30% on application; £30% on 7/11/83; £31.50% on 12/12/83. Next interest payment £1.3137% on 16/10/84. Indexation as 2% Index-Linked Treasury 1996. Base month (Feb. 1983) = 327.3. RPI gain to date = 7.5%

SPECIAL Ex DIVIDEND YIELDS

112 110$^{13}_{32}$ 3/11/82	80$^{9}_{16}$ 26/10/81	109$\frac{1}{2}$ (106$\frac{5}{8}$ Net)	5.7.21	**1000**	**12$\frac{1}{2}$% Exchequer 22 Mar.,** **1990**
113 117$^{5}_{32}$ 3/11/82	83$^{11}_{32}$ 26/10/81	116 (112$^{11}_{32}$ Net)	8.1.21	**1757**	**13$\frac{1}{2}$% Exchequer 22 Sept.,** **1992**
114 96 4/10/65	38$^{21}_{32}$ 3/1/75	78$\frac{1}{4}$ (76$\frac{1}{2}$ Net)	9.1.14	a **600**	**6% Funding 15 Sept.,** **199**
115 108$^{31}_{32}$ 27/1/72	51$^{27}_{32}$ 3/1/75	93$\frac{1}{4}$ (90$\frac{5}{8}$ Net)	11.7.14	a **750**	**9% Treasury 15 Mar.,** **92/9**
116 114$^{11}_{16}$ 19/10/82	76$^{7}_{32}$ 26/10/81	115$\frac{1}{4}$ (112$\frac{5}{8}$ Net)	14.7.25	**2900**	**12$\frac{1}{4}$% Exchequer 26 Mar.,** **1999**
117 112$^{1}_{32}$ 	73$^{3}_{16}$ 	113$\frac{1}{2}$	19.7.18	**1400**	**11$\frac{1}{2}$% Treasury 19 Mar.,** **2001/0**

Price and next ex. div. date	Accrued interest + or - * (days)	Price excluding accrued interest	GROSS Yield Interest	GROSS Yield Redemption #	GROSS var. in price = in Red. Yield	INTEREST AND REDEMPTION GAIN OR LOSS TAXED AT 40.0% Net Redemption Yield	Grossed-up Net Red. Yield	var. in price = in Grossed-up Red. Yield	Net price allowing for tax on accrued	INTEREST TAXED AT 37.5% Net Yield Interest	Net Yield Redemption #	var. in price = in Red. Yield	Grossed-up Net Red. Yield	5p var. in tax = in Net Red. Yield
	£		£	£	p	£	£	£		£	£	p	£	p
101¼	+0.783 (124)	101.250	2.278	4.866● 5.399■	3.6	3.933● 4.457■	6.555 7.428	5.9	101.544	1.419	3.991● 4.516■	3.5	6.386 7.225	11.6
85	0.040	84.960	2.475	5.103● 5.466■	2.9 (1.7)	4.244● 4.578■	7.040 7.630	4.8	84.975	1.546	4.279● 4.634■	2.8 (1.7)	6.846 7.414	11.0
98⅞	0.960	97.915	2.594	4.243● 4.421■	1.2 (1.4)	3.294● 3.461■	5.489 5.769	2.0	98.275	1.615	3.353● 3.521■	1.2 (1.4)	5.365 5.633	11.8
82⅜	0.045	82.330	3.310	3.568● 3.657■	0.7 (0.9)	2.412● 2.488■	4.020 4.147	1.2	82.347	2.068	2.484● 2.561■	0.6 (0.7)	3.974 4.097	14.4
81¼	0.770	80.480	3.265	3.527● 3.612■	0.7 (0.8)	2.350● 2.420■	3.917 4.034	1.2	80.769	2.033	2.423● 2.494■	0.6 (0.7)	3.877 3.991	14.6
96⅛ xd 16th Aug.	-1.781	97.906	12.767	13.084	3.3 (1.6)	7.922	13.203	3.5	97.238	8.034	8.459	2.9 (1.4)	13.534	61.7
100⅛ xd 16th Aug.	-1.923	102.048	13.229	13.114	2.5 (1.3)	7.898	13.163	2.7	101.327	8.327	8.221	2.1 (1.1)	13.154	65.2
68⅝ xd 9th Aug.	-0.740	69.365	8.650	11.525	2.9 (1.0)	7.319	12.199	3.3	69.087	5.428	8.742	2.5 (0.9)	13.988	37.1
79¼ 9th Aug.	-1.110	80.360	11.200	12.229 (1996)	2.4 (1.9)	7.579	12.632	2.7	79.943	7.036	8.365	2.0 (1.6)	13.384	51.5
98½ xd 20th Aug.	-1.879	100.379	12.204	12.221	1.9 (1.8)	7.378	12.296	2.0	99.675	7.681	7.704	1.4 (1.4)	12.326	60.2
97 xd 13th Aug.	-1.544	98.544	11.670	11.711 (2004)	1.7 (1.6)	7.074	11.790	1.8	97.965	7.337	7.393	1.2 (1.2)	11.828	57.6

The purchaser of these stocks pays the gross accrued interest in addition to the consideration except where the books are closed when the interest from the settlement date to the next interest date is deducted from the consideration.

Redemption gain or loss taxed at 30.0%.

The amount in brackets is the effect of the commission, allowing for VAT at 15% thereon, on the yield for a money value of £1,000,000.

On application principal and interest are exempt from all British taxes (including Capital Transfer Tax) if the owner, wherever domiciled, is not ordinarily resident in the U.K. These exemptions will not apply so as to exclude the interest from any computation for taxation purposes of the profits of any trade or business carried on in the U.K. Stock may be bought by the public.

＃ Yields to the earliest and latest dates of redemption are shown in both gross yields are within 25p of the nominal rate; otherwise yields are shown to the presumptive date only, but those not shown are available on request.

● Prospective real rate of return based on projected inflation of 10%.

■ Prospective real rate of return based on projected inflation of 7%.

both cash holdings and future institutional cash flow, thus reducing the number of times they need to seek a new yield level. Third, they enable the authorities to exploit superior information, or a judgement on an event that is different from the market's, by selling stock even if they have no immediate need for cash. Fourth, they can reduce the risk of a vicious circle of expectations (or a 'buyers' strike') developing. This can occur if an initial failure to sell stock causes an overrun in monetary growth. If calls are outstanding, partially covering financing needs in the following one or two banking months, institutions will be less likely to judge the authorities to be anxious sellers contemplating the need for a rise in yields, and to delay their purchases. Finally, the smaller amounts of cash that initially need to be found by buyers reduces the impact on the market.

Convertible stocks

Stocks with the right to convert on specified dates, at the holder's option, into longer-dated stocks have been used frequently since January 1981. Convertibles have been of two types. First, those that have provided the right to convert at a single date after some years. There has been only one recent example; this was issued in 1973 with both redemption and the conversion option in 1980. Second, those that provide an option to convert on four or five dates at six-monthly intervals and on deteriorating terms (see Table 7.2). The longer stock has been either an entirely new issue, or a further tranche of an existing issue.

Table 7.2   *12¼% Treasury Convertible 1986*

	Nominal amount of 13% Treasury 2000 per £100 nominal of 12¼%	Implied redemption yield on 13% Treasury 2000
	£750m. issued 9th June 1982 at 97·75 to yield 12·99% (to 1986) Redemption 14 July 1986 at 100 or:	
Date of conversion	*Treasury Convertible 1986*	*(% p.a.)*
14 January 1983	97	12·86
14 July 1983	95	12·58
14 January 1984	93	12·32
14 July 1984	91	12·09
14 January 1985	89	11·89

Source: BEQB, September 1982, p. 349.

In the example, the gross redemption yield on 13% Treasury 2000 at the close of business on 4 June 1982, when the issue was announced, was 13·304 per cent. The running yield was 13·261 per cent. The gross redemption yield on the nearest equivalent short-dated stock (12% Treasury 1986) at the close of business on 4 June was 12·943 per cent whilst the running yield was 12·355 per cent. Thus the stock was broadly comparable in yield to similar short-dated stocks, but yielded about $\frac{1}{2}$ per cent less than the existing issue of 13% Treasury 2000.

The advantage of convertibles to the investor is that they provide a short-dated and therefore less volatile stock with some protection against yields falling sharply. However, there may be costs associated with this protection. Although the authorities have issued convertibles so that they are attractive as shorts in their own right, they have sometimes been expensive in the secondary market so that the investor has had to accept a lower yield as the price of the option to switch longer. In addition, the shape of the yield curve may be such that the investor sacrifices yield whilst holding the shorter stock rather than the longer. The market also is free to move ahead before the option begins to provide protection since conversion terms have normally offered a yield on the longer stock that is lower than that available at the time the issue is announced. In the example of $12\frac{1}{4}$% Treasury Convertible 1986 this drop in yield was $\frac{1}{2}$ per cent, or about 4 points in the price.

There may be several advantages to the authorities of issuing convertibles. First, they provide a slightly different asset to the private sector. This may be saleable, or judged to be saleable, more cheaply to the government when portfolios are already heavy with conventional paper. Second, there may be times when there is no appetite for either longs or shorts *per se*, although buyers who are natural investors in long stocks may be tempted by the safety of a short that provides some protection against a fall in long yields. Third, the authorities may not want to be seen borrowing in the long end. A convertible can be presented primarily as a short, whilst a small drop in yields will mean that the government has actually sold a long. Fourth, the authorities avoid direct pressure on long yields. Lastly, in issuing a convertible rather than a long, the authorities indicate to the market that they will not borrow in the long end at existing yields, although they will at the specified, lower, yields.

Index-linked stocks

A stock whose interest payments and principal are linked to the rate of retail price inflation was first issued in March 1981. The method of calculating yields on index-linked stocks is discussed in Chapter 11.

Until the March 1982 Budget, ownership of the first three index-linked stocks was confined to UK pension funds, UK life companies in respect of their pension liabilities, and registered friendly societies. There were at least four reasons for this. There was an aversion in official circles to index-linking as it suggested a long-term acceptance of inflation. The Wilson Report had commented that 'It is arguable that the issue of index-linked stock by the government would be regarded as of particular significance in implying that it had abandoned its efforts to curb inflation and could generate a wave of heightened fears concerning inflation in the future' (Committee to Review the Functioning of Financial Institutions, 1980a, p. 236). For similar reasons there was official West German and American pressure on the UK authorities. An additional fear was that there would be upward pressure on the exchange rate since index-linked stocks were thought to be attractive to overseas buyers. Non-residents could be forbidden to purchase such stocks, but this would be difficult to police if ownership was open to all UK residents. Finally, limiting ownership avoided the problem of the tax treatment of the index-linking since the stocks could be held only against pensions liabilities where returns from assets were chargeable neither to income tax nor to capital gains tax.

The authorities have sought to develop the market in the new instrument by issuing small amounts of stock with differing maturities, rather than by making one or two large issues, and by facilitating switching between conventional and index-linked stocks. Marketability has improved greatly since the first issue, but it is still poor in comparison with the conventional market. This had been foreseen:

Index-linked long-term government securities might perhaps be less heavily traded than long-dated gilts are at present, partly because they would be better suited to the needs of the long-term institutions and partly because the low nominal interest rate would reduce the tax incentive for deals involving gross and net funds. On the other hand, new opportunities for profitable switching might arise as between indexed and non-indexed securities. (Committee to Review the Functioning of Financial Institutions, 1980a, p. 236)

The authorities' success can be judged by the growth in the number of holders of the stocks. Table 7.3 gives the most recent published data. The personal sector, which has been allowed to buy index-linked stocks since March 1982, clearly finds the 1988 stock, with its advantages as a relatively money-certain instrument offering good returns for high tax-payers, to be attractive. It also appears that there is increasing personal sector interest in the 1996 stock. The remaining issues are held mainly by institutions.

The yields on index-linked stocks have swung widely since their introduction (see Figure 7.1). This volatility has been a result not of changes in real returns in the economy, but of other, more technical, reasons.

Table 7.3   *Number of holdings of index-linked stocks, 1982–3*

Maturity	Nominal outstanding £m.	Number of holdings[1]			
		Early Oct. '82	Mid-Nov. '82	Mid-Feb. '83	Mid-May '83
1988	750[2]	10,800 (8,800)	13,400 (10,700)	21,000 (15,800)	24,900 (18,200)
1996	1,000	2,100 (900)	2,300 (1,000)	3,600 (1,900)	4,400 (2,600)
1999[3]					
2001	250	[4]	700 (500)	1,000 (700)	1,100 (800)
2003	250		[4]	800 (500)	900 (600)
2006	1,000	900 (300)	900 (300)	1,100 (400)	1,000 (400)
2009	400		200	400 (100)	400 (100)
2011	750	800 (200)	800 (200)	800 (200)	800 (300)
2016	750			[5]	900 (500)

Notes: [1] The figures in brackets show the number of holdings identified as holdings of private funds and private trusts. All figures rounded to the nearest hundred.
[2] The amount of the 1988 stock outstanding was increased to £1,000m. in December 1982.
[3] No figures were available for the 1999 convertible stock because it was still in allotment letter form at mid-May 1983.
[4] Official holdings not exhausted.
[5] No figure quoted because the stock was still in allotment letter form.

Source: BEQB, June 1983, p. 180.

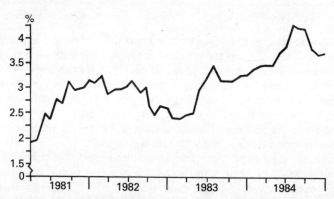

Figure 7.1   *Yield on 2% Index-Linked Treasury Stock 1996 (based on the assumption of a constant 10% rate of inflation)*

Initially investors were very uncertain how to value index-linked stocks. Portfolios contained no comparable asset and the first issue probably represented only 1¼ per cent of the funds eligible for investment. Even by the end of 1983 the nominal £6,480m. of stock in issue represented only 3 per cent of life company, pension fund and general insurance company portfolios. Thus there was an element of non-repeatable stock adjustment as institutions built up their holdings. The extension of eligibility in March 1982 produced a similar increase in demand and acted as a temporary depressant of yields. Applications for the first index-linked stock demonstrated this stock-adjustment demand: fund managers judged there would be further issues, but dared not assume it; they judged the price would not move sharply upward, but they had to protect themselves against the possibility; in many cases they had insufficient time to canvass the views of their investment advisers and panels; on balance it was thought politic to ensure that at least some was put in portfolio. The result was a wide spread of prices at the tender and a thin yield of 2·00 per cent (see Table 7.4).

Table 7.4   *Tenders for 2% Index-Linked Treasury Stock 1996*

Price tendered per £100 stock (£)	% of tenders received	% of total value of tenders
130 or more	0·3	0·1
120–129·75	1·5	1·3
110–119·75	24·8	18·5
100–109·75	55·0	43·4
90– 99·75	15·7	29·1
80– 89·75	2·7	7·6

Source: BEQB, June 1981, p. 176.

Yields have also been affected by changes in the authorities' handling of the market. They adopted the tender method of issue with no minimum price because, like the investor, they had uncertain views on how to value the new instrument. On the first issue they accepted the market's view of the clearing price; on the second issue they struck a price well below that implied by the existing index-linked stock; subsequently they appear to have accepted the judgement of the market and cut off tenders at levels that have provided yields in line with existing issues.

Finally, the market has been thin and undeveloped. There have been small amounts of stock in issue and on occasions prices have reacted strongly to relatively small buying and selling.

In spite of the problems of finding a sustainable yield basis, the introduction of index-linked stocks has brought considerable advantages.

The servicing costs in the early years and (depending on inflation) perhaps also in later years, are lower than those on conventional stocks of the same term. The government's assessment of the prospects for inflation may at times differ from that of investors; in this case it may consider the real cost of borrowing on index-linked stocks to be lower than that on conventional stocks. This may happen, for example, if inflation is on a declining trend, so that inflationary expectations, formed over several years, are lagging the lower rates of more recent periods.

At times the real cost of borrowing may be pushed up because portfolios have become over-heavy with conventional stocks. In this case index-linked stocks 'avoid the problem of persuading institutional investors to increase the proportion of a comparatively unsuitable asset in their port-folios and . . . eliminate the risk premium required for holding securities of a fixed nominal value' (Committee to Review the Functioning of Financial Institutions, 1980a, p. 235). At an operational level they provide an alternative to selling conventional stocks; in particular they make the investor's calculations of the volume of conventional stock the authorities need to sell, and therefore his judgement of the appropriate level of yields, more uncertain.

The usefulness of index-linked stocks has been reduced because the authorities have found it difficult to engineer demand through the tradi-tional techniques of market management. They have found themselves responding to unpredictable surges in investment, aiding liquidity by switching, nursing incipient rallies, carefully judging the balance between price improvement and official supply. They, like investors, note the co-incidences and timing of investment, but there is insufficient experience for there to be more than hypotheses about the causes of demand. There are three such hypotheses: that it is a redirection of cash flow, and redistribution of portfolios, as other markets reach new high levels; that it is a response to a new level of index-linked yields; and that it is a demand for security as inflationary expectations rise.

The growth in the index-linked market is too recent for its behaviour over the financial cycle to provide evidence yet for the first hypothesis.

The authorities have not yet pushed up yields on index-linked stocks in an aggressive fashion to win monetary control over short periods, although a taste was provided by the second issue – 2% Index-Linked Treasury 2006 – in July 1981. This was allotted at a price lower than most market participants expected and as a result was sold out on the first day of dealing. The existing index-linked stock fell about 4 points. There has been no additional experience of the response to a level of yields that are regarded as unsustainably high and of the sensitivity to capital gains expectations, which have enabled the large funding operations in con-ventional stocks to take place in the past.

The view that demand responds to rises in inflationary expectations is widely held, but it often leaves one of two assumptions unstated. If nominal yields rise in line with inflationary expectations so that real yields remain constant there should be continued demand for conventional stocks; the hypothesis therefore assumes that nominal yields will be slow to respond, that real interest rates on conventional stocks will fall and that this will direct investment towards the higher relative returns on index-linked stocks. The alternative assumption is that as inflationary expectations rise, they will also become more volatile – perceived real returns on conventional stocks will become less certain. This will redirect demand to index-linked stocks if nominal yields do not rise by an additional premium to compensate for this uncertainty.

Index-linked convertibles

An index-linked convertible is an index-linked stock with the option to convert into a conventional stock of the same maturity at six-monthly intervals. There has been only one such issue: £1,000m. of 2½% Index-Linked Treasury Convertible 1999, issued on 5 May 1983 at 97·50 to yield 2·71 per cent. The stock was convertible into 10¼% Conversion 1999 on the basis of £100 nominal into £100 nominal on 22 November 1983, 22 May 1984 and 22 November 1984. The yield on the conventional stock if the stock was converted at the first opportunity was 10·12 per cent. Although the conversion option was exercisable on the same terms at each date, the implied terms deteriorated. This was because the holders who converted later suffered the lower yield on their index-linked holdings for longer than those who converted at the earlier dates.

The authorities issued the stock since they thought there would be a demand, before a general election, for a hedge against both a rise and a fall in inflation. There was considerable uncertainty about the price that should be paid for this hedge. In the event, at the issue price, the stock yielded about £0·10 per cent less than the level implied by comparable index-linked stocks and about £3/8 per cent less than comparable conventional stocks on conversion on the first option date (*BEQB*, June 1983, p. 180). Not all the stock was sold on issue, however, and the authorities subsequently cut the price by 5 3/4 of a point from the level at which stock had been previously supplied (see Table 6.1). At this lower price it yielded about £0.17 per cent less than comparable index-linked stocks and, if converted, was in line with conventional stocks.

Low coupon stocks

Stocks with low coupons have been issued at large discounts. They have provided low gross redemption yields, but attractive net yields to higher rate tax-payers (see Table 7.5).

Table 7.5   *Additional tranche of 3% Treasury 1987*

Amount created £m.	Date announced	Date created	Presumed issue price	Gross redemption yield %	Net redemption yield[1] %	Grossed up net redemption yield[1] %
150	13 April 1984	13 April 1984	83	9·158	6·976	17·441

Note: [1] At 60% income tax and 0% CGT.

Deep discount bonds, often with zero coupons, were issued in the foreign currency bond markets by private borrowers from the beginning of 1982. These were bought by residents of countries whose revenue authorities did not treat the capital gain as income for tax purposes. In the UK the tax position is simplified since capital gains tax is payable only on gilt-edged stocks held for less than twelve months.

The lower yields have not been the incentive to make low coupon issues. This is because the cost to the government of an issue is the interest payments *plus* the difference between the issue and redemption price *less* the tax paid by the investor to the Inland Revenue. The total cost of any issue over its life therefore depends on the average tax position of the holders. This cost of making low coupon issues – interest, capital payment and tax forgone – is constantly monitored by the authorities.

The annual cost to the government may be seen by comparing a low coupon stock with other money-certain five-year assets, assuming the investor pays 60 per cent income tax and no CGT (see Table 7.6).

Table 7.6   *Total 'cost' of borrowing on selected instruments*

	(a) Paid by the the borrower %	(b) Received by the Inland Revenue %	(c) Received by the investor %	(a–b) 'Cost' to the government %
3% Transport 1978/88 (created 26 June 1984 at 79 9/16)	9·210	2·349	6·861	6·861
National Savings 27th issue[1]	7·126	0	7·126[2]	7·126
10% Exchequer 1987[3] (at 95 19/32 on 26 June 1984)	11·798	6·256	5·542	5·542

Notes: [1] Holdings could be up to £5,000.
[2] 7·51% compound annual interest rate.
[3] A taplet of £200m. was created on 4 June 1984 and was reported to have run out on 19 June 1984 at 96 1/2.

A major drawback to these issues is that they can rarely be sold quickly. In July 1980, £600m. 3% Treasury 1985 was sold out in thirty-seven days, but this was exceptional. In general, the issues have the same limitation as index-linked stocks – investors buy them sporadically and unenthusiastically. They are thus difficult to use in any predictable fashion for month-to-month monetary control. Low coupon stocks have been declining as a proportion of the conventional coupon market. They are now used to replace maturing low coupon stocks, keeping existing high tax-paying funds in the market, rather than for raising new money.

Variable coupon stocks

Variable coupon stocks were designed to provide greater price stability than conventional stocks and thus be attractive when the prospects for conventional stocks were uncertain. They did this by bearing a coupon that varied each week with the return on Treasury bills. The method of calculating the return on variables is described in Chapter 11.

The first variable rate stock since 1920 – Variable Rate Treasury Stock 1981 – was issued in May 1977, in part as an official response to criticism that innovation and flexibility were lacking in the authorities' handling of the market. The £400m. issue was made to the Issue Department, which responded to market bids; this permitted a flexibility in the pricing of the new instrument which was considered necessary since the authorities had little idea of the price that investors would be prepared to pay and needed the maximum freedom to find a suitable level. The issue sold out in just over three weeks, with about half being bought by investors outside the banking system (*BEQB*, September 1977, p. 302).

A second issue, also of £400m. but maturing in 1982, was issued in July 1977. Demand was slow, however, and it took until May 1978 for the issue to run out. A third issue of £400m., maturing in 1983, was made in January 1979. This ran out in May.

Variable rate stocks provided a competitive return over their life in comparison with conventional stocks of a similar term. Thus the Bank of England calculates that the first variable rate stock, if bought in May 1977 at a price of 98, would have provided an annual return of 11·8 per cent, compared with 10·6 per cent on 12¾% Exchequer 1981, which matured six days after it (see Figure 7.2). In addition there was superior short-term price stability; for example, between September 1977 and December 1978 the return on this variable rate stock was 17·5 per cent and the return on the conventional high coupon stock –3·1 per cent (*BEQB*, December 1981, p. 474).

There have been no replacements for the three issues as they matured. There appear to be six reasons for the failure of the experiment. First, they

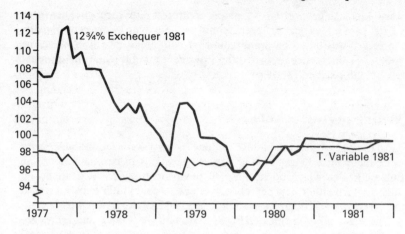

Figure 7.2   *Price of Variable Rate Treasury 1981 and 12¾% Exchequer 1981*

were intended to attract demand when the authorities were unable to sell conventional coupon stocks. This, to some extent, turned out to be the case. After the first issue, which was sold mainly on its novelty, official sales coincided with periods of uncertainty. It was not appreciated, however, that when the outlook is uncertain investors want money-certain assets. It is not sufficient to provide an asset that loses value less fast than other gilt-edged stocks, especially if marketability is poor or unproven. It would have required a considerable yield advantage over money market instruments to compensate for this disadvantage. Second, they were intended to attract demand from non-bank investors. In this they signally failed after the first issue. 'None of the [variable stocks] has attracted non-bank holders on a regular, substantial basis ... The value of these stocks in helping to restrain the growth of sterling M3 has therefore been modest'. Third, they were an attractive asset for the discount market and banks since they provided a secure yield above the rate at which they could always borrow from the Bank of England (*BEQB*, December 1981, p. 474). It was not intended, however, that they should provide a relaxed life for discount houses. Fourth, their price was not in fact stable. They were unattractive when yields on conventional stocks were falling and capital values rising. The Bank tried to make them more marketable by itself buying them against sales of conventional stocks, often reversing the switch later. This process was limited, however, since the authorities usually needed to be net sellers of stock and were not interested in providing open-ended support so investors could avoid the penalty of misjudgement. Fifth, the ½ per cent margin over the Treasury bill discount rate became worth less, as a proportion of the rate, as interest rates rose: $\frac{1}{2}$ per cent over a 7 per cent rate is very different from $\frac{1}{2}$ per cent over 14 per cent. Finally, the return was based on the discount rate on Treasury bills and not the yield. The difference absorbed the $\frac{1}{2}$ per cent margin when the discount rate on bills reached 13·914 per cent.

Timing and method of issues

Until the early 1980s the pattern for new issues was for the announcement to be made on a Friday at 3.30 p.m., applications to be received on the following Thursday and dealings to begin on the Friday. This delay, during which either new perceptions or events could intervene, increased the authorities' difficulties in judging the yield basis for new issues.

There are now no rules (*BEQB*, March 1982, p. 32n) and issues are made at times and by methods that suit the circumstances. In particular, there can be rapid issuing when demand has suddenly arisen, the Issue Department's portfolio lacks a suitable volume or type of stock, and the authorities wish to tap the enthusiasm while it lasts.

The main changes in the pattern have been:

- Issues are often announced on a Monday at 3.30 p.m. for application on Thursday and dealing on Friday.
- An issue can be announced, and placed with the Issue Department, to be available to the market some days later. Taplets are now usually announced and created on a Friday or Monday and made available to the market on the immediately following Monday or Wednesday.
- An issue, either tap or taplet, can be created and announced on one working day, placed with the Issue Department on the same day, and be available for supply to the market the next day. The announcement is normally at 3.30 p.m., but can be later.
- There can be long periods between the announcement of an issue and its availability to the public. This happens when a new type of instrument is being created and it is thought that investors need more time than usual to assess it. This period was fourteen days in the case of the first variable rate stock, seventeen days in the case of the first index-linked stock and seven days in the case of the index-linked convertible stock.

Spread of dates

A spread of maturity dates gives the authorities the choice of when, within the dates, to redeem the stock. It is thus an option against the investor, who will find his stock redeemed at the earlier date if the government can issue a new stock at a lower yield. A spread of dates, as well as potentially depriving an investor of the higher yield during the period of the spread, makes the stock less useful as a match against liabilities.

The authorities have increasingly conceded narrower spreads and single dates. Since 1972 there has been only one single-dated issue maturing wholly after the year 2000, other than those created by investors accepting a conversion option on shorter stocks. The exception was 10½% Exchequer 2005 issued in January 1985. The authorities have been able to retain a spread of dates for stocks maturing in the next century, or with one date in the next century, since they are needed by the life companies and pension funds to meet their long-term liabilities.

Example 7.2 *12% Exchequer 2013/17*

£1,000m. issued 15 June 1978 at 96 to yield 12·50%

Redemption: 'If not previously redeemed, the stock will be repaid at par on 12th December 2017, but Her Majesty's Treasury reserve to themselves the right to redeem the stock, in whole or in part, by drawings or otherwise, at par on or at any time after 12th December 2013 on giving not less than three months' notice in the London Gazette.' (Prospectus).

Maturities
The matching needs of the life companies and pension funds provide a natural market for long-dated stocks. In recent years the authorities have been reluctant to issue such stocks, which lock them into high nominal, and unknown real yields for long periods. The pressure of events and the need to sell the planned volume of stock have often made it necessary, however.

This reluctance has been the reason why a period of heavy official sales of long-dated stocks has sometimes culminated in the issue of a somewhat shorter stock as the authorities felt their immediate needs to have been satisfied. On a larger scale, the contraction in borrowing and reduced pressure to sell in 1982, 1983 and 1984 allowed a reduction, and at times total cessation, in issues of twenty-first-century stocks.

'Year and a day'
Only stock held for less than twelve months is liable to CGT. Until 1985, when new rules were announced for treating interest as accruing on a day-to-day basis, the authorities sometimes encouraged buyers by issuing new stocks and taplets in such a way that they could be held for more than twelve months but only one interest payment need be received. This involved issuing either a medium- or long-dated stock that was dealable both cum-dividend and special ex-dividend (see Chapter 9) or a further

tranche of a short-dated stock with more than six months until its first ex-dividend date. In both cases there was only a short window in which a purchase was possible that left more than twelve months until the next ex-dividend date. This technique improved the authorities' control over the timing of sales, at the cost to the Inland Revenue of permitting investors a single untaxed interest payment.

Example 7.3   *10½% Exchequer Convertible 1986*

£1,100m. issued to the Issue Department on 14 March 1983
at 98·75 to yield £10·99% (to 1986)
First dealings 16 March 1983

Calls: £25% on application, £40% on 29 April 1983 and £33·75%
on 23 May 1983

In this example the first interest payment was £5·9676 per cent on 19 November 1983. This covered 250 days, accruing by different amounts as each call was paid. The stock went ex-dividend on 12 April 1984. An investor had from 16 March 1983, when the stock was first available in the market, to 11 April 1983 to buy if he was to hold it for at least twelve months and be able to sell before it became ex-dividend on 12 April 1984. In practice the investor will wish to buy earlier rather than later during this period since this leaves more time to choose a suitable selling opportunity before the 1984 ex-dividend date.

Assuming no change in yield and purchase on the first day of dealings on 16 March 1983, the return if sold on 11 April 1984 would have been as shown in Table 7.7. The return has three elements: a capital gain of £0.36, which bears no tax; the coupon of £5.9676 paid on 19 November 1983, which was taxed at the specified rate; and the 145 days of accrued interest attached to the stock (£4.17123) when it was sold on 11 April 1984, which bore no tax.

Table 7.7   *Return on 10½% Exchequer Convertible 1986*

Income tax %	Tax rate CGT %	Net yield %	Grossed-up yield %
0	0	11·02	11·02
30	0	9·12	13·03
37 1/2	0	8·64	13·82
40	0	8·48	14·13

Example 7.4   *12% Treasury 1995*

£250m. issued to the Issue Department on 29 May 1981 at 90 1/4 cd to yield 14.34%. At the time also dealable special ex-dividend at 84 7/8 to yield 14·27%. First day of dealing 1 June 1981. Ex-dividend on 18 June 1982.

In this example an investor could have bought special ex-dividend between 1 June and 17 June 1981, and sold before the ex-dividend date on 18 June 1982, having held for at least twelve months and received only one 6 per cent coupon.

If the stock was purchased special ex-dividend on 1 June 1981 and sold cum dividend on 17 June 1982 the return on the assumption of an unchanged yield of 14·34 per cent would have been as shown in Table 7.8.

Table 7.8 *Return on 12% Treasury 1995*

Tax rate			
Income tax %	*CGT* %	*Net yield* %	*Grossed-up yield* %
0	0	13·72	13·72
30	0	11·69	16·70
37 1/2	0	11·18	17·89
40	0	11·01	18·35

Pricing an issue – tendering

The authorities now use four methods of pricing new issues:

(i) Conventional new issues are made at a minimum tender price. This ensures that the benefit of a rise in the market between the announcement of an issue and applications is gained by the government (*BEQB*, June 1979, p. 128). This method of issue was adopted after February 1979 when it was found that the authorities' judgement on the price at which they could sell stock could be overtaken by events, or improving sentiment, between the time of the announcement and applications. This admission of the problems of correctly pricing an issue several days ahead of applications has not been followed by that of its corollary – that if a stock can be priced too low in the light of new events it can also be priced too high. Thus the 'minimum' price stays.

(ii) Taplets are placed directly with the Issue Department of the Bank of England at the price ruling in the market at 3.30 p.m. on the day of issue.

(iii) New issues of index-linked stocks are made without any minimum tender price, although the authorities reserve the right to reject bids. This provides them with maximum pricing flexibility: they are able to consider the pattern of bidding; they can see precisely how much more they can borrow for each reduction in the price; they are informed of the quality of many of the applications and can perhaps form a judgement of applicants' willingness to pay higher prices later in the market; finally, they can alter their minimum price in line with the immediacy of their need to borrow.

(iv)   A new stock may be placed directly with the Issue Department and is then available to meet bids from the market makers. There is no indication of the price at which bids will be considered or met. This method was used to issue the three variable rate stocks.

All stock in a minimum tender price issue is allotted at the minimum accepted price (the 'allotment price'). If there are insufficient applications at or above the minimum tender price, the balance is allotted to the Issue Department at the minimum tender price. If the stock is oversubscribed, applications at the highest price are allotted in full; applications at each lower price are also allotted in full until the whole issue is covered. Those applying at the minimum accepted price will be scaled down to ensure that the issue is covered exactly. Applications have to be in units of a $\frac{1}{4}$ point. An example might be a £1,000m. issue at a minimum tender price of 96$\frac{1}{4}$:

£250m. applied for at 97$\frac{3}{4}$
£150m. applied for at 97$\frac{1}{2}$
£500m. applied for at 97$\frac{1}{4}$
£400m. applied for at 97.

The applications at 97$\frac{3}{4}$, 97$\frac{1}{2}$ and 97$\frac{1}{4}$ are allotted in full; they total £900m. Those applying at 97 are allotted 25 per cent of their application so that the issue is exactly covered at the minimum accepted price of 97, a premium of $\frac{3}{4}$ point to the minimum tender price.

Index-linked issues are made on a similar basis, except there is no minimum tender price which is only selected by the authorities after applications have been received.

8 Futures: The Twenty-Year Contract

History

The market in interest rate futures developed in Chicago where there was already a tradition of trading in commodity futures. In October 1975 one of the exchanges, the Chicago Board of Trade (CBT), began trading in Government National Mortgage Association (GNMA or 'Ginnie Mae') pass-throughs.* At the beginning of 1976 a rival exchange, the International Monetary Market (IMM), began trading in futures contracts for 90-day Treasury bills. The initial reception by the bond community was lukewarm, partly because the concept of interest rate futures was little understood and partly because there seemed to be something indecent about trading government debt alongside wheat, soya beans and pork bellies. None the less, it took only two and a half years for trading volume to soar.

The success of the contract led to many imitations – to contracts in other fixed-interest instruments and to the establishment of financial futures markets in other centres. The IMM now has contracts in 90-day certificates of deposit and 90-day eurodollar time deposits, as well as the original 90-day Treasury bill. The CBT has contracts in a ten-year Treasury note, and a long Treasury bond,† as well as the original GNMA. The most successful of these has been the Treasury bond. This was introduced in 1977 and volume began to climb rapidly nine months later. The volume of Treasury stock traded in the futures market in the first quarter of 1984 was $1,347,715m., compared with $597,284m. traded in the cash market by all reporting and recognised dealers.

In 1981 the New York Futures Exchange (NYFE) opened and began trading in bonds, bills and foreign currencies. It has not succeeded in

---

* Pass-throughs are mortgage-backed marketable securities where the interest and principal on the underlying mortgages are collected by an agent and 'passed through' to the holder of the security in the same proportion as they are received by the pool.

† The contract is a notional 8% Treasury bond; delivery can be made of any bond, of whatever coupon, that if callable cannot be called for fifteen years from the date of delivery and if not callable does not mature for at least fifteen years from the date of delivery.

threatening the established markets in Chicago. The London International Financial Futures Exchange (LIFFE) opened in September 1982 and over the following two years introduced contracts in four currencies (against the US dollar), three-month eurodollar time deposits, three-month sterling time deposits, a US Treasury bond, a twenty-year gilt-edged stock and the FT-SE 100 share index.

Forward transactions and futures

Transactions where a seller contracts to deliver a specified volume of a specified item to a buyer at some date in the future at a price fixed now have been common for many years, especially in the commodities and foreign exchange markets. A futures contract is similar to a forward transaction except in three ways. First, the article traded, the contract, is standardised and may not actually exist, although its relationship to the underlying asset is strictly defined, whereas most forward transactions are individually tailored to the particular item and need of the buyer or seller. Second, futures contracts are revalued each day and gains and losses are credited and debited to the clients' accounts. Forward transactions do not usually entail any receipt or payment until maturity. Third, a futures contract is normally closed off with a transaction in the opposite direction before delivery has to be made, whereas in a forward transaction it is usually the intention of the seller to deliver. The small number of contracts that are settled by delivery means that futures markets are often considered to be more speculative than cash markets.

End-users and speculators

There are two types of participant in any market – the end-user and the speculator. The end-user, or hedger, tries to ensure that he will make a gain or loss on his futures contract to offset as exactly as possible a gain or loss on his actual or intended cash position. An example might be an industrial company that knows that it will be in receipt of a specified sum in three months' time for which it will have no use for another three months. In order to ensure that the company receives today's interest rate on its money, starting three months hence, it can buy three-month futures contracts. If interest rates fall, it will make a profit on its contracts that will compensate it (hopefully exactly) for the lower interest rate it will be receiving for three months when its money becomes available three months hence. Equally, if interest rates rise it will make a loss on its contracts, but it will receive a higher return when it comes to investing its money (see Example 8.2 below). Thus the end-user seeks protection from a price movement, avoiding both profit and loss on his combined cash and futures positions.

The speculator hopes to profit from either a movement in prices (see Example 8.3 below), or a movement in relative prices. Since he does not want, or does not own, the underlying article, he will close out his positions before delivery. Conceptually, the speculator has four roles that contribute to efficiently functioning markets.

First, it is unlikely that an end-user wishing to execute a bargain in one direction will simultaneously find another end-user wanting to execute a bargain in the opposite direction. The speculator carries the risk in the period between the two end-users' dealing. The speculator is paid because the transactions cannot be carried out by the two hedgers except at prices that the speculator judges will make him a profit to compensate him for the risk.

Second, it is unlikely that the two end-users will want to deal in the same number of contracts, even if they want to deal at the same time. The speculator again intervenes, carrying the balance of the contracts, and thus allows the end-users to hedge.

Third, an end-user wanting to trade in a large number of contracts might have difficulty in persuading another end-user to trade in the opposite direction without a large movement in prices. This could be needed to persuade the other end-user to deal at a time, or in a size, that did not really suit him. The speculators, however, will deal as soon as the price has moved by more than they judge to be justified in the circumstances. The speculators therefore minimise the price movements needed to absorb hedging transactions.

Fourth, speculators spread risk through arbitrage – buying something that is cheap and simultaneously selling something that is expensive. Arbitrage can refer to the purchase of one security and the sale of another, or to the purchase and sale of the same security for delivery at different dates, in expectation that the prices will move to the speculator's advantage. An example of the first type of arbitrage might be that between actual gilt-edged stocks in the cash market and futures contracts (see Example 8.1 below). An example of the second might be that between gilt-edged futures contracts deliverable in, say, September and December (see Example 8.4 below).

Arbitrage transfers some of the effects of a transaction in one market into other markets. Thus a large buyer of gilt-edged stock in the cash market will need to push up prices until sellers are found. Arbitrageurs will sell stock in the cash market and buy gilt futures contracts as soon as it becomes profitable. In this way a transaction in the cash market is partly or wholly satisfied by transactions in the futures market. If there are participants in the futures market who would not operate in the cash market there is increased liquidity. Inasmuch as the expenses of dealing in the futures market are less than those of dealing in the cash market the price movement required to bring the arbitrageur into action, and therefore the price movement produced by end-user activity, is reduced.

The gilt contract

Turnover in the gilt contract is relatively small (see Figure 8.1) and the market lacks liquidity. Moreover, activity is mainly in a single contract: that for the nearest delivery month when it is not in the spot month (see 'A note on details' at the end of this chapter). Thus the discussion of arbitrage between contracts for different delivery months is at present largely theoretical as far as the London market is concerned.

There are several reasons why the gilt contract has had a slow start. Prices have entered a period of comparative stability after the shocks and fiscal debaucheries of the 1970s. Of the natural end-users of a long contract, the life companies have the advantages in the cash market of the one year CGT concession and the opportunities of buying stock special ex-dividend; they can see limited advantage in buying a contract that might entail taking delivery of a stock that undoes carefully engineered positions. At the same time, natural conservatism has made them unwilling to sell futures to lock in profits on these positions. The pension funds at first were uncertain whether profits from futures trading would be taxable or, indeed, whether trading would threaten their whole tax-free status (see Chapter 9). Even after it was made clear at the end of 1983 that profits would be free of tax and participation would not affect their tax privileges, they were slow to become active. Inertia, lack of skills in a new market, the lengthy process of obtaining trustees' understanding and consent, and the need to gear up bureaucracies and accounting procedures have contributed to this. In addition trustees have become more cautious. A public debate has been in progress about the accountability of funds and there has been a change in the official attitude to fiscal privilege. This change was demonstrated by the ending of Life Assurance Premium Relief in the 1984 Budget and the change at the beginning of 1984 in the tax treatment of the profits made by building societies in the gilt-edged market.

The contract has become a useful tool for the market makers – the jobbers. There are no data on turnover by type of user, but it would appear that at times the jobbers dominate the market; they are always important participants. There are two reasons for this. First, it is not normal practice for the major jobbers to deal with each other in the cash market since it entails showing their positions to their competitors. However, by using floor brokers they are able to deal anonymously with each other in the futures market. In this way they can pass all or part of a cash market bargain on to others, instead of taking the whole risk themselves.

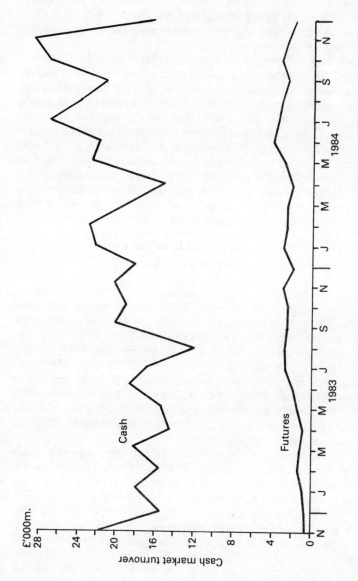

Figure 8.1   Value of gilt interest rate contracts traded and the volume of transactions in the cash market

Sources: The Stock Exchange; LIFFE.

Second, the jobbers cannot initiate business in the cash market by approaching a broker and asking him to find them buyers or sellers, without advertising their position or intentions. The futures market allows them to take the initiative and anonymously to alter their risk according to their judgement of the market.

Although the usefulness of the futures market is limited by its lack of liquidity and the existence of a single contract – the jobbers cannot hedge positions in short- and medium-dated stocks or make themselves a long position in one maturity against a short position in another – the market does help them to alter their overall long-dated position at their own initiative, to deal anonymously, and to transfer part of the risk of a single or cumulative cash market bargain to others. In thus aiding the efficient working of the cash market it has something in common with the role of the brokers' screens in the US Treasury market – a system that enables the three dozen recognised dealers in government securities to trade anonymously with each other at their own initiative, positioning their books as they wish and transferring some of the risk to other dealers.

Connecting the cash and futures markets

In principle, relative prices in the gilt-edged market and the futures market should change only if the cost of carry changes – that is, if the level of short-term interest rates changes. Otherwise, if the cash market price rises relative to the futures price, arbitrageurs will sell stock in the cash market, earn interest on the money thus raised, and buy in the futures market. Such an opportunity is displayed in Example 8.1 below. If the cash market price falls relative to the futures price arbitrageurs will buy stock in the cash market, paying interest on the money needed to settle the bargain, and sell in the futures market. This arbitrage will continue until it has brought the relationship between the cash market and futures back to a position where it is no longer profitable.

A rise in short-term interest rates will increase the cost of owning a cash stock so that the price of the cash stock will need to fall relative to the futures price if equilibrium is to be maintained. A fall in short-term interest rates, on the other hand, will reduce the cost of owning a stock and equilibrium will be maintained only if its price rises relative to the futures price. Given the level of short-term interest rates and expenses, arbitrage should ensure that prices of stocks in the cash and futures markets will always be such that they provide equal returns.

When arbitrageurs consider profit opportunities involving the cash and futures markets, they base their calculations on the cheapest deliverable stock. An arbitrageur selling futures to buy a cash stock will buy the cash stock that is the cheapest for him to deliver into the futures contract when the time comes for the futures sale to be settled. An arbitrageur selling in the cash market and buying in the futures market will expect that his futures purchase will be settled by the vendor delivering the stock that he finds the cheapest. Thus the cheapest deliverable stock is the one that can be bought in the cash market in the normal way and then delivered in the futures market with the greatest profit or the least loss.

Identifying the cheapest stock partly depends on the level of short-term interest rates, because the cost of financing the purchase has to be allowed for. The interest rate cost (the cost of carry) is the difference between the cost of borrowing to finance the purchase over the period of the arbitrage and the rate of interest accruing on the purchased stock, since this belongs to the buyer of the cash stock.

If c = the coupon on the cash stock expressed as a percentage per annum, r = the financing rate expressed as a percentage per annum, p = the cash price of the stock expressed as a fraction of par and t = the number of days of carry, the cost of carry is

$$(c - pr)t/365.$$

The cheapest deliverable stock is that which provides the largest result from:

$$\text{(futures price)} \times \text{(price factor)} + \text{(cost of carry)} - \text{(clean price)}$$

Example 8.1
On 30 May 1984 the price of 13¾% Treasury 2000/03 was 119 7/8 and that of 13% Treasury 2000 was 115. The clean prices on the two stocks were 115·091 and 110·085. The price of the June futures contract was 102 4/32. The rate of interest for thirty days was 8 5/8 per cent. Table 8.1 shows the profit from buying each stock and delivering into the futures market on the final possible delivery day. The profit on delivering 13¾% Treasury 2000/03 was 0·016 per cent, compared with a loss of 0·442 per cent on delivering 13% Treasury 2000. The first stock was therefore the cheaper to deliver. The expression is only approximate; an exact calculation would have to include any interest payments, interest reinvestment rates, taxes, commissions and the interest cost of the margin on the futures position.

Since lower coupon stocks are generally more attractive to tax payers than higher coupon stocks they are low yielding when looked at from the point of view of a non-tax payer. Thus the cheapest deliverable stock, which is calculated ignoring taxes, is usually one of those with the highest coupon and the highest gross yield.

In practice, arbitrage does not pull the returns on the two markets to complete equality. The prices at which it is profitable to arbitrage depend on the interest rate that borrowers pay for the period of the arbitrage (if selling the futures and buying the cash stock) or earn (if selling in the cash market and buying in the futures). There is, moreover, no single identifiable borrowing and lending rate for the period of an arbitrage: bank borrowers effectively borrow at the bid end of the LIBOR (London Interbank Offered Rate) spread; some foreign-currency-based banks are able to create cheap sterling; some institutions have money placed with them at below market rates for prudential or other non-commercial reasons. The same peculiarities can apply to the lending rates enjoyed by those watching for arbitrage opportunities.

Table 8.1   *Identifying the cheapest deliverable stock*

	Futures price	Price factor	Product of futures price and price factor	Cost of carry for 30 days	Clean price	Profit (loss)
13¾% Treasury 2000/03	102 4/32	1·1243779	114·827	0·280	115·091	0·016
13% Treasury 2000	102 4/32	1·0711398	109·390	0·253	110·085	(0·442)

There was also a marked bias towards the futures contract being cheap once the market settled down in the middle of 1983 (see Figure 8.2). This had largely disappeared by the middle of 1984 as a few pension funds became free to deal in the contract and began arbitraging out of cash stocks. The cheapness of the contract in the earlier period was in part because many institutions had tax and accounting reasons for not buying futures in preference to cash stocks, even if futures were the cheaper. This would not have mattered if arbitrageurs were free to deal in unlimited size. In practice, however, there were only a limited number of participants, mainly the jobbers, who could borrow stock freely and who were thus able to sell in the cash market and buy futures. Moreover, even those participants had prudential limits placed on their exposure. On the other hand, there were no practical limits to arbitrageurs selling futures to buy cash stocks; they merely needed access to money.

Expectations, forward/forward rates

It is usual for interest rates to rise as the term to maturity increases (see Chapter 10). In futures market jargon this upward sloping yield curve is known as positive cost of carry. Positive cost of carry implies that futures prices should become progressively lower for each lengthening in the

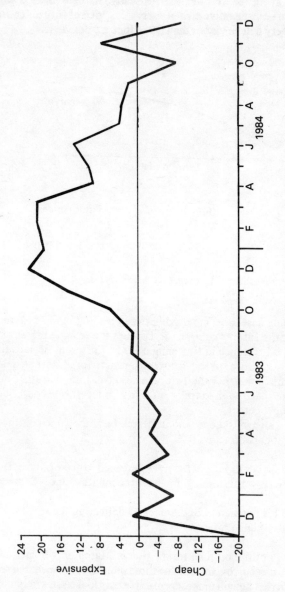

Figure 8.2 The cheapness or dearness of the cheapest deliverable cash stock compared with the price of futures in the near-month

contract – money has to be borrowed, or can be lent, at progressively higher interest rates (see Figure 8.3). Equally, if there is a downward sloping yield curve or negative cost of carry, the price of futures contracts for distant delivery will be higher than those for near delivery.

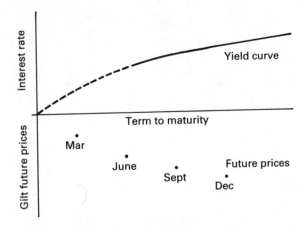

Figure 8.3   *Yield curves and futures prices*

If the financing cost for the period between dealing in the cash market and delivery of the futures contract determines the relative prices of cash and futures, the difference in financing costs for different periods determines the relationship between futures contracts for different delivery dates. It is at this point that the futures market in interest rates and the expectations approach to the term structure of interest rates described in Chapter 10 come together.

For example, an arbitrageur who in March buys the June contract and sells the September contract will:

(i)   receive delivery in June of his stock and need to make payment;
(ii)   need to borrow this money for the three months June – September, until
(iii) he closes his position in September by delivering the stock that was delivered to him in June.

He will carry out the original transaction in March only if the interest rate at which he can borrow in June for three months to finance delivery of his stock is such that he will make a profit. He may look at this in two ways. First, in March he may have calculated the rate at which he would need to borrow in June to break even and concluded that the rate was unlikely to be higher. Second, in March he may have had a specific expectation about the level of interest rates that would prevail in June and this was such as to promise him a profit. In either case he would have had a view on the level of interest rates – the forward/forward rate – for a three-month period beginning in June.

There are three practical points. First, it is unlikely that the arbitrageur will ever take delivery or deliver – he will close out his positions with bargains in the opposite direction when the change in relative interest rates or the return to the normal relationships he was anticipating has taken place. Second, he may close off his interest rate risk by dealing in the three-month sterling deposit contract; this opens up a whole further area of arbitrage. Third, although the arbitrage described here is a major source of activity in Chicago, the London market is new and there is little activity in any month except that nearest to delivery.

Examples

Example 8.2
An industrial company knows it will be in receipt of £1m. in three months' time for which it will have no use for another three months. It wants to ensure it obtains today's interest rate on its money, although it will not actually have the cash for three months.

The three-month sterling interest rate contract is for £250,000 (from March 1985 £500,000) and is quoted on an index basis. Settlement is at LIBOR *less* 0·25 per cent. If the annual rate of interest were 10 per cent, for example, the quote would be 100 *minus* 10 *plus* 0·25, giving a price of 90·25. If interest rates fell to 8 per cent, the price would be 100 *minus* 8 *plus* 0·25 giving a price of 92·25. One tick (see 'A note on details' below) is 1/100 of 1 per cent; in other words a change in the price from 92·00 to 92·01. The value of one tick is therefore:

$$1/100 \times 1\% \times \text{one-quarter of a year} \times \text{the face value of the contract}$$
$$(\pounds 250,000) = \pounds 6.25$$

The company carries out the following transactions:

	Cash	*Futures*
10 March	Expects to have £1m. available in June. The 3-month CD rate is 10%.	Buys four September £250,000 3-month sterling time deposit contracts at 90·00 (interest rate 10·00%).

10 June

Company receives £1m. and buys a CD giving an interest rate of 8%.	Sells four September contracts at 92·00 (interest rate 8·00%).
Loss	Gain
2% for one quarter on £1m. = £5,000.	200 ticks × £6.25 × 4 contracts = £5,000.

Interest rates may have moved in the opposite direction. In this case there would have been a loss on the futures position to set against the higher interest rate earned on the cash.

In this example the loss on the cash market transaction exactly equals the profit on the futures. This happens because the interest rate in the cash market falls from 10 per cent to 8 per cent, which is the same as the interest rate movement experienced on the September contracts between March and June. There was thus no change in the 'basis' – the spread between the cash and futures interest rate. In practice, a hedge transaction is rarely so convenient. The actual result achieved will differ from the result of this example if the basis changes. The hedger might, for example, find himself in June selling the four September contracts at 91·00, implying an interest rate of 9 per cent. In this case the profit is only £2,500 (100 ticks × £6.25 × 4 contracts).

Example 8.3

The speculator hopes to profit from a movement in prices. Since he does not want, or does not own, the underlying article, he will close out his position before delivery.

The twenty-year gilt contract is for £50,000. One tick is 1/32 of 1 per cent, so the value of one tick is:

$$1/32 \times 0·01 \times £50,000 = £15.625.$$

In October, the speculator buys twenty December contracts at 96 8/32. He sells them six weeks later at 98 2/32. His profit or loss is: 20 contracts × 58 ticks (98 2/32 – 96 8/32) × £15.625 = £18,125, less the interest cost of the margin of £1,500 per contract (the LIFFE minimum initial margin) on twenty contracts for six weeks.

Example 8.4

Arbitrage that involves selling a contract in one instrument and simultaneously buying another contract in a different but related instrument is known as spread trading. An example might be taking a position between a three-month Treasury bill and a three-month CD contract in expectation that the relationship between the two will alter. The emphasis is on *relationship*.

Arbitrage that involves selling and buying the same contract, but for different delivery months, is known as a straddle. The section on how the cheapest deliverable stock is identified shows how arbitrage distributes price pressures between the cash and futures market. Straddles carry this process one stage further by distributing price pressures between different delivery months.

This is an example to show how a straddle should work. Straddles are rarely possible in the gilt contract because there is little liquidity except in the near-month (see Glossary).

10 June
>   Arbitrageur sells twenty September gilt futures contracts at 96 18/32 and buys twenty December gilt futures contracts at 97 8/32.
>   The spread is 96 18/32 – 97 8/32 = 22/32 or 22 ticks.

10 July
>   He buys twenty September gilt futures contracts at 106 9/32 and sells twenty December gilt futures contracts at 107 7/32.
>   The spread is 106 9/32 – 107 7/32 = 30/32 or 30 ticks.

>   The profit is 30/32 – 22/32 = 8/32, or 8 ticks × 20 contracts × £15.625 = £2,500, less the interest cost of the margin required by LIFFE for one month.

A note on details

The contract

The contract is a notional stock with a term to maturity of twenty years at the first day of the relevant delivery month. The coupon is 12 per cent, interest is payable at half-yearly intervals as on most real stocks and there is assumed to be no accrued interest at the date of delivery.

The nominal value of each contract is £50,000. This was chosen as being large enough to avoid unwieldy numbers of contracts being traded, but small enough to enable a number of contracts to be chosen that would closely match exposure in other markets.

Contracts are traded for delivery in March, June, September and December. Contracts are traded for five delivery months at any one time so that when transactions in a new contract begin the furthest delivery date is fifteen months into the future.

Settlement can be on any business day up to the final business day in the delivery month. The day is chosen by the seller, who must give two days' notice of delivery.

A stock can be delivered that has a term to maturity of not less than fifteen years and not more than twenty-five years on the first day of the delivery month. Stocks with double dates are assumed to mature on the earliest date. The stock cannot be partly paid, be in bearer form (see Glossary), or be convertible or index-linked. It must be delivered in multiples of £50,000 nominal. In order to avoid a clash with the procedures of the Inland Revenue and The Stock Exchange that control the creation and avoidance of interest payments, stocks may not be delivered during their special ex-dividend period.

The last trading day for contracts in a delivery month is two business days before the last business day.

Note
LIFFE will provide a legal definition of all the contracts on request. A description of the contract is provided in Pézier (1983).

Paying for the delivery of real stock
LIFFE publishes a list of stocks that may be delivered on each of the business days in a delivery month. This is necessary since some stocks become special ex-dividend or go ex-dividend during the month and are therefore only eligible for delivery on some days. They also publish a price factor and the accrued interest for each deliverable stock; this relates each deliverable stock to the notional contract and enables a calculation to be made of the amount a buyer will pay a seller on the settlement day for the real stock that is being delivered. This price factor is defined as 'the price per £1 nominal value of the specific real stock at which this stock has a gross redemption yield of 12 per cent, minus the undiscounted amount of accrued interest' (Pézier, 1983, p. 27). The details of the calculation are provided in Chapter 11.

Details of the accrued interest provided by LIFFE are for the sum payable on each £50,000 value of deliverable stock as at the last day of the month before the delivery month; they also publish the size of the accrued interest that needs to be added for each additional day until delivery.

The data in Table 8.2 are published by LIFFE.

Quotations
Quotations are in 1/32 of £100 nominal of the notional stock. This is worth £15.625 on a contract of £50,000.

Exchange Delivery Price
The price used to calculate the sum payable on delivery is the LIFFE official closing price on the second business day prior to delivery.

Table 8.2 Twenty-year interest rate contract – price factors and accrued interests (Contract month: June 1984)

	Stock	Price factor	Daily accrued	Initial accrued	Delivery days
1	Treasury 13% 14 Jul 2000	1·0711398	17·8082	−783·56	X†††XXXX78††12345††89012††56789†
2	Treasury 13¾% 25 Jul 2000–03	1·1243779	18·8356	−1,035·96	X†††XXXXX††89012††XXXXX††89012††56789†
3	Treasury 11½% 19 Mar 2001–04	·9616062	15·7534	1,150·00	1††45678††12345††89012††56789†
4	Funding 3½% 14 July 1999–2004	·3597397	4·7945	−210·96	X††XXX78††12345††89012††56789†
5	Treasury 12½% 21 Nov 2003–05	1·0367569	17·1233	171·23	1††45678††12345††89012††56789†
6	Treasury 8% 5 Oct 2002–06	·6909664	10·9589	613·70	1††45678††12345††89012††56789†
7	Treasury 11¾% 22 Jan 2003–07	·9812586	16·0959	−836·99	X††XXXXX††XXXX5††89012††56789†
8	Treasury 13¾% 26 Mar 2004–08	1·1115844	18·4932	1,220·55	1††45678††12345††89012††56789†
9	Treasury 5½% 10 Sep 2008–12	·4779819	7·5342	617·81	1††45678††12345††89012††56789†

Key:
Daily accrued – accrued interest per day on £50,000 face value.
Price factor – price factor expressed as a fraction of par.
Initial accrued – accrued interest on £50,000 face value as of the last day of the month prior to the delivery month.
Delivery days – † = non-business day; X = 3-week special ex-dividend period and preceding business day.
Invoicing formula – invoicing amount = (settlement price) × (price factor) × 500 + initial accrued + (daily accrued) × delivery day in month.

Source: LIFFE.

Initial margin

The minimum initial margin required by LIFFE is 3 per cent or £1,500 per contract except in the spot month. The actual margin required by a member of LIFFE from his client may be higher. Profits and losses are calculated each day, with prices based on the LIFFE official closing prices, and payments are made to those with profits and required from those with losses. The daily payments needed to maintain the initial margins are known as 'variation margin'.

A straddle – a simultaneous long and short position in the same contract for different delivery months – is charged a margin of £250 per contract, except in the spot month.

Required LIFFE margins for both straight positions and straddles are doubled for the spot month.

See the section 'Limit to price movement'.

When spot

The spot period for any delivery month begins five days prior to the first day on which the seller can give notice of delivery. During this period initial margins are assessed in isolation from margins in other contract months.

Gross redemption yields

The gross redemption yield to which a price in the contract is equivalent can be calculated using tables provided by LIFFE. The actual equivalent yield will depend on when, during a delivery month, the stock is delivered and on expenses such as commissions and interest on margins. The yields also assume that the seller settles with one of the cheapest stocks to deliver.

LIFFE supplies two tables. The first, 'Long Gilt Price Versus Yield', shows for each 1/32 price in the futures contract the equivalent GRY on a 12 per cent notional stock with twenty years to maturity and no accrued interest at delivery. The second, 'The Long Gilt Yield Correction Factor', shows how different the actual yield will be from the theoretical yield on the notional stock given in the first table. It shows the amount by which the yield on the notional stock needs to be corrected in order to find the yield on a real stock. The correction factors until June 1985 are those applicable to 13¾% Treasury 2000/03 since this is normally the stock that is the cheapest to deliver.

Limit to price movement

There is a limit to the price movement of 2 points in either direction from the previous working day's LIFFE official closing (settlement) price. If this is breached there is a pause in trading. This limit is a protection made necessary by the fact that users are only required by LIFFE to pay an initial margin equivalent to 3 points. The pause in trading enables new margin payments to be called.

There is no price limit in the spot period or in the four weeks before the first delivery date for a contract.

Tick

A tick is the value (in pounds and pence) of the smallest movement permitted in each contract. It is specified by LIFFE.

9 Interest Payments and Taxation

Interest on gilt-edged stocks is paid half-yearly. The only exceptions are $2\frac{1}{2}\%$ Consols and Annuities, where it is paid four times a year.

Accrued interest is the amount of interest that would be paid if the interest was paid each day. The accrued interest on stocks with a life of five years or less from the dealing date is accounted for separately: a buyer pays the market price plus the accrued interest and a seller is paid the market price plus the accrued interest.

Example 9.1   *12% Treasury 1986*

Dealing date	Settlement date	Last coupon payment	Next coupon payment	Accrued interest %	Price	Amount paid/ received per £100 nominal of stock
2 September (Friday)	5 September (Monday)	12 June	12 December	2·795 (85 days)	100 3/4	103·545

In this example the number of days is found as follows:

June	July	August	September	Total
18	31	31	5	85

The accrued interest can then be calculated as:

$$\frac{\text{coupon} \times \text{number of days}}{365} \text{ or } \frac{12 \times 85}{365} = 2\cdot795\%$$

The calculation also uses 365 days in a leap year.

The accrued interest on stocks with a life of over five years from the dealing date is included in the price of the stock. The subtraction of the accrued interest from the market price gives the 'clean' or 'net' price.

Example 9.2 10½% Treasury 1999

Dealing date	Settlement date	Last coupon payment	Next coupon payment	Accrued interest %	Price	Clean price	Amount paid/received per £100 nominal of stock
2 September (Friday)	5 September (Monday)	19 May	19 November	3·136 (109 days)	98 1/2	95·364	98 1/2

Ex-dividend

Payment to the actual holders on the interest payment date would be delayed if stock continued to change ownership and required registration into new names up to the date of the coupon. The Bank of England therefore ceases to register stock, with entitlement to the next coupon, about thirty-seven days before the coupon is actually paid. These thirty-seven days are known as the ex-dividend period and stock is quoted 'xd'. When stock is transferable with entitlement to the next interest payment in the period immediately prior to being ex-dividend, it is sometimes designated cum-dividend or 'cd'.

The accrued interest is negative during this period. This is necessary because a seller would otherwise receive both the use of the buyer's money and the interest payment, payable to him as the registered holder, part of which represents interest accruing during the ex-dividend period when he was not the actual owner. This negative accrued is counted back from the next interest payment date to the settlement date excluding the day on which the interest is actually paid.

The negative accrued is accounted for separately on stocks with a life of five years or less from the dealing date, the buyer paying the market price less the accrued interest and the seller being paid the market price less the accrued interest.

Example 9.3   *12% Exchequer Convertible 1985*

Dealing date	Settlement date	Next coupon date	Accrued interest	Price	Amount paid/ received per £100 nominal of stock
2 September (Friday)	5 September (Monday)	22 September	−0·559 (minus 17 days)	101 5/16 xd	100·7535

The negative accrued on stocks with a life of over five years from the dealing date is included in the price of the stock. The addition of this accrued to the market price gives the clean price.

Example 9.4   *12¼% Exchequer 1999*

Dealing date	Settlement date	Next coupon date	Accrued interest	Price	Price plus accrued interest (clean price)
2 September (Friday)	5 September (Monday)	26 September	−0·705 (21 days)	105 1/4 xd	105·955

Rules for producing ex-dividend dates

The Bank of England's rules for producing ex-dividend dates are:

(i) 'For British Government and Government-Guaranteed stocks on which dividends are payable half-yearly, ignore the dividend due date and count back 37 calendar days. The 37th day is the ex-dividend date unless it falls on a non-business day, when the ex-dividend date is the first business day closer to the dividend date, i.e. the 36th, 35th, etc., day.'

(ii) 'For British Government stocks on which dividends are payable quarterly the ex-dividend dates are the first of the month preceding the month in which the dividend is due unless that day should fall on a non-business day, when the ex-dividend period is shortened as in (i) above.'

(iii) 'Where "half-year" stocks (as in (i) above) have dividend dates coincident with the quarterly dates covered in (ii) above, the ex-dividend dates for the "quarterly" stocks are adopted for the "half-yearly" stocks.'

(iv) '10½% Exchequer 1987 has the same ex-dividend dates as British Government quarterly stocks with dividends due on 5 April and 5 October.'

(Bank of England, December 1978 and February 1984)

Special ex-dividend

Under Stock Exchange rules (Rule 545.2(b)) all stocks except shorts and 3½% War Loan can be dealt in both ex-dividend and cum-dividend for three weeks before the official ex-dividend date (see Figure 9.1). This is known as the special ex-dividend (sxd) period. Since the rule forbids such dealings for longer than three weeks from the ex-dividend date, the start of the period is found by counting forward to the first business day if the three week period would otherwise fall on a holiday.

When dealt in special ex-dividend accrued interest is calculated in the same way as stocks dealt in ex-dividend. In Example 9.5, the difference between the prices cum-dividend and ex-dividend is only 6 1/8 points, although the interest payment is worth 6 3/4 points to a gross fund. Since it is worth less than 6 3/4 points to net funds, they are prepared to pay a premium to buy the stock special ex-dividend and avoid a taxed interest payment. For the same reason, a fund that pays no tax will normally sell special ex-dividend, and receive the gross interest payment.

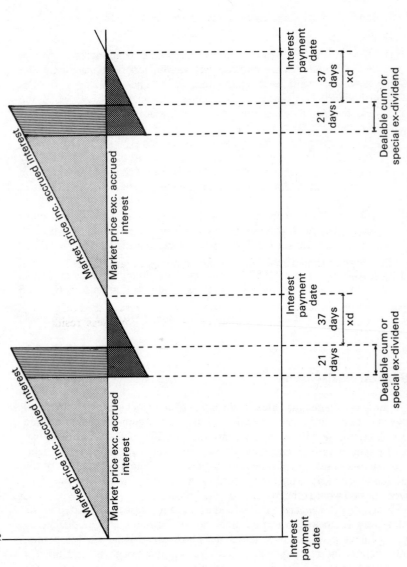

Figure 9.1 Accrued interest on medium- and long-dated British Government and government-guaranteed stocks other than 3½% War Loan

Example 9.5   *13½% Exchequer 1994*

Dealing date	Settlement date	Last coupon payment	Next coupon payment	Accrued interest %	Price	Price plus accrued interest (clean price)
2 September (Friday)	5 September (Monday)	27 April	27 October	4·845 (131 days)	113 7/8 cd	109·030

or:

			27 April	−1·923 (minus 52 days)	107 3/4 sxd	109·673

Payment of interest

The Bank of England pays interest net of the basic rate of tax. The exceptions are:

- Persons not ordinarily resident in the UK who have successfully applied for interest to be paid gross (see section on overseas residents for details).
- Holders of 3½% War Loan, unless otherwise requested. The interest still needs to be declared by UK residents for tax purposes.
- Stocks on the National Savings Register. Most gilt-edged stocks can be bought and sold by applying on a form obtainable from post offices. The application is sent to the Bonds and Stock Office of the Department of National Savings. The investor does not know the exact price at which he will deal or when the Government Broker will carry out the transaction. Commissions are considerably lower on small bargains than those charged by ordinary stockbrokers. Up to £10,000 may be invested in any one stock on any one day and there is no limit to the amount of each stock that may be held. Stock held on this register needs to be sold through the Bonds and Stock Office, although it can be transferred to the regular Bank of England register. In this case it may be sold in the normal fashion through a stockbroker. Interest on stock held on this register is paid gross, although it needs to be declared for tax purposes.
- Approved pension funds. Pension funds can write to their Inspector of Taxes, who will request the Bank of England to pay interest without deduction of tax. This arrangement needs to be renewed every time a new holding is acquired or reacquired. For this reason many funds

retain, as a permanent holding, a small amount of every stock, or every stock in which they are likely to invest.

- Holdings that produce interest of less than £2.50 gross per half year.

Taxation in general

Banks, accepting houses, trustee savings banks and discount houses pay the relevant rate of corporation tax on their profits, of which those made in the gilt-edged market are part. The concession that CGT is only paid on gilt-edged stock held for less than one year is not therefore applicable to them. Income and capital gains are taxed equally.

General insurance funds are taxed in a similar fashion to banks.

Life assurance funds
(a)   In respect of life business they pay a maximum of $37\frac{1}{2}$ per cent on policy holders' unfranked income (income other than from dividends). Under current proposals this will be reduced to 35 per cent from the 1986/7 financial year. Since they are generally taxed on investment income and realised capital gains less management expenses most funds pay less than the maximum, especially if business is growing rapidly, since the start-up costs of new policies are heavy. Industrial life business tends to grow slowly and this may cause these businesses to pay rates nearer the maximum. The rate of CGT on policy holders' funds is the lower of that for individuals (30 per cent) and $37\frac{1}{2}$ per cent. The standard CGT concession on gilt-edged gains and losses applies.
(b)   In respect of approved pensions business there is exemption from tax on both income and capital gains. Realised book profits (without the standard CGT concession) and income form part of the profits of the pensions business. These are taxable except to the extent they are reserved for pension annuitants.
(c)   In respect of general annuity business there is no tax payable on investment income provided that payments to annuitants in the tax year are equal to or greater than the income. Realised book profits, without the standard CGT concession, form part of the profits of the business.

Building societies pay a special 40 per cent rate of corporation tax on investment income and capital gains. Until 1984 societies enjoyed the standard CGT concession on their gilt-edged holdings.

Approved pension funds pay tax on neither investment income nor capital gains. The Inland Revenue has the right to make an assessment if it considers that the purpose of a fund's policy has been to make trading profits rather than long-term investments (Finance Act 1970, s. 21). This power has rarely been used.

Authorised gilt-edged unit trusts pay 30 per cent on income and are exempt from CGT. CGT is payable by the underlying holder on disposal.

Investment trusts pay corporation tax on income and are exempt from CGT. CGT is payable by the underlying holder on disposal.

Personal sector. Interest is treated as income for income tax purposes. The standard CGT concession applies.

Jobbers. Both interest and capital gains are part of the profits of the business and are treated according to the legal status (partnership or company) of the business.

Tax treatment of accrued interest

At present, when calculating income tax and CGT accrued interest is treated as part of the cost of a stock. The whole of the interest, when paid, is assessed on the holder as income (Wigmore v Thomas Summerson and Sons Ltd, 1925; Inland Revenue Commissioners v Oakley, 1925; Schaffer v Catermole, 1980).

Excessive and systematic shedding of interest payments before stock goes ex-dividend should be avoided since the Inland Revenue has considerable powers; these are specified in the Income and Corporation Taxes Act 1970, s. 460 – s. 470. This caution applies to both institutions and persons. If the Inland Revenue thinks that individuals have reduced their higher rate income tax by more than 10 per cent, the interest can be taxed as if it accrues daily. This does not apply if it can be shown that the behaviour was exceptional, was not systematic and that there was no such avoidance in the previous three years (Income and Corporation Taxes Act 1970, s. 30).

These practices are scheduled to change in February 1986 when interest between interest payment dates will be treated as accruing on a day-to-day basis and be charged to income tax. When a transaction takes place, the seller will have the interest that has accrued from the preceding interest payment date to the transaction date treated as income, and the buyer will be allowed an equal deduction. The charges and deductions will be excluded from computations of CGT. Ex-dividend transactions will involve the negative interest being charged to income tax in the case of purchases and being treated as a deduction from income tax in the case of sales (Press Release, Inland Revenue, 28 February 1985).

Bond washing rules

The special ex-dividend period has in the past provided opportunities for profitable exploitation. Tax laws and Stock Exchange rules have been developed to counter these. The latest and most radical are to be introduced in February 1986, when interest will be treated as accruing on a day-to-day basis and thus will be subject to income tax.

The earliest moves, in the Finance Act 1937, ch. 54, were against high tax-paying individuals selling cum-dividend and simultaneously buying back ex-dividend, thus avoiding (washing) a coupon taxed as income. Later, rules were necessary to stop gross funds selling special ex-dividend and buying back cum-dividend. This was profitable for two reasons. First, it was worth net funds paying a higher price special ex-dividend than the cum-dividend price less the gross interest payment. This effectively enabled the gross funds to sell a coupon at a premium. Second, it also meant there were buyers of stock special ex-dividend from gross fund sellers who were switching into stock cum-dividend. The government thus found itself repaying withholding tax to gross funds that had created an interest payment. This ploy reached such a point in the late 1950s that it was rumoured that the tax reclaimed from the Inland Revenue on an interest payment on 4% Funding 1960/90 was greater than the value of the interest payment itself.

The rules and laws regulating dealing during the special ex-dividend period can be distinguished by their two functions: there are those aimed at ensuring that interest payments are not created by gross funds; and there are those aimed at controlling the amount of income a net fund can shed by selling cum-dividend.

Creation of coupons

In the case of special ex-dividend sales The Stock Exchange requires that the brokers supply the buying jobber with a certificate stating:

> we have made all enquiries necessary to satisfy ourselves including obtaining a written assurance from our principal that the principal has been the beneficial owner of this stock for more than one month prior to the date of this sale or that he has bought the stock ex-dividend previously during the current three week period. (Council of The Stock Exchange, 1984, Rule 675.1 and Permanent Notice No. 13–18)

The certificates and the written assurances have to be retained for at least six years and provided for The Stock Exchange or Inland Revenue if requested.

Stock Exchange rules also require that the certified transfer for any special ex-dividend purchases over £50,000 be deposited with the Quotations Department of The Stock Exchange. It is not released until the day the stock officially goes ex-dividend unless it is needed to settle, in its entirety, a special ex-dividend sale. In this case the stock is redeposited with the Quotations Department by the new owner.

The Inland Revenue can charge gross funds most of the basic rate of tax if they sell without having held the stock for at least one calendar month and receive a dividend (Income and Corporation Taxes Act 1970, s. 471 and s. 473).

The effect of the first Stock Exchange rule is to ensure that a seller has not sold special ex-dividend to repurchase cum-dividend, thus creating an interest payment, unless he has been the owner of the sold stock for at least one month. The effect of the second rule is to ensure that all special ex-dividend stock is frozen in the Quotations Department and cannot be used to settle a switch into cum-dividend stock. The charge made by the Inland Revenue removes the incentive for a gross fund to buy stock cum-dividend, claiming the gross interest payment, having sold special ex-dividend.

Avoidance of income tax
The Stock Exchange rules require that when a stock is bought special ex-dividend, brokers supply the jobbers with a certificate stating:

we have made all enquiries necessary to satisfy ourselves including obtaining a written assurance from our principal that this purchase neither reverses a cum-dividend short sale already effected nor will be reversed by a cum-dividend sale done simultaneously or yet to be effected before the payment of the dividend . . . should he wish to sell this stock ex-dividend during the current three week period such sale will be carried out through a Member of The Stock Exchange with a jobber. (Council of The Stock Exchange, 1984, Rule 675.1 and Permanent Notice No. 13–18)

An effect of the rule is that a net fund cannot sell a stock cum-dividend and buy back special ex-dividend.

Tax concessions

The Capital Gains Tax Act 1979, sch. 2, para. 1, defines gilt-edged securities as the existing stocks listed in Part II of the schedule, together with 'stocks and bonds issued under section 12 of the National Loans Act 1968' and those 'guaranteed by the Treasury and issued under the electricity (Scotland) Acts 1943 to 1954, the Electricity Acts 1947 and 1957 and the Gas Act 1972'. They do not, therefore, include local authority debt.

Holders of such stocks enjoy two tax concessions:

(i)   There is no stamp duty payable on transfers of stock. This privilege is shared with other public sector debt and, since 1976, with debentures and loan stocks. Equities, and other property over a certain value, attract 1 per cent duty.

(ii) Only stocks held for less than twelve months attract CGT. This was introduced in 1969. Losses can be used to offset other gains. Stocks held for longer periods pay no CGT. Equally, losses on stocks held for more than a year cannot be used to reduce the CGT charge on profits made elsewhere.

Both these concessions aid liquidity and this enables the government to sell stock on a lower yield, or more stock on the same yield. It also encourages switching and thus enables the authorities to influence the whole market by dealing in only one or two stocks (Committee to Review the Functioning of Financial Institutions, 1980a, p. 204).

Capital gains tax

The provision that only capital gains on stocks held for less than one year are liable to CGT and that losses on such holdings are allowable (Capital Gains Tax Act 1979, s. 67(1)) is a valuable incentive for net funds to hold gilt-edged stock. It is equally expensive to the Inland Revenue. The manner in which allowable losses and tax-free gains can be taken are therefore closely regulated. The provisions are:

• A loss is not allowable if a stock is reacquired within one month of its disposal, or within six months if the reacquisition is not carried out through a stock exchange, except against a subsequent chargeable gain on the reacquired stock. This is sometimes known as 'the one-month-repurchase rule'. It is not allowable against gains on other asset disposals. A loss on the reacquired stock, if taken within a year, is allowable (Capital Gains Tax Act 1979, s. 70).

• The one-month repurchase rule also applies if a further holding of a stock is acquired and then disposed of within one month. This is to stop the rule being circumvented by, effectively, reacquiring a stock before it is sold (Capital Gains Tax Act 1979, s. 70).

- A stock sold more than one year after its acquisition cannot be reacquired on the same day if it is to be regarded as a new investment; nor can it be reacquired for cash settlement on the day following the sale (Finance Act 1982, s. 88).
- A position open and closed on the same day is matched (Finance Act 1982, s. 88).
- A sale is matched against the first acquisition made within one year of the sale. If there is insufficient stock acquired on the first date to cover the disposal, the next acquisition is used (Capital Gains Tax Act 1979, s. 68).
- The acquisition date on stocks that have been obtained by conversion is deemed to be that of the acquisition of the original stock (Income and Corporation Taxes Act 1970, s. 326 and Capital Gains Tax Act 1979, s. 82).

Overseas residents

Interest on $3\frac{1}{2}$% War Loan in registered form is paid gross to all holders, unless otherwise requested. Interest on War Loan in bearer form, and interest on other gilt-edged stocks in this form, is paid net of UK tax at the basic rate. However, payments are made gross on bearer stocks (including War Loan) if the application for payment of each coupon is accompanied by an exemption claim form with the name of the beneficial owner and proof of tax-exempt status.

Until 1977 it was usual for new issues to include the facility of having their interest paid gross to persons not ordinarily resident in the UK and for the stock to be available in bearer form. These are known as FOTRA (Free of Tax to Residents Abroad) stocks. Such issues were discontinued as a measure to make sterling assets less attractive to non-residents when the exchange rate was under upward pressure. The issue of FOTRA stocks has not been resumed (except on one occasion in 1984 – $10\frac{1}{4}$% Treasury Convertible 1992), although taplets that add to existing FOTRA issues are created. FOTRA stocks (including $3\frac{1}{2}$% War Loan) amounted to 87 per cent of nominal gilt-edged stocks outstanding at the end of February 1977 compared with 20 per cent at the end of 1984.

There are two ways of arranging payment gross on stocks held in registered form.

First, by completing form A3 and applying to the Inspector of Foreign Dividends, Lynwood Road, Thames Ditton, Surrey, KT7 ODP. If the Inspector is satisfied that the beneficial owner is a person not ordinarily resident in the UK he will authorise the Bank of England to make payments without deduction of tax. Each holding needs to be identified and the Bank of England sets up separate exempt accounts for each stock. The amount of stock can be altered without new application once such an account has been opened. For this reason some overseas funds retain permanent holdings of small amounts of every stock in which they are likely to invest. The Inspector automatically reviews exemption, the frequency depending upon the circumstances of each case; review is more frequent if there are a large number of beneficiaries. It usually takes about one month after the Inspector receives form A3 for the exemption arrangements to be made. Thus purchase of stocks shortly before they go ex-dividend should be avoided if the first interest payment is to be made without deduction of tax. If a net payment is received on a FOTRA stock the tax can be reclaimed by completing form A1 and applying to the Inspector of Foreign Dividends. This form, like form A3, also requires that the name and address of the beneficial owner be given. Repayment usually takes about four weeks.

Strict interpretation of the Income and Corporation Taxes Act 1970 (s. 99 (1)) would mean that relief from tax would not be due unless the stock was actually held on the interest payment date. As a concession to long-term holders, however, relief may be allowed if the stock is sold during the ex-dividend period. 'Long-term holder' usually means a person who has owned the stock for some time, the period being at the discretion of the Inspector. In practice claims have been allowed when the security has been held for more than one month but consideration is given to the individual circumstances of each case. The concession does not apply to stock sold prior to the ex-dividend date.

The requirement that the name and address of the beneficial owner be declared on both form A1 and form A3 means that gilt-edged holdings should be avoided unless the owner is a person not ordinarily resident in the UK, or is a legal entity managed and controlled outside the UK, and is prepared to divulge the required information.

Second, an 'E' arrangement. This is an Inland Revenue concession enabling interest to be paid on FOTRA stocks beneficially owned by a person not ordinarily resident in the UK and registered in the nominee companies of banks and approved stockbrokers. The aim of the concession is to reduce the number of individual claims for exemption. The UK nominee submits a list of holdings, together with an indemnity against any interest being mistakenly paid gross to a person ordinarily resident in the UK, to the Inspector of Foreign Dividends (form 217 A/FD). The authority to pay gross is normally issued to the Bank of England within seven days. The Bank will then open an exempt account; this takes about six weeks. The agent has fourteen days from the payment of the interest to submit a list of beneficial owners and their holdings to the Inspector (form C9). The exemption authority is cancelled if the holding falls to nil. An 'E' arrangement is intended only for long-term holdings, which are described as those spanning two or three interest dates. Stocks that form part of a trust or an estate in the course of administration must not be included in the 'E' arrangement; instead exemption should be claimed by the beneficiaries on form A3.

All gilt-edged stocks, irrespective of whether they are FOTRA, may have their interest paid gross in two circumstances. First, to those with sovereign immunity. Claims for exemption should be made to the Inland Revenue, Policy Division 5 (International), Somerset House, Strand, London, WC2R 1LB. Second, where a double taxation agreement allows. The agreement between the UK and the overseas government differs in every case and there are no agreements with some countries. Some agreements provide for the rate of UK tax to be limited to a rate less than the basic rate. A specific claim form for each country is provided by the Inspector of Foreign Dividends. This has to be completed by the claimant and then certified by the tax authorities of the relevant country. If he is satisfied, the Inspector will arrange for the interest either to be paid gross, or to be taxed at the relevant reduced rate.

The scheme to treat interest as accruing on a day-to-day basis will not apply to those who are not ordinarily resident in the UK, unless they are trading in the country through a branch or agency.

Contract Stamp

Contract stamp is payable on contracts issued by members of The Stock Exchange for gilt-edged bargains. The bands are: up to £100 (0), £100.01 to £500 (£0.10), £500.01 to £1,500 (£0.30) and a flat £0.60 thereafter.

Value Added Tax

Value Added Tax at 15 per cent is paid on commission charged on gilt-edged bargains for UK residents and private individuals resident in the rest of the EEC. Residents of the Channel Islands, corporate residents of the non-UK European Community acting in a business capacity and residents of the rest of the world are zero-rated. Some UK fund managers with overseas clients are charged VAT in the normal fashion and may be able to reclaim from HM Customs and Excise.

10 The Term Structure of Interest Rates

All stocks in the gilt-edged market are the ultimate liability of a single borrower; they have equal creditworthiness; nearly all enjoy good, if not totally equal, liquidity; and few stocks have complications such as sinking funds to affect their value. It is rare, however, for stocks to have the same redemption yields even if they have the same coupons. The differences in yields are a result of different maturity dates. The relationship between yield (see Chapter 11) and maturity is described as the term structure and the graphical illustration is the yield curve (see Figure 10.1).

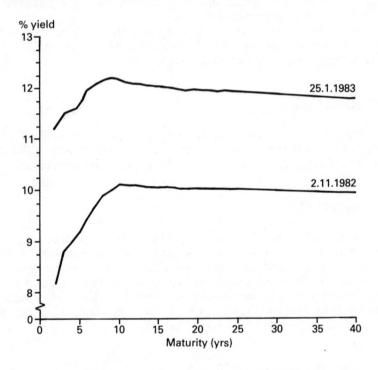

Figure 10.1 *Fitted yield curves as at 2 November 1982 and 25 January 1983*
Source: Bank of England.

There are at least three explanations of the way the term structure is determined. The lack of agreement leaves the authorities unclear about their ability to influence the gilt-edged market in the direction desired by policy.

Thus, if investors are more averse to changes in capital values than to changes in income levels, they will normally need to be offered a higher yield to buy longer and more volatile stocks. If they are more worried about fluctuations in income they may be persuaded to switch longer without any increase in yield or even for a reduction. If investors regard all stocks as the same, or all stocks within a certain range of maturities as the same, an increase in supply and yield in one part of the market will cause them to switch into it until yields are equalised. It follows that if investors are prepared to substitute stocks of differing terms in this manner the authorities cannot alter the shape of the yield curve by changing the term to maturity of their sales; they have no power to twist the yield curve to influence the exchange rate or to reduce interest rates in specific maturities to help industrial or local authority borrowers.

If investors have liabilities of specific terms they will prefer assets to match. In this case stocks of different maturities may not be substitutes and the authorities can twist the curve by changing the maturity of the issues they supply. The extent of the authorities' influence will depend on the freedom with which investors can risk moving from their matched positions.

If the yields at each term are merely the short-term interest rate that investors expect to prevail at that point in the future, an increase in the supply of a particular maturity will cause investors, all other things being equal, to switch longer or shorter into that stock until its yield returns to the previous relationship with yields on other maturities. In this case the increase in government supplies may affect the level of the yield curve, but not its shape, and the ability to twist the curve is lost.

Explanations of the term structure

Convention describes three explanations of the term structure: the pure expectations theory; the liquidity premium theory; and the institutional or segmented markets theory. Market practitioners have a tendency to view these theories as assuming such certainties or simplifications that they border on the absurd. However, the simplifications of theory aid understanding of a more complicated reality and help ensure that practitioners are conscious of perhaps otherwise unstated assumptions that underlie their views.

Expectations

The expectations approach appeals to economists because of its con- sistency with the way that pricing is viewed in futures markets (see Chapter 8). The approach sees the term structure as representing at each point the level of short-term (spot) interest rates that are expected to prevail at that point in the future. There is then implicit in the term structure the expected interest rate for every maturity at every point in the future. The term structure changes as views of the future level of spot rates change.

The mechanism for this may be seen by assuming an investor has funds available for a specified period and surveys the whole spectrum of yields from cash to forty-year stock. The investor will choose to buy the stock, or series of stocks, that he believes will provide him with the best return during the period he has the funds. He may hold cash, or a series of short stocks and reinvest the maturity proceeds, or stocks longer than the period for which he has the use of the funds and sell in the secondary market. Whenever the investor makes a decision, even if the decision is to do nothing, there is implicit an expectation about the level of interest rates for each term at every point during which he has the use of the funds.

A simplified example might assume an investor with funds available for two years and opportunities consisting of a short-term deposit and one-, two- and three-year stocks. The investor can make a decision once a year. The example ignores expenses and compounding. The investor may:

- hold short-term money for one year and then buy either a one- or two-or three-year stock;
- hold short-term money for two years;
- hold a one-year stock and then reinvest in either short-term money or a one- or two- or three-year stock;
- hold a two-year stock for two years;
- hold a three-year stock for one year and reinvest in either short-term money or a one-year or two- or three-year stock;
- hold a three-year stock for two years.

The decision to hold money rather than stock involves expectations of the level of short rates. The decision to hold a series of stocks involves expecta- tions of the level of one- and two-year yields in one year's time. The decision to hold a three-year stock for two years involves expectation of the level of one-year yields at the end of two years. If the investor had no such expectations he would be unable to decide at the beginning of his two-year holding period whether he should buy the one-year stock and then reinvest in the two- or three-year stocks or buy the three-year stock and sell after two years. Thus, if the yield on the one-year stock at the beginning of the investor's two-year period is 2 per cent and that on the two-year stock is 3 per cent, the yield on the one-year stock in one year's time is expected to be 4 per cent.

If it is assumed that there are arbitrageurs who can borrow money (to buy stock) or stock (to sell short) so they can freely deal in stocks of any maturity, it follows that (a) the future yield on every stock at each point in the future can be assumed to be contained within the term structure, and (b) all yields contain expectations about the level of spot interest rates at every point in the future.

Most participants in the gilt-edged market would regard the expectations theory as implausible. They would doubt that they invest in accordance with expected future short rates, might doubt its relevance in the case of institutions with measurable future liabilities and would certainly doubt their ability to forecast day-to-day changes in the term structure. The pre-condition of a good investment manager is scepticism about anything pretending to certainty. He would applaud the oft-repeated comment that to believe in the expectations theory was to believe that any buyer of Consols must 'think that he knows exactly what the rates of interest will be every day from to-day till Kingdom Come' (Robinson, 1951, p. 102n).

Tests have shown that the level of forward spot rates predicted by the term structure systematically exceeds realised spot rates. In an uncertain world, failure of realised spot rates to coincide with those predicted earlier by the market would prove little, but there should be no systematic bias (Kessel, 1965). As a result, theorists now regard the explanation as inadequate (e.g. Shiller *et al.*, 1983).

Liquidity preference
Liquidity preference explains why forward interest rates predicted by the term structure have an upward bias and thus explains why the yield curve is usually upward sloping.

The explanation rests on two assumptions: first, it assumes that investors are more averse to capital risk than to fluctuations in income and therefore prefer shorter stocks; second, it assumes that borrowers prefer to match the assets they are buying by issuing long-dated liabilities on which the cost is certain. These opposing preferences mean that interest rates will normally be higher on longer-dated stocks than on shorter-dated.

It follows that the return from buying a longer-dated stock will exceed the return from buying a series of shorter-dated stocks even if short-term interest rates are not expected to change. This higher yield may be regarded as compensating risk-averse investors for the greater capital risk of holding longer-dated stocks. If investors are risk-averse the authorities have the power to alter the shape of the yield curve by increasing supplies of longer-dated stocks, which will only be saleable at higher yields. Thus this theory has some of the same implications for policy as the segmented markets approach, but for different reasons.

The higher yield earned on longer stocks is a result of their greater volatility – longer stocks will show greater depreciation than shorter stocks if interest rates rise uniformly at every term (see Chapter 11). The increase in volatility for a given lengthening of term is greater on shorter than on longer stocks. The steepness of the yield curve will therefore be greatest at the short end of the market and the curve will gradually flatten out (see Table 10.1).

Table 10.1   *Percentage fall in price for each three-year lengthening in term on an 8% stock moving to a 9% yield*

	% change in price from par	% change in price for lengthening
Three years	−2·6	–
Six years	−4·6	−2·0
Nine years	−6·1	−1·5
Twelve years	−7·3	−1·2
Fifteen years	−8·2	−0·9

The yield curve will slope upwards except when it is expected that short-term interest rates are at high and unsustainable levels. In this case investors will be prepared to hold longer and more vulnerable paper either to capture certainty of income for longer or to take advantage of greater capital appreciation when interest rates fall. The liquidity preference approach is therefore often combined with the expectations approach (Hicks, 1939).

The segmented markets approach

The institutional or segmented markets approach assumes that investors have greater aversion to income fluctuations than to capital risk. It therefore comes to different conclusions from the liquidity preference approach, with its opposite assumptions.

Examples of institutions with a preference for certain maturities are easy to find. Life funds have at least some measurable liabilities, and they can match these by buying assets with a fixed stream of income and by assuming a rate at which these can be reinvested. They also normally write their policies with such conditions that payment on early surrender is at a discount to contributions so that the fund is protected even when stock values are low. Pension funds have liabilities as long as or even longer than the longest-dated stocks, so they match, or at least minimise, the period of income uncertainty by holding the longest stocks. Building societies and banks have short-dated liabilities and buy short-dated and more capital-certain stocks. These are simplifications of the institutional behaviour described in Chapters 3 and 4, but amount to a preference for certain maturities.

The approach emphasises that such institutions do not regard all stocks as similar irrespective of term; they do not substitute in response to higher yields; they do not invest purely in response to an expectation of future interest rates. It follows that increases in supply in one part of the market, raising yields, will not cause switching between maturities sufficient to re-establish the previous relationship between yields; that investors can be persuaded to be permanent holders of longer and more volatile stocks on lower yields than shorter stocks; and that the authorities have the ability to influence the term structure by altering the maturity of their sales.

Behaviour in the UK

Much of the evidence used to explain the term structure has been American. Practice in the UK suggests additional points:

- The tax system encourages individuals to hold financial wealth through institutions and acquire long-term assets such as life assurance policies and pension rights. These long-term liabilities mean that institutions are less sensitive to changes in yields on long-dated stock relative to those on short- or medium-dated.
- The response of the term structure to changes in supply alters as innovation affects the nature of institutional liabilities. For example, unitisation of pension and life assets with the accompanying need for performance is reducing the preference for income-certain assets. This is partly because the underlying policy holder is now bearing more of the risk and partly because capital performance is required over short periods. The emphasis is moving from considering a switch out of long-dated stocks as speculative to considering a movement into them as speculative.
- The freedom with which institutions can speculate by moving out of their matched positions depends on their capital, reserves and surpluses. These fluctuate with financial values.
- The response to higher yields in another part of the market is not linear. Each speculative switch exposes reserves and surpluses and reduces the ability to make further moves. Thus the response to each new change in relative yields can be expected to diminish.

The Bank of England's par yield curve

Most conventional gilt-edged stocks will stand at large discounts when yields have risen to new highs. For many investors capital gains are taxed at a lower rate than income, so a new stock priced at par would need a higher gross redemption yield than that indicated by a yield curve fitted to existing stocks. The Bank of England needed to show the GRY on stocks priced at par 'to assist in judging the appropriate terms for new government issues (which are usually made at a price close to par), and in advising on the rates of interest to be charged by the central government for lending to public corporations and local authorities' (*BEQB*, December 1972, p. 470).

The Bank's par yield curve (see Figure 10.2) was developed by J. P. Burman and W. R. White in the Bank's economic section. It was first described in the *BEQB* for December 1972, and subsequent modifications were reported in articles in the *BEQB* for September 1973, June 1976 and June 1982.

The par yield curve is derived from a model of the term structure in the gilt-edged market. The theory underlying the model is derived from a view of the way the market works. It is assumed that the market is divided into two segments: the shorter segment contains investors with expectations about the level of prices one year hence; the longer contains investors with expectations about prices five years hence. These points in the future for which there are expectations are called 'planning horizons'. The time between the present and the horizon is called the 'decision period'.

Investors are assumed not to form a view of interest rates beyond their horizons and to expect yields to continue unchanged from their expected levels at each horizon. If investors can switch freely, the expected return (income plus capital gain or loss) over the decision period will be equal on every stock in the market. The only exceptions are stocks with less than one year of life – that is, stocks maturing before the shorter horizon is reached. It follows that if yields at the horizon are expected to rise from existing levels the yield curve will slope upwards – a higher present yield is needed on longer stocks to compensate for the expected capital loss. If, on the other hand, yields are expected to fall, the yield curve will slope downwards because investors are prepared to hold longer stocks on lower present yields and be compensated by capital gains.

The two segments are spliced together. All stocks maturing between one and five years belong to the shorter segment and all those maturing after ten years to the longer segment. Prices for the intervening period are derived from combining the shorter and longer segments, with weights depending on each stock's position within the band.

Differences in GRY on stocks of the same term are a result of coupon and therefore of tax. The level is determined by a combination of net and

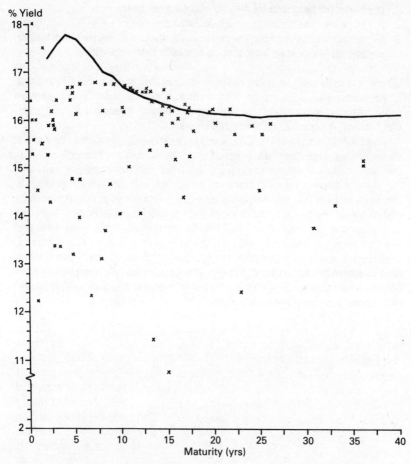

Figure 10.2   *Actual yields and the par yield curve as at 26 October 1981*

Source: par yield curve – Bank of England.

gross investors; the importance of the net investor decreases and that of the gross investors increases as the coupon rises. This continues up to a level where gross investors dominate and changes in coupon have little effect on GRYs. This is known as the 'gross zone' and varies with maturity. The expected price at each horizon is a weighted average for gross and net investors, who are assumed to be of different importance in each segment.

The model therefore defines the term structure in terms of:

- the one-year and five-year planning horizons;

- the expected net yields at the two planning horizons;
- the expected net return over the decision periods;
- the effective tax rate on low coupon stocks in the shorter and longer segments, and that on high coupon stocks in both segments.

There was originally an additional parameter; this was a premium related to volatility, which increased with term and capital risk. It was discontinued when it was found impossible to distinguish expectations of higher yields from compensation for increased risk.

The model uses the expectations and segmentation approaches described above. These, together with its handling of the tax and coupon effects, give four advantages. First, by breaking the market into two parts it admits the importance of institutions that seek to match liabilities and do not regard all stocks as substitutes. Second, by breaking expectations into short and long it allows a more realistic modelling of the very different behaviour of, say, life funds and discount houses. Third, it admits what every fund manager knows – total ignorance beyond a certain point in the future; this contrasts with the normal assumption that expectations of future interest rates exist for the entire term structure. Finally, it estimates tax and coupon effects. Many curves ignore these and force themselves to encompass a wide range of coupons without allowance for tax.

11 Value

Treasury bill rates

Tenders for 91-day bills are received at the Bank of England on the last business day each week. They are made through a London banker, discount house or broker in terms of a price per £100 nominal. 'Treasury Bill Rate is the average rate of discount on 91-day Treasury bills allotted pursuant to tenders, weighted by the nominal value of bills allotted at each price and expressed as an annual percentage rate of discount calculated to four places of decimals rounded' (Bank of England, Prospectus, 27 May 1977).

The relevant formulae are, where P = price, R = rate of discount, y = yield:

$$R = \frac{(100-P) \times 365}{91}$$

$$y = \frac{R \times 100}{P} \%$$

or

$$y = \frac{100-P}{P} \times \frac{365}{91} \times 100\%.$$

The yield is therefore not compounded.

Variable rate Treasury stocks

Interest payments on variable rate Treasury stocks were made half-yearly. Each payment was calculated as half the sum of an indicator rate plus a fixed margin of $\frac{1}{2}$ per cent.

The indicator rate was the daily average over a reference period of Treasury Bill Rate. This reference period ran from the ex-dividend date for the preceding interest payment up to the ex-dividend date for the next interest payment. The rate for each interest payment was rounded to two places of decimals. It was announced by the Bank of England on the business day preceding the day on which the stock became ex-dividend.

Running yields

The running, or income, yield on a stock is the annual coupon as a percentage of the price. It is calculated on the clean price. It uses the market price in short-dated stocks (since it excludes the accrued interest) and the market price adjusted for the accrued interest in medium- and long-dated stocks (since it includes the accrued interest).

Thus, on short-dated stocks:

$$\text{running yield} = \frac{\text{coupon}}{\text{price}} \times 100$$

and on medium- and long-dated stocks:

$$\text{running yield} = \frac{\text{coupon}}{\text{price minus accrued interest}} \times 100.$$

Gross redemption yields

The most common method of valuing a gilt-edged stock is by calculating its gross redemption yield or yield to maturity.

A dated stock consists of a stream of coupons, normally payable every six months, and final redemption proceeds payable on maturity. A payment received earlier has greater present value than an equal payment received later. A redemption yield values both coupons and redemption proceeds according to when, during a stock's life, they are payable.

A redemption yield may be defined as 'the rate of interest at which the value of the interest payments discounted to the present time plus the value of the redemption proceeds discounted to the present time equal the price' (Day and Jamieson, 1980, vol. II, p. 28).

If $i = \dfrac{1}{100}$ of the semi-annual yield, P = the total price (including accrued interest on short-dated stocks), C = the annual coupon, C_1 = the actual coupon receivable at the next coupon date, k = the fraction of the half-year period from the settlement date to the next coupon payment date, n = the number of periods from the next coupon date to the maturity date, and v = the present value of 1 due at the end of one period or $\dfrac{1}{(1+i)}$, then:

$$P = v^k [C_1 + \frac{C}{2}(v + v^2 + \ldots + v^n)] + 100 v^{n+k}$$

$$= v^k [C_1 + \frac{C}{2} \times v \times \frac{1 - v^n}{1 - v}] + 100 v^{n+k}$$

$$= v^k [C_1 + \frac{C}{2} \times \frac{1 - v^n}{i}] + 100 v^{n+k}.$$

The redemption yield convertible half-yearly is $200 \times i$ per cent.

In the case of a partly paid stock, when s = the number of future calls payable, B_j = the amounts of the various future calls and b_j = the fractional period from the settlement date to the future call dates, then the redemption yield, convertible half-yearly, is $200 \times i$ per cent where:

$$P = v^k [C_1 + \frac{C}{2}(v + v^2 + \ldots v^n)] + 100v^{n+k} - \sum_{j=1}^{s} B_j v^{bj}$$

$$= v^k [C_1 + \frac{C}{2} \times \frac{1 - v^n}{i}] + 100v^{n+k} - \sum_{j=1}^{s} B_j v^{bj}$$

Net redemption yields

A net redemption yield is the yield after the relevant amounts of income tax and CGT have been paid.

If t = the percentage rate of tax on income and t_c = the percentage rate of tax on capital gains, then the net redemption yield is found by solving:

$$P = v^k [(1 - \frac{t}{100}) C_1 + (1 - \frac{t}{100}) \times \frac{C}{2} \times \frac{1 - v^n}{i}] + [100 - \frac{t_c}{100}(100 - P)]v^{n+k}.$$

Grossed-up net redemption yields

A grossed-up net redemption yield is the gross yield to which a net yield is equivalent at specified rates of income tax. This enables comparison to be made with interest rates on other fixed-interest instruments.

If $i\%$ = the net redemption yield at the tax rate $t\%$, the grossed-up net redemption yield is:

$$\left(\frac{i}{1 - \frac{t}{100}} \right) \%.$$

Redemption yields in practice

Gross redemption yields shown on brokers' and jobbers' lists sometimes differ. There are two reasons. First, the method of determining the length of each coupon period differs. Some methods use the actual number of days in each coupon period as they appear on a calendar. Some methods assume every coupon covers an exact half-year period. In some cases allowance is made for the shortening and lengthening of periods caused by coupon dates falling on weekends and holidays. In each case the present value of the coupon is altered by the change in the number of days lying between payment for the stock and payment of the coupons. Second, some methods assume that the broken period continues to the next coupon date so that there is an even number of periods to the date of redemption. The advantage is that the two coupons in each calendar year will cover a whole year, whereas an odd coupon period could be different from an exact half-year.

Redemption yields are criticised. Some criticisms are valid, but others either should be aimed at inappropriate use or are based on misunderstandings about what redemption yields mean or assume.

Thus, the comment is made that redemption yields mislead since stock is rarely held to redemption and at any other time the price may have varied from that needed to give the original yield. The comment is true, but the original redemption yield on purchase remains correct on the assumptions made in its calculation, and it still provides a consistent basis for comparison between stocks.

Another criticism assumes that a redemption yield is valid only if it is possible to reinvest every coupon at the same redemption yield. The purchaser, however, is buying only the right to a stream of coupons and the final redemption proceeds. Only these payments are certain; there is no assumption in a redemption yield that they can be reinvested at the same yield as the initial purchase. To make such an assumption is to confuse the interest rate that is used to provide a present value for future payments with the ability to invest that stream at that interest rate.

It is also pointed out that as long as the yield curve is not flat (see Chapter 10) a different value is put on similar coupons paid on the same day on stocks in different parts of the market (Day and Jamieson, 1980, vol. II, p. 71). Thus on 2 September 1983, 7¾% Treasury 1985/88 yielded 10·76 per cent and 7¾% Treasury 2012/15 yielded 10·10 per cent. As a result the present value being placed on the coupons on the first stock was lower than that being placed on the second, although the coupons are payable on the same day. It is for this reason that some critics advocate valuing each coupon at a different interest rate; in some cases this is derived from the point on the yield curve at which it is payable.

Volatility

Market convention describes volatility as the change in the price of a stock in response to a change in its gross redemption yield. Volatility depends on maturity and coupon. Thus, on a ten-year stock:

| | Price to yield | | |
Coupon %	8%	9%	10%
5	79·61	73·98	68·84
10	113·59	106·50	100·00
15	147·57	139·02	131·15

and on a stock with a 10 per cent coupon:

| Term to | Price required to yield | | |
maturity	8%	9%	10%
5	108·11	103·96	100·00
10	113·59	106·50	100·00
15	117·29	108·14	100·00

These examples show (a) that, on stocks of similar maturity, the higher the coupon the smaller will be the percentage change in price required to produce a given change in yield, and (b) that, on stocks with similar coupons, the longer the stock the greater will be the percentage change in price required to produce a given change in yield.

The reason for this is to be found in the calculation of the gross redemption yield. Other things being equal, the higher is the coupon the less important is the contribution of the final redemption proceeds, and the longer is the life of the stock the greater is the reduction in the value of the final redemption proceeds due to the effect of compound interest.

It follows that:

- Volatility is a mixture of coupon and nominal life; it can be seen from Table 11.1, for example, that 6% Funding 1993 had greater volatility than 13¼% Treasury 1997 although it is the shorter stock in calendar terms.
- A higher coupon shortens the effective life of a stock since interest payments represent a larger proportion of the total return; volatility therefore varies with effective life rather than with calendar life. This was discussed in Chapter 1 when the maturity and duration of outstanding gilt-edged stocks were being contrasted.
- A higher level of yields reduces the value of the final redemption proceeds relative to the coupons; volatility therefore varies with the level of yields.
- At high yield levels, where coupons contribute a higher proportion of the return, undated stocks become shorter than long-dated stocks; they thus become less volatile than dated stocks.

Table 11.1   *Volatility of selected gilt-edged stocks on 31 October 1983*

Stock	Price	Gross redemption yield %	Volatility[1] %
10½% Treasury 1989	102 3/8	11·074	4·15
12½% Exchequer 1990	107 1/8	11·206	4·40
13¾% Exchequer 1992	113 1/8	11·368	5·33
12¼% Treasury 1993	111	11·237	5·72
6% Funding 1993	76 3/4	9·853	6·86
13½% Exchequer 1994	113 1/8	11·354	5·84
12½% Exchequer 1994	109 7/8	11·273	6·05
12% Treasury 1995	107 3/4	11·264	6·22
13¼% Treasury 1997	118 1/4	11·105	6·62
10½% Exchequer 1997	99 3/4	10·818	7·01
8¾% Treasury 1997	88 5/8	10·522	7·48
15% Exchequer 1997	125 7/8	11·299	6·59
12% Exchequer 1998	106 7/8	10·972	7·15
10½% Treasury 1999	98 1/8	10·687	7·51
12% Exchequer 1999/02	111 7/8	10·828	7·27
3½% Funding 1999/04	49	9·143	11·33
12½% Treasury 2003/05	114 7/8	10·612	8·01
13½% Treasury 2004/08	124 3/4	10·658	7·95
5½% Treasury 2008/12	61 3/8	9·524	10·60
12% Exchequer 2013/17	121 3/8	10·199	9·15
3½% War Loan	34 7/8	9·954	10·01

Note: [1] % change in price for 1 point change in GRY.

Shorts

Yields on very short stocks that have gone ex-dividend for the penultimate time are calculated on a simple interest basis; this is in part to facilitate comparison with Treasury bills.

Reinvestment yields

A reinvestment yield quantifies the risk that is being taken when switching a stock into a part of the market that is not the switcher's natural home or when the shape of the yield curve is particularly unusual and unlikely to persist.

Assume a switch from a longer to a shorter stock where the shorter stock is held to maturity. A reinvestment yield is the yield on which the longer stock would need to stand at the time of the redemption of the shorter stock if the return from holding the shorter stock and repurchasing the longer stock is to equal the return from holding the longer stock for the same period.

Year and a day

A 'year and a day' yield is the yield on a stock held for just longer than one year so that there is no CGT payable. The calculation is usually applied to situations where only one interest payment is receivable (see Chapters 7 and 9), with the second interest payment being taken as capital in the form of accrued interest. The calculation usually assumes that the GRY on the stock is the same at the end of the period, but it may assume that the yield changes in line with the existing yield curve.

Year and a day yields may be grossed-up to show, at a specified rate of tax on income, the gross yield to which the net yield is equivalent.

Index-linked stocks

The coupons and redemption price of index-linked stocks are related to the movement in the general index of retail prices (RPI) over the life of the stock. These are calculated by multiplying the nominal coupon or nominal redemption (100) by the factor:

$$\frac{\text{the index figure applicable}}{\text{the index figure for the base month}}.$$

The index figure applicable is the index figure published seven months before the month in which the coupon is paid or redemption due. This means that it is the actual figure for eight months previously since there is a gap of a month before the figure for a given month is published. This lag enables the amount of the next coupon to be known before the start of the six-month period to which it applies and the daily accrued to be calculated. The extra month was added in case there is ever a delay in the publication of the index (*BEQB*, December 1983, p. 484).

Depending on the stock, the payments are calculated to either two or four places of decimals rounded down.

Example 11.1   *2% Index-Linked Treasury 2006*

£1,000m., issued 8 July 1981 at 86.
Coupon payments: 19 January and 19 July.
Calls: £30% on application, £30% on 14 August 1981 and £26% on
11 September 1981
Index-linking: RPI in base month (November 1980) = 274·1.

The index number applicable for the half-yearly coupon payable on 19 January 1984 was that for May 1983 (333·9). The coupon payable was therefore:

$$1 \times \frac{333 \cdot 9}{274 \cdot 1} = \pounds 1.21\%.$$

There is no agreed method of calculating the real yields on index-linked stocks, and the yields published on brokers' lists and in the newspapers vary widely.

The most important differences lie in the assumptions made about the future rate of inflation. The eight-month lag with which the movement in the RPI applies means that the redemption value and interest payments are affected by the change in the RPI in the eight months before a stock's issue; this change is known. Equally, the redemption value is not affected by the change in the RPI in the final eight months of a stock's life; this change is not known. Different assumptions about the movement in the RPI during this final eight months alter the real value of the final redemption proceeds and thus the real yield.

There are two approaches to finding an assumption for future inflation: the 'explicit' method assumes inflation will continue from some chosen date at a constant rate; the alternative method assumes that inflation will continue at the level experienced over some selected recent period – perhaps the year-on-year rate or the annualised rate over six months. The drawback of the first approach is that the rate of change may look realistic at the time it was chosen, but look hopelessly inappropriate five or ten years later – the rate of inflation has been very volatile during the last decade. To avoid this, some brokers calculate yields on a range of assumed RPI changes and allow the users to make their own choices. The second approach avoids this problem, but has the drawback that the assumed change in the RPI can alter every month with the publication of new data. As a result, yields can show disconcerting changes although there has been no movement in the price of the stock.

Given an assumption about future inflation, there are two approaches to calculating the real yield. First, the assumed inflation rate is applied to the stream of coupons and the redemption proceeds so that their value is found in money terms. A nominal GRY is then calculated for these payments and deflated by the assumed change in the RPI. Second, the real value of the coupons and redemption proceeds are projected and a real yield calculated from them. The two approaches should provide the same results if the assumed inflation rates are constant.

A further difference in methodology lies in the treatment of the period between the last known RPI figure and the settlement day for a transaction. Calculations can either use the assumed future rate of inflation or assume a continuation of the rate experienced over some recent period.

The Fixed Interest Subcommittee of the Joint Index and Classification Committee of the Institute of Actuaries and the Faculty of Actuaries has been working to produce a standardised methodology. It is probable that this will involve the explicit method with the assumed constant rate of inflation also applying to the period between the last known RPI figure and settlement day for the transaction. This method, with a 5 per cent assumed inflation rate, has been used in the *BEQB* since March 1984. The *BEQB* had previously assumed that the rate experienced during the six months to the most recently published figure would continue at a constant rate over the remaining life of the stock.

The calculation of index-linked yields would still have shortcomings even if these differences were resolved. The RPI is struck at some point in the middle of the month, whilst interest payments and redemption proceeds are paid at any time within a month, the exact dates depending on the issue. The effect may be as much as 5 or 10 pence in the yield. The assumed rate of inflation may be very different from that being currently experienced; in this case it is unrealistic to pretend that the assumed inflation rate will begin on the settlement day for the transaction for which the calculation is being made. Last, inflation itself has a seasonality.

A formula to find a real gross yield when it is assumed that the RPI changes at a uniform rate over the remaining life of a stock would be: if P is the price including accrued interest, d = the number of days from the settlement date to the next interest payment date, d_1 = the number of days from the last published index date to the settlement date, r = the assumption of the annual rate of inflation from the settlement date to the maturity date of the stock, I = the last published index figure, I_1 = the index figure at the base date, C = the nominal interest payment per annum (e.g. 2 for 2% Index-Linked Treasury 1996 and 2·5 for 2½% Index-Linked Treasury 2012), C_1 = the actual interest payment due at the next payment date (0 if the stock is xd), n = the integral number of periods (half years) from the next interest payment date to the redemption of the stock, v = the present value of 1 at a rate i% for one period, i.e. $v = 1/[1 + \dfrac{i}{100}]$, B_j = the outstanding calls on a partly paid stock (say s in number), and bj = the number of days from the settlement date to the jth call, then:

$$P = v^{d/182\cdot5}\left[C_1(1+r)^{-d/365} + \frac{I}{I_1}(1+r)^{-8/12}(1+r)^{d_1/365}\left(\cdot5C\sum_{j=1}^{n}v^j + 100v^n\right)\right]$$

$$- \sum_{j=1}^{s} B_j(1+r)^{-bj/365}\,v^{bj/182\cdot5}$$

The real yield convertible half-yearly is found by doubling i.

Futures

Twenty-year gilt price factor formula
LIFFE (Pézier, 1983a, p. 27) defines the gilt price factor formula as:

> ... the price per £1 nominal value of the specific stock at which this stock has a gross redemption yield of 12%, minus the undiscounted amount of accrued interest.

The price factor is calculated for each deliverable gilt at the first day of each delivery month according to the formula:

$$F = \frac{1}{(1.06)^{\left(\frac{x}{182.5}\right)}} \left[c_1 + \frac{c}{0.12} \left(1 - \frac{1}{1.06^n} \right) + \frac{1}{1.06^n} \right] - \frac{c}{2} \left(\frac{y - x}{182.5} \right)$$

where:

c = coupon per £1 nominal, payable half-yearly;

c_1 = coupon per £1 nominal stock payable at the next payment date which will usually be $c/2$ unless the stock is ex-dividend on settlement day in which case it will be zero;

n = number of half years from the next payment date to the relevant redemption date;

x = number of days from and including the first day of the delivery month up to the next payment date;

y = number of days after the previous payment date up to and including the next payment date.

If the stock is ex-dividend on settlement day, the final term in the formula is:

$$+ \frac{c}{2} \left(\frac{x}{182 \cdot 5} \right).$$

Appendix 1 *Switching*

Switching is the sale of one stock and the simultaneous purchase of another. 'Simultaneous' should be emphasised – the characteristic of switching is that the profit is expected to result not directly from a general change in market levels but from a change in the relative prices of the two stocks.

Switching is an important part of the management of institutional portfolios, especially those of life and pension funds. There are two reasons for this. To the extent that an institution's liabilities are of an identifiable length and money value it will need to stay in its required maturity; improvements in yield can be earned only by moving between stocks in the same part of the market. To the extent permitted by the laws and rules described in Chapter 9, institutions can improve returns by using the one-year CGT concession, special ex-dividend situations and the facility that enables them to hold stock for one year, taking the final interest payment as capital.

This type of switching will gradually die out until it finally ceases in February 1986 when interest on gilt-edged stocks will begin to be treated for tax purposes as accruing on a day-to-day basis between interest payment dates.

The advantages to the investor of these switches are at the expense of the Inland Revenue. As with the issue of low coupon stocks discussed in Chapter 7, they represent examples of how the cost of selling and servicing the national debt is not only the direct cost of interest but also any revenue forgone. There are three compensations for these revenue costs. First, switching ensures that there is liquidity in nearly all issues. Market makers are prepared to deal in mature issues, taking positions, because they know that small movements in relative prices or the incentive to switch provided by tax positions will unlock investors' holdings and enable them to restore balance to their books. This marketability increases the volume of stock that the authorities can sell at a given yield level. Second, switching enables the authorities to influence a range of stocks by dealing in only one. For example, a tap stock or unofficial line will need to become only slightly cheap to stimulate switches from comparable issues. Third, marketability in all stocks means that the yield curve can adjust quickly to new circumstances, enabling the authorities to renew official sales.

Switches are conventionally divided into three kinds: anomaly or jobbing switches; policy switches; and tax switches. In practice, the three categories frequently overlap.

Anomaly switches

An anomaly switch is traditionally described as being able to make a profit even if there is a change in the level of the market. It therefore involves stocks whose mixture of term and coupon gives them similar volatilities (see Chapter 11). The increase in market movements during the last fifteen years has shown the inadequacy of this shorthand description from a different era. Volatility changes with the level of yields and nowadays an investment manager assessing the potential profitability of an anomaly switch will take into account the effects of a general change in the yield level.

An anomaly switch involves selling a stock that is considered expensive and buying a stock that is considered cheap. The judgement is usually based on historical criteria involving either the relationship between the two stocks under consideration or comparison with a construct embracing all or part of the other stocks in the market:

- Yield differences, or the difference between the GRY or NRY of the two stocks.
- Price ratios, or the percentage of one stock represented by another. This is usually calculated using clean prices (see Chapter 9). Ratios may be misleading over long periods if stocks with very different running yields are being compared. This is because the interest on the two stocks is accruing at different rates and counteracting the profit made as the price ratio moves in the desired direction. Various techniques have been developed to take account of this, usually involving adding back to the clean price a proportion of the accrued interest so that the calculated ratio history takes some account of the different rates at which the two stocks accumulate income.
- Positions relative to a fitted yield curve (see Chapter 10) or a model that enables each stock's cheapness or dearness to be described in terms of a normal position. The histories of a stock's normal position are sometimes weighted so that the more distant past is given less importance than the more recent experience.

Most securities firms keep these records on a computer and histories are quickly available. The speed and ease with which anomalies can now be identified makes such switching opportunities rarer than previously.

Figure A.1 is reproduced from a volume of yield and ratio histories produced each month by a securities firm. It shows in graphical form the relationship between 9% Treasury 1992/96 and 10½% Exchequer 1997. The history shows:

(i) The difference between the GRYs on the two stocks. This is the yield on the first stock minus the yield on the second. The range of the differences in each month is indicated by the extremes of the vertical line and the average for the month by the crossing line. The differences include special ex-dividend prices, when stocks are dealable in this form.

(ii) The difference between the NRYs, calculated in the same way, with tax on interest payments charged at 37½ per cent and with no CGT.

(iii) The gross stock ratio. This shows the nominal amount of the first stock that is produced by £100 nominal of the second. The prices used are clean.

(iv) The net stock ratio. This is the same as (iii), except that 62½ per cent (100% − 37·5%) of the accrued interest is retained in the prices on which the ratios are calculated.

Figure A.1 *9% Treasury 1992/6 v 10½% Exchequer 1997*

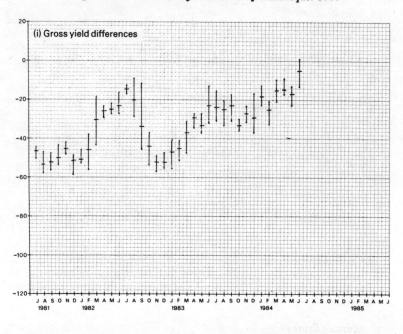

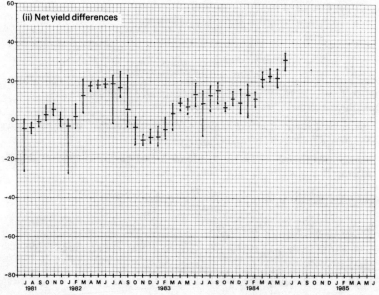

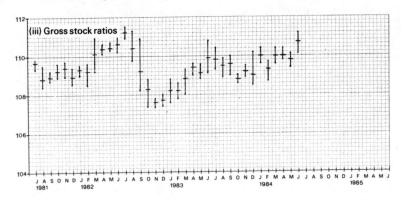

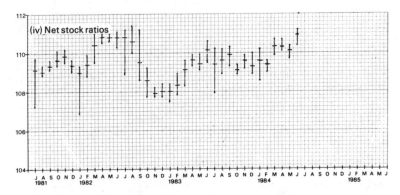

Example A.1   *Anomaly switch*

Sell 9% Treasury 1992/96; buy 10¼% Exchequer 1997. Fund pays no tax.
Open the switch on 14 February 1983 by:

selling 9% Treasury 1992/96 at 85 3/4 xd. Accrued interest –0·690; clean price 86·440; GRY 10·980%; volatility 7·09;

buying 10¼% Exchequer 1997 at 93 1/2 xd. Accrued interest –0·173; clean price 93·673; GRY 11·417%; volatility 7·06.

Yield difference 43.7p; ratio $100 \times \dfrac{93 \cdot 673}{86 \cdot 440} = 108 \cdot 37.$

Close the switch on 22 April 1983 by:

selling 10¼% Exchequer 1997 at 100. Accrued interest +1·812; clean price 98·188; GRY 10·746%;

buying 9% Treasury 1992/96 at 90 3/4. Accrued interest +1·011; clean price 89·739; GRY 10·458%.

Yield difference 28.8p; ratio $100 \times \dfrac{98 \cdot 188}{89 \cdot 739} = 109 \cdot 42.$

The profit is calculated as:

Nominal of stock			Consideration
Opening			
£			£
−1,166,181	9% Treasury 1992/96	at 85 3/4	1,000,000
+1,069,519	10½% Exchequer 1997	at 93 1/2	1,000,000
			0
Closing			
−1,069,519	10½% Exchequer 1997	at 100	1,069,519
+1,166,181	9% Treasury 1992/96	at 90 3/4	1,058,309
		Profit	11,210
			(1·12%)

The profit of £11,210 is calculated before expenses. These are 120p CSI (Council for the Securities Industry) levy on both the opening and closing, plus any commission that may be payable.

Policy switches

Policy switches involve the sale of one stock and simultaneous purchase of another where the volatility of the two stocks is very different. The aim is to profit from a general movement in market yields that will affect the prices of the two stocks by different amounts. A policy switch can mean:

(i) Switching between stocks of similar terms, but very different coupons. There may be two reasons: first, the investor may wish to remain matched, but to alter volatility to profit from an expected change in the level of interest rates; second, the investor may want to take advantage of a change in the supply of stocks of one level of coupon relative to that of another. This might be expected to happen if the general market level has changed and the authorities, who normally supply stocks with prices near par, are expected to begin supplying stocks at the new yields.

(ii) Switching between different terms. Again, there may be two reasons: first, a change in the general level of interest rates is anticipated; or, second, it is hoped to profit from a change in the shape of the yield curve.

In practice, policy switches overlap with anomaly switches: a stock that is expensive on yield and ratio histories is chosen for sale and a stock that is cheap is chosen for purchase.

Tax switches

Tax switches are made by tax-paying funds to avoid interest payments and to take advantage of the CGT concession and the tax treatment of accrued interest. These switches in turn provide opportunities for gross funds to buy interest payments. The switches in each case have to be consistent with the rules and laws described in Chapter 9 and will cease after February 1986 when the new rules on the tax treatment of accrued interest become effective.

A tax-paying fund will wish to create the opportunity to hold a stock for about a year and then decide whether to sell within the year if there is a loss, or hold for more than a year if there is a gain. It will wish to do this in such a way that it takes only one of the six-monthly interest payments, receiving the second in the form of capital. The fund can do this by buying a stock special ex-dividend and selling cum-dividend a year later.

Figure A.2   *12% Treasury 1995 v 13¼% Treasury 1997*

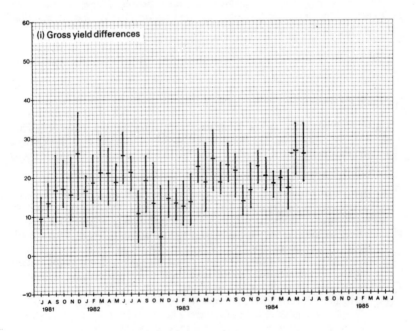

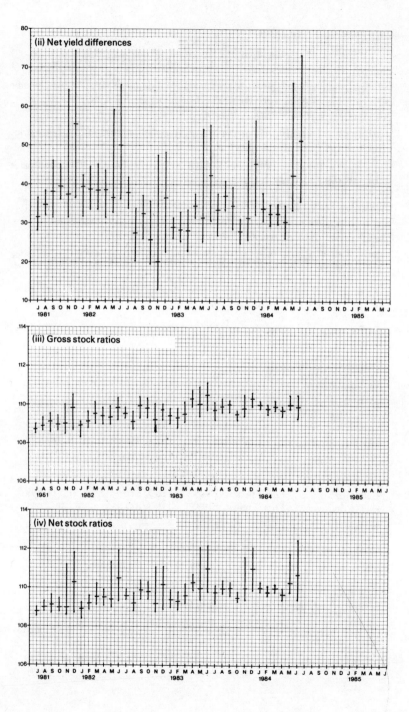

Example A.2   *Tax switch (Figure A.2)*

Sell 13¼% Treasury 1997; buy 12% Treasury 1995. Fund pays tax at 37½% on income and zero on capital gains when the stock is held for a year or longer.
Open the switch on 29 November 1982 by:

selling 13¼% Treasury 1997 at 114 1/2 cd. Accrued interest +4·755, clean price 109·745; GRY 11·798; volatility 6·70;

buying 12% Treasury 1995 at 99 1/2 sxd. Accrued interest −1·841; clean price 101·341; GRY 11·810%; volatility 6·41.

Yield difference 1.2p; ratio $100 \times \dfrac{109 \cdot 745}{101 \cdot 341} = 108 \cdot 29$.

Close the switch on 30 November 1983 by:

selling 12% Treasury 1995 at 110 5/8 cd. Accrued interest +4·241; clean price 106·384; GRY 10·975; volatility 6·27.

buying 13¼% Treasury 1997 at 115 3/8 sxd. Accrued interest − 1·888; clean price 117·263; GRY 10·777; volatility 6·66.

Yield difference 19.8p; ratio $100 \times \dfrac{117 \cdot 263}{106 \cdot 384} = 110 \cdot 23$.

The profit is calculated as:

Nominal of stock			*Consideration*
Opening			
£			£
− 873,362	13¼% Treasury 1997	114 1/2 cd	1,000,000
+1,005,025	12% Treasury 1995	99 1/2 sxd	1,000,000
			0
Closing			
−1,005,025	12% Treasury 1995	110 5/8 cd	1,111,809
+ 873,362	13¼% Treasury 1997	115 3/8 sxd	1,007,641
			+104,168

Loss of three coupons on 13¼% Treasury 1997:

$$3 \times \frac{13 \cdot 25}{2} \times 0 \cdot 625 \times \frac{\text{nominal}}{100} \qquad\qquad -108,488$$

Receipt of one coupon on 12% Treasury 1995:

$$1 \times \frac{12}{2} \times 0 \cdot 625 \times \frac{\text{nominal}}{100} \qquad\qquad +37,688$$

Profit   33,368
(3·34%)

There is no CGT payable since the stock has been held for more than a year. In this example the switch has been profitable although the sold stock became more expensive relative to the stock purchased.

As far as possible a tax switch will be combined with an anomaly switch, in that the cheapest suitable stock will be purchased – cheapest being determined with the aids to judgement used in anomaly switching. It may also be combined with a policy switch. In this case the investor will choose the stock:

- that is the cheapest, judged on anomaly criteria;
- of the term or coupon already selected on policy grounds;
- whose accrued interest suits the fund's tax position.

Appendix 2 *Prospectuses*

TENDERS MUST BE LODGED AT THE BANK OF ENGLAND, NEW ISSUES (B), WATLING STREET, LONDON, EC4M 9AA NOT LATER THAN 10.00 A.M. ON THURSDAY, 26TH AUGUST 1982, OR AT ANY OF THE BRANCHES OF THE BANK OF ENGLAND OR AT THE GLASGOW AGENCY OF THE BANK OF ENGLAND NOT LATER THAN 3.30 P.M. ON WEDNESDAY, 25TH AUGUST 1982.

ISSUE BY TENDER OF £250,000,000

$2\frac{1}{2}$ per cent INDEX-LINKED TREASURY STOCK, 2001

PAYABLE IN FULL WITH TENDER

INTEREST PAYABLE HALF-YEARLY ON 24TH MARCH AND 24TH SEPTEMBER

1.   The Stock is an investment falling within Part II of the First Schedule to the Trustee Investments Act 1961. Application has been made to the Council of The Stock Exchange for the Stock to be admitted to the Official List.

2.   THE GOVERNOR AND COMPANY OF THE BANK OF ENGLAND are authorised to receive tenders for the above Stock.

3.   The principal of and interest on the Stock will be a charge on the National Loans Fund, with recourse to the Consolidated Fund of the United Kingdom.

4.   The Stock will be registered at the Bank of England or at the Bank of Ireland, Belfast, and will be transferable, in multiples of one penny, by instrument in writing in accordance with the Stock Transfer Act 1963. Transfers will be free of stamp duty.

5.   If not previously redeemed under the provisions of paragraph 14, the Stock will be repaid on 24th September 2001. The value of the principal on repayment will be related, subject to the terms of this prospectus, to the movement, during the life of the Stock, of the United Kingdom General Index of Retail Prices maintained by the Department of Employment, or any Index which may replace that Index for the purposes of this propectus, such movement being indicated by the Index figure issued monthly and subsequently published in the London, Edinburgh and Belfast Gazettes.

6.   For the purposes of this prospectus, the Index figure applicable to any month will be the Index figure issued seven months prior to the relevant month and relating to the month before that prior month; "month" means calendar month; and the Index ratio applicable to any month will be equal to the Index figure applicable to that month divided by the Index figure applicable to August 1982.

7.   The amount due on repayment, per £100 nominal of Stock, will be £100 multiplied by the Index ratio applicable to the month in which repayment takes place. This amount, expressed in pounds sterling to four places of decimals rounded to the nearest figure below, will be announced by the Bank of England not later than the business day immediately preceding the date of the penultimate interest payment.

8.   Interest will be payable half-yearly on 24th March and 24th September. Income tax will be deducted from payments of more than £5 per annum. Interest warrants will be transmitted by post.

9. The first interest payment will be made on 24th March 1983 at the rate of £1.5044 per £100 nominal of Stock.

10. Each subsequent half-yearly interest payment will be at a rate, per £100 nominal of Stock, of £1.25 multiplied by the Index ratio applicable to the month in which the payment falls due.

11. The rate of interest for each interest payment other than the first, expressed as a percentage in pounds sterling to four places of decimals rounded to the nearest figure below, will be announced by the Bank of England not later than the business day immediately preceding the date of the previous interest payment.

12. If the Index is revised to a new base after the Stock is issued, it will be necessary, for the purposes of the preceding paragraphs, to calculate and use a notional Index figure in substitution for the Index figure applicable to the month in which repayment takes place and/or an interest payment falls due ("the month of payment"). This notional Index figure will be calculated by multiplying the actual Index figure applicable to the month of payment by the Index figure on the old base for the month on which the revised Index is based and dividing the product by the new base figure for the same month. This procedure will be used for each occasion on which a revision is made during the life of the Stock.

13. If the Index is not published for a month for which it is relevant for the purposes of this prospectus, the Bank of England, after appropriate consultation with the relevant Government Department, will publish a substitute Index figure which shall be an estimate of the Index figure which would have been applicable to the month of payment, and such substitute Index figure shall be used for all purposes for which the actual Index figure would have been relevant. The calculation by the Bank of England of the amounts of principal and/or interest payable on the basis of a substitute Index figure shall be conclusive and binding upon all stockholders. No subsequent adjustment to such amounts will be made in the event of subsequent publication of the Index figure which would have been applicable to the month of payment.

14. If any change should be made to the coverage or the basic calculation of the Index which, in the opinion of the Bank of England, constitutes a fundamental change in the Index which would be materially detrimental to the interests of stockholders, Her Majesty's Treasury will publish a notice in the London, Edinburgh and Belfast Gazettes immediately following the announcement by the relevant Government Department of the change, informing stockholders and offering them the right to require Her Majesty's Treasury to redeem their stock. For the purposes of this paragraph, repayment to stockholders who exercise this right will be effected, on a date to be chosen by Her Majesty's Treasury, not later than seven months from the last month of publication of the old Index. The amount of principal due on repayment and of any interest which has accrued will be calculated on the basis of the Index ratio applicable to the month in which repayment takes place. A notice setting out the administrative arrangements will be sent to stockholders at their registered address by the Bank of England at the appropriate time.

15. Tenders must be lodged at the Bank of England, New Issues (B), Watling Street, London, EC4M 9AA not later than 10.00 A.M. ON THURSDAY, 26TH AUGUST 1982, or at any of the Branches of the Bank of England or at the Glasgow Agency of the Bank of England not later than 3.30 P.M. ON WEDNESDAY, 25TH AUGUST 1982. Each tender must be for one amount and at one price which is a multiple of 25p. Tenders will not be revocable between 10.00 a.m. on Thursday, 26th August 1982 and 10.00 a.m. on Wednesday, 1st September 1982. TENDERS LODGED WITHOUT A PRICE BEING STATED WILL BE REJECTED.

16. Tenders must be accompanied by payment in full, i.e. the price tendered for every £100 of the nominal amount of Stock tendered for. A separate cheque must accompany each tender; cheques must be drawn on a bank in, and be payable in, the United Kingdom, the Channel Islands or the Isle of Man.

17.   **Tenders must be for a minimum of £100 nominal of Stock and for multiples of Stock as follows:**

Amount of Stock tendered for	Multiple
£100—£1,000	£100
£1,000—£3,000	£500
£3,000—£10,000	£1,000
£10,000—£50,000	£5,000
£50,000 or greater	£25,000

18.   Her Majesty's Treasury reserve the right to reject any tender or to allot a less amount of Stock than that tendered for. Valid tenders will be ranked in descending order of price and allotments will be made to tenderers whose tenders are at or above the lowest price at which Her Majesty's Treasury decide that any tender should be accepted (the allotment price). All allotments will be made at the allotment price and tenders which are accepted and which are made at prices above the allotment price will be allotted in full. Any balance of Stock not allotted to tenderers will be allotted at the allotment price to the Governor and Company of the Bank of England, Issue Department.

19.   Letters of allotment in respect of Stock allotted, being the only form in which the Stock may be transferred prior to registration, will be despatched by post at the risk of the tenderer, but the despatch of any letter of allotment, and any refund of any excess amount paid, may at the discretion of the Bank of England be withheld until the tenderer's cheque has been paid. In the event of such withholding, the tenderer will be notified by letter by the Bank of England of the acceptance of his tender and of the amount of Stock allocated to him, subject in each case to payment of his cheque, but such notification will confer no right on the tenderer to transfer the Stock so allocated.

20.   No allotment will be made for a less amount than £100 Stock. In the event of partial allotment, or of tenders at prices above the allotment price, the excess amount paid will, when refunded, be remitted by cheque despatched by post at the risk of the tenderer; if no allotment is made the amount paid with tender will be returned likewise. Non-payment on presentation of a cheque in respect of any Stock allotted will render the allotment of such Stock liable to cancellation. Interest at a rate equal to the London Inter-Bank Offered Rate for seven day deposits in sterling ("LIBOR") plus 1 per cent per annum may, however, be charged on the amount payable in respect of any allotment of Stock for which payment is accepted after the due date. Such rate will be determined by the Bank of England by reference to market quotations, on the due date for such payment, for LIBOR obtained from such source or sources as the Bank of England shall consider appropriate.

21.   Letters of allotment may be split into denominations of multiples of £100 on written request received by the Bank of England, New Issues, Watling Street, London, EC4M 9AA, or by any of the Branches of the Bank of England, on any date not later than 29th September 1982. Such requests must be signed and must be accompanied by the letters of allotment. Letters of allotment, accompanied by a completed registration form, may be lodged for registration forthwith and in any case they must be lodged for registration not later than 1st October 1982.

22.   Tender forms and copies of this prospectus may be obtained at the Bank of England, New Issues, Watling Street, London, EC4M 9AA. or at any of the Branches of the Bank of England, or at the Glasgow Agency of the Bank of England, 25 St. Vincent Place, Glasgow, Gl 2EB; at the Bank of Ireland, Moyne Buildings, 1st Floor, 20 Callender Street, Belfast, BTI 5BN; at Mullens & Co., 15 Moorgate, London, EC2R 6AN; or at any office of The Stock Exchange in the United Kingdom.

BANK OF ENGLAND
LONDON

20th August 1982

A separate cheque representing a deposit at the rate of £35.00 for every £100 of the *nominal* amount of Stock tendered for must accompany each tender; cheques must be drawn on a bank in, and be payable in, the United Kingdom, the Channel Islands or the Isle of Man.

Tenders must be for a minimum of £100 Stock and for multiples of Stock as follows:—

Amount of Stock tendered for	Multiple
£100—£1,000	£100
£1,000—£3,000	£500
£3,000—£10,000	£1,000
£10,000—£50,000	£5,000
£50,000 or greater	£25,000

Her Majesty's Treasury reserve the right to reject any tender or part of any tender and may therefore allot to tenderers less than the full amount of the Stock. Tenders will be ranked in descending order of price and allotments will be made to tenderers whose tenders are at or above the lowest price at which Her Majesty's Treasury decide that any tender should be accepted (the allotment price), which will be not less than the minimum tender price. All allotments will be made at the allotment price: tenders which are accepted and which are made at prices above the allotment price will be allotted in full; tenders made at the allotment price may be allotted in full or in part only. Any balance of Stock not allotted to tenderers will be allotted at the allotment price to the Governor and Company of the Bank of England, Issue Department.

Letters of allotment in respect of Stock allotted, being the only form in which the Stock may be transferred prior to registration, will be despatched by post at the risk of the tenderer, but the despatch of any letter of allotment, and any refund of the balance of the amount paid as deposit, may at the discretion of the Bank of England be withheld until the tenderer's cheque has been paid. In the event of such withholding, the tenderer will be notified by letter by the Bank of England of the acceptance of his tender and of the amount of Stock allocated to him, subject in each case to payment of his cheque, but such notification will confer no right on the tenderer to transfer the Stock so allocated.

No allotment will be made for a less amount than £100 Stock. In the event of partial allotment, the balance of the amount paid as deposit will, when refunded, be remitted by cheque despatched by post at the risk of the tenderer; if no allotment is made the amount paid as deposit will be returned likewise. Payment in full may be made at any time after allotment but no discount will be allowed on such payment. Interest may be charged on a day-to-day basis on any overdue amount which may be accepted at a rate equal to the London Inter-Bank Offered Rate for seven day deposits in sterling ("LIBOR") plus 1 per cent per annum. Such rate will be determined by the Bank of England by reference to market quotations, on the due date for the relevant payment, for LIBOR obtained from such source or sources as the Bank of England shall consider appropriate. Default in due payment of any amount in respect of the Stock will render the allotment of such Stock liable to cancellation and any amount previously paid liable to forfeiture.

Letters of allotment may be split into denominations of multiples of £100 on written request received by the Bank of England, New Issues, Watling Street, London, EC4M 9AA on any date not later than 13th September 1984. Such requests must be signed and must be accompanied by the letters of allotment.

Letters of allotment must be surrendered for registration, accompanied by a completed registration form, when the balance of the purchase money is paid, unless payment in full has been made before the due date, in which case they must be surrendered for registration not later than 17th September 1984.

TENDERS MUST BE LODGED AT THE BANK OF ENGLAND, NEW ISSUES (A), WATLING STREET, LONDON, EC4M 9AA NOT LATER THAN 10.00 A.M. ON WEDNESDAY, 8TH AUGUST 1984, OR AT ANY OF THE BRANCHES OF THE BANK OF ENGLAND OR AT THE GLASGOW AGENCY OF THE BANK OF ENGLAND NOT LATER THAN 3.30 P.M. ON TUESDAY, 7TH AUGUST 1984.

ISSUE OF £1,200,000,000

11 per cent EXCHEQUER STOCK, 1989

MINIMUM TENDER PRICE £94.25 PER CENT

PAYABLE AS FOLLOWS:

Deposit with tender	£35.00 per cent
On Monday, 17th September 1984	Balance of purchase money

INTEREST PAYABLE HALF-YEARLY ON 29TH MARCH AND 29TH SEPTEMBER

This Stock is an investment falling within Part II of the First Schedule to the Trustee Investments Act 1961. Application has been made to the Council of The Stock Exchange for the Stock to be admitted to the Official List.

THE GOVERNOR AND COMPANY OF THE BANK OF ENGLAND are authorised to receive tenders for £1,000,000,000 of the above Stock; the balance of £200,000,000 has been reserved for the National Debt Commissioners for public funds under their management.

The principal of and interest on the Stock will be a charge on the National Loans Fund, with recourse to the Consolidated Fund of the United Kingdom.

The Stock will be repaid at par on 29th September 1989.

The Stock will be registered at the Bank of England or at the Bank of Ireland, Belfast, and will be transferable, in multiples of one penny, by instrument in writing in accordance with the Stock Transfer Act 1963. Transfers will be free of stamp duty.

Interest will be payable half-yearly on 29th March and 29th September. Income tax will be deducted from payments of more than £5 per annum. Interest warrants will be transmitted by post. The first interest payment will be made on 29th March 1985 at the rate of £6.2641 per £100 of the Stock.

Tenders must be lodged at the Bank of England, New Issues (A), Watling Street, London, EC4M 9AA not later than 10.00 A.M. ON WEDNESDAY, 8TH AUGUST 1984, or at any of the Branches of the Bank of England or at the Glasgow Agency of the Bank of England not later than 3.30 P.M. ON TUESDAY, 7TH AUGUST 1984. Tenders will not be revocable between 10.00 a.m. on Wednesday, 8th August 1984 and 10.00 a.m. on Monday, 13th August 1984

Each tender must be for one amount and at one price. The minimum price, below which tenders will not be accepted, is £94.25 per cent. Tenders must be made at the minimum price or at higher prices which are multiples of 25p. Tenders lodged without a price being stated will be deemed to have been made at the minimum price.

Tender forms and copies of this prospectus may be obtained at the Bank of England, New Issues, Watling Street, London, EC4M 9AA, or at any of the Branches of the Bank of England, or at the Glasgow Agency of the Bank of England, 25 St. Vincent Place, Glasgow, G1 2EB; at the Bank of Ireland, Moyne Buildings, 1st Floor, 20 Callender Street, Belfast, BT1 5BN; at Mullens & Co., 15 Moorgate, London, EC2R 6AN; or at any office of The Stock Exchange in the United Kingdom.

BANK OF ENGLAND
LONDON

3rd August 1984

Glossary

accrued interest the amount of interest that would be paid if interest were payable daily. It is calculated (even in a leap year) on the basis of a 365-day year. It is included in the price of the stock in the case of *mediums* and *longs*; it is accounted for separately in the *shorts*.

assented/non-assented acceptance of an option to convert into another stock is usually required about one week before the actual conversion date. In this period there are two separate quotations: 'assented', where the option to convert has been chosen, and 'non-assented', where the holder has retained an unconverted holding.

authorities the Treasury, Bank of England and relevant ministers who are responsible for the conduct of monetary policy and for managing the gilt-edged market. Also referred to as 'the government', 'the Bank' and, since their agent in the market is the Government Broker, the 'GB'.

bear term used to describe an operator who has sold stock. Used by investors when they have sold stock they own; in this case they have 'covered bears'. Used by *market makers* when they have sold stock they do not own; in this case it is used to describe either a position in a single stock or an overall position.

bearer securities where title passes without a transfer or registration. Gilt-edged securities designated 'loan' can be held in either registered or bearer form. Those designated 'stock' can be held only in registered form.

book an institution's or *market maker's* inventory of marketable assets and liabilities.

broker an agent in a *single-capacity* securities market.

bull term used to describe an operator who has bought stock. *Market makers* use it to describe either a position in a single stock or an overall position.

bulldog debt denominated in sterling of a non-resident borrower listed on The Stock Exchange.

call the capital sum, payable on a specified day, on a *partly paid* new issue.

callable a US term for a bond where the issuer has the right to redeem before maturity at a specified price.

cash market the name given by participants in the futures market to the gilt-edged market, where bargains are normally settled on the business day following the transaction.

cd cum-dividend.

certificate of deposit (CD) 'A London interest bearing Sterling C.D. is a negotiable instrument in bearer form issued by an institution authorised to take deposits under the Banking Act 1979 certifying that a specified sum has been deposited with the issuing institution at a stated rate of interest, to be repaid on a specified date' (British Bankers' Association, 1984). Allowed for the first time by the Finance Act 1968. Sterling CDs are mainly issued for periods of one to three months. The Bank of England does not allow CDs to be issued with lives of less than twenty-eight days or more than five years. Interest is normally paid on the principal; there are a small number of *discount* issues. The Finance Act 1983 permitted building societies to issue sterling CDs.

clean the term used to describe short-dated stocks when *xd*.

clean price the price of a stock after deducting the *accrued interest*.

commercial bills a bill of exchange is an unconditional order, signed by the person giving it (the creditor or drawer) requiring the person to whom it is addressed (the debtor or acceptor) to pay a specified sum on a stated date. When a bill is signed by a debtor it is accepted. 'Eligible' bills are eligible for rediscount (sale) at the Bank of England; they are eligible when they have been accepted by one other party, a bank on the Bank of England's list, have an original term of 187 days or less and have a remaining term of 91 days or less.

'Ineligible' bills are accepted by a bank that is not on the Bank of England's list. They can be for any term.

'Trade' bills are drawn on companies. They can be for any term.

conventional stock a stock whose interest payment is fixed in money terms and that is not convertible.

coupon (i) the rate of interest payable on £100 nominal of stock, whether fixed or variable; (ii) a single half-year or quarterly payment; (iii) the 'coupon' attached to bearer securities that have to be presented for payment of the interest.

discount the amount by which a stock stands beneath its *par* value. In trading it can also refer to the amount it stands below its issue price.

domestic credit expansion a measure of the domestic sources of bank deposit creation. DCE is defined as the *Public Sector Borrowing Requirement* less sales of public sector debt to the non-bank private sector plus bank lending in sterling to the UK private and overseas sectors. DCE was a performance criterion (a condition) quantified in the letters of intent that accompanied UK drawings on the IMF in 1969 and 1976.

domestic non-bank sector or non-bank private sector the *personal sector* plus the industrial and commercial sector plus *financial institutions* not included in the *monetary sector*.

dual capacity a securities market where the agent (the *broker*), acting for clients, and the *market maker* (the *jobber*) are the same.

eligible bills see *commercial bills*.

Exchange Equalisation Account (EEA) a fund originally set up under the 1932 Finance Act. It is controlled by the Treasury and managed by the Bank of England as agent. The account holds the UK gold and foreign currency reserves, using them in the foreign exchange market to buy and sell sterling. The sterling with which the Account buys foreign currencies is provided by the *National Loans Fund*.

financial institutions 'obtain, convert (for instance by borrowing short in small amounts and lending long in large amounts) and distribute available funds as their main activity. They are separately distinguished from industrial and commercial companies . . . they are sub-divided . . . between the monetary sector and other financial institutions' (*Financial Statistics, Explanatory Handbook*, 1983 edn, p. 69). The most important are banks, insurance companies, pension funds and building societies.

fraction prices of gilt-edged stocks are quoted in fractions. The smallest fraction commonly encountered in medium- and long-dated stocks is 1/16 and in short-dated stocks 1/64. Smaller fractions may be encountered with actively traded stocks, particularly *partly paid* new issues, and when two bargains are matched.

gross funds those funds whose income is not subject to tax and who have no liability to tax on capital gains. Occasionally applied to funds that are liable to the same rate of tax on income and capital gains.

gross national product (GNP) at factor cost, expenditure based the sum of: consumers' expenditure, general government final consumption, gross domestic capital formation, net exports of goods and services and net property income from abroad. It is equal to the income of UK residents, before providing for depreciation. 'Factor cost' means that it is estimated at market prices less taxes on expenditure plus subsidies.

International Monetary Fund (IMF) agreed upon at the Bretton Woods conference in 1944, starting operations in 1947. Aimed to counter disorderly exchange rates and competitive devaluations and to provide temporary financing for nations in balance of payments difficulties. Finance is provided by members' subscriptions in the form of their own currencies and convertible reserve assets. Thus the IMF will normally have holdings of sterling in the form of Interest-Free Treasury Notes.

irredeemables, undateds stocks with no final date of *redemption*, but that have a date before which they cannot be redeemed. This date has passed in every case. Strictly they should not be referred to as irredeemables as they can be redeemed at any time on notice from the government.

jobber a *market maker* in a *single-capacity* securities market.

LIBOR London Interbank Offered Rate. The rate of interest at which deposits are freely offered in the interbank market by first-class names to first-class names.

liquid market a market is said to be liquid when large amounts can be bought or sold on narrow price spreads.

London International Financial Futures Exchange (LIFFE) the exchange in London, established in 1982, where contracts in financial futures are traded.

long (of stock) see *bull*.

longs stocks with a remaining life of over ten or over fifteen years from the date of dealing.

market maker a business entity that, acting as principal, buys and sells securities.

mature issues issues that have been in existence for some time.

mediums stocks with a remaining life of over five and less than ten or fifteen years from the date of dealing.

monetary sector 'comprises the UK offices of institutions either recognised as banks or licensed to take deposits under the Banking Act 1979, together with the National Girobank, the trustee savings banks, the Banking Department of the Bank of England, and those institutions in the Channel Islands and the Isle of Man which have opted to adhere to the new monetary control arrangements introduced in August 1981. [Before 1981], statistics relate to the banking sector, which consisted of the UK offices of all banks that agreed to observe a common reserve ratio and other credit control arrangements, together with the financial transactions of the Banking Department of the Bank of England and the institutions which make up the discount market' (*Financial Statistics, Explanatory Handbook*, 1983 edn, p. 56).

National Loans Fund a Treasury account at the Bank of England set up under the National Loans Act 1968. The inflows are the proceeds of government borrowing. The main payments are those to the Consolidated Fund to meet any deficit; loans to nationalised industries and local authorities; and sterling required by the *Exchange Equalisation Account*.

near-month, nearby month the nearest contract for delivery on the *London International Financial Futures Exchange*.

net funds funds whose income is subject to tax but that have no liability to capital gains tax on gilt-edged stocks held for one year or more.

net net funds funds subject to tax on both income and capital gains.

NILO stands for National Investment and Loans Office. The name for additional tranches of existing issues created for the National Debt Commissioners for the investment of funds under their management. The tranches are not listed on The Stock Exchange and are not transferable except to the Issue Department.

nominal

(1) the nominal value of a holding: fixes an investor's share of an issue and is the unit on which the *redemption* and interest payments are based;

(2) the nominal value of the national debt: the sum of the nominal values of individual instruments that comprise the national debt. In the case of index-linked stocks this includes both the original nominal amounts and the capital uplift accrued to date;

(3) nominal quote: a price made by a *market maker* in a small amount of stock;

(4) nominal holding: a small holding;

(5) nominal GNP: the GNP in current prices in contrast to the GNP in constant prices.

open market operations purchases and sales of public or private sector paper in the domestic markets by the authorities.

paper a general term for marketable financial assets, with the implication that it is debt.

par the *nominal* or face value. Normally £100, but with new issues it may be used to refer to the issue price.

partly paid securities on which there is a liability to pay a *call*, or calls, of a specified amount on a specified day.

penny stocks stocks that are quoted in pence instead of fractions. A stock is quoted in pence for the first time on the first Monday following the day on which it has 91 days to *redemption*.

personal sector consists of private individuals resident in the UK, unincorporated businesses, sole traders, partnerships, private trusts, educational establishments, churches and trade unions. Since few data are collected from the sector directly, it often includes the 'residual' – anything that cannot be identified and allocated to the other sectors.

premium the amount by which a stock stands above its *par* value. In trading it also refers to the amount by which it stands above its issue price.

primary market the original sale to a buyer by the borrower or his agent.

Public Sector Borrowing Requirement (PSBR) the amount the public sector has to borrow from other sectors to finance the balance between its cash receipts and expenditure. There are three sub-sectors of the public sector: the central government, the local authorities and public corporations.

recognised or primary dealer a dealer in US Treasury debt with whom the Federal Reserve Bank of New York will transact business. A 'reporting' dealer is one that wishes to become a recognised dealer; the dealer is asked to report transactions and positions until the Fed is satisfied that it meets its criteria for a full dealer.

redemption the exchange of stock for cash (normally £100 of cash per £100 of stock) on the day specified in the prospectus. The redemption date coincides with the last interest payment. The redemption price of an index-linked stock is calculated by a formula given in the prospectus.

redemption – last dealings the last full day of dealing in a stock due for redemption is six days after the final *xd* date, unless this falls on a non-business day. In this case it is the first earlier business day.

retail price index (RPI) the general index of retail prices measures the percentage change each month in the average level of prices of commodities and services purchased by households. The weights are adjusted each February in accordance with the Family Expenditure Survey for the year to the previous June. It is calculated for a Tuesday near the middle of the month.

secondary market the market in existing securities, representing claims on borrowers or the ownership of a company.

short (of stock) see *bear*.

shorts stocks with a remaining life of five years or less from the date of dealing.

single capacity a securities market where the agent (the *broker*), acting for clients, and the *market maker* (the *jobber*), are separated.

sinking fund a sum that may be set aside, either to cancel stock by its purchase in the market, or to be invested in other securities to accumulate and be available to redeem the stock for cash. There are only two stocks with sinking funds. Conversion 3½% 1961 or after, has a fund maintained by payments equivalent to not less than 1 per cent of the *nominal value* of the loan outstanding at the end of each half year during which the average daily price has been below 90. This is used to cancel stock by purchase in the following half year. Redemption 3% 1986/96 has a fund maintained by half-yearly payments sufficient to provide for *redemption* of all the stock by 1996. It may be redeemed after 1986. The sinking fund is subject to review every five years.

sxd special ex-dividend.

tap issues strictly speaking issues where the subscription lists remain open after listing has become effective. Usually used of a new issue where the Issue Department has taken up stock and is making it available to meet demand in the *secondary market*.

taplets issues of additional small tranches of existing stocks to the Issue Department of the Bank of England.

terminable annuities issued to the National Debt Commissioners between 1943 and 1950 as an investment for the Post Office Savings Bank and Trustee Savings Banks. They had an original term to maturity of between twenty-seven and thirty-two years. The last issue was redeemed on 15 December 1979.

Treasury bills short-term government marketable liabilities normally with a life of 91 days. Offered for sale on the last working day of each week for payment on any business day in the following week. Treasury bills are issued on tap to the *Exchange Equalisation Account*, the Issue Department, the National Debt Commissioners and other government departments. No interest is paid as such. They are issued at a *discount*.

unofficial line (of stock) a stock that is not a *tap* or *taplet* sold into the market from the Issue Department's portfolio.

Ways and Means Advances deposits of surplus funds lent back to the Treasury by other parts of the public sector.

xd ex-dividend.

Bibliography

Books and articles

Admission of Securities to Listing ('The Yellow Book') (1984–), Issued by Authority of The Stock Exchange.

Bank of England (1984), *The future structure of the gilt-edged market: The Bank of England's dealing and supervisory relationships with certain participants*, London: Bank of England.

Bootle, R. (1985), *Index-Linked Gilts: a practical investment guide*, Cambridge: Woodhead-Faulkner.

British Bankers' Association (1984), *Sterling Certificates of Deposit*, London.

Butterworths Yellow Tax Handbook: Income Tax, Corporation Tax, Capital Gains Tax (1984), London: Butterworth.

Chalmers, E. (1967), *The Gilt-Edged Market: A study of the background factors*, London: Griffiths.

Clapham, Sir John (1944), *The Bank of England: A History*, 2 vols, Cambridge University Press.

Committee on the Working of the Monetary System ('Radcliffe') (1959), *Report*, Cmnd 827, London: HMSO.

Committee on the Working of the Monetary System ('Radcliffe') (1960a) *Minutes of Evidence*, London: HMSO.

Committee on the Working of the Monetary System ('Radcliffe') (1960b) *Principal Memoranda of Evidence*, London: HMSO.

Committee to Review the Functioning of Financial Institutions ('Wilson') (1977–8), *Evidence*, London: HMSO.

Committee to Review the Functioning of Financial Institutions ('Wilson') (1978–9), *Research Reports*, London: HMSO.

Committee to Review the Functioning of Financial Institutions ('Wilson') (1979), *Second Stage Evidence*, London: HMSO.

Committee to Review the Functioning of Financial Institutions ('Wilson') (1980a), *Report*, Cmnd 7937, London: HMSO.

Committee to Review the Functioning of Financial Institutions ('Wilson') (1980b), *Appendices*, London: HMSO.

Council of The Stock Exchange (1984–), *Stock Exchange Rules*, London.

Day, J. G. and Jamieson, A. T. (1980), *Institutional Investment*, 6 vols, Institute of Actuaries and the Faculty of Actuaries. vol. I: *General Introduction to Investment*; vol II: *Gilt-Edged Securities*.

Department for National Savings (1984), *Investing in National Savings: A reference guide for professional advisers*, London: the Department.

Dodds, J. C. and Ford J. L. (1974), *Expectations, Uncertainty and the Term Structure of Interest Rates*, London: Martin Robertson.

Downton, C. V. (1977), 'The trend of the national debt in relation to national income', *Bank of England Quarterly Bulletin*, September.

Gemmil, G. and Fitzgerald, D. (1982), *Hedging Techniques*, London: LIFFE Ltd.

Gemmil, G. and Fitzgerald, D. (1983), *Trading Techniques*, London: LIFFE Ltd.

Goodhart, C. A. E. (1975), *Money, Information and Uncertainty,* London: Macmillan.

Goodhart, C. A. E. (1984), *Monetary Theory and Practice: the UK experience,* London: Macmillan.

Hargreaves, E. L. (1930), *The National Debt,* London: Edward Arnold & Co.

Hicks, J. R. (1939), *Value and Capital, An Inquiry into some Fundamental Principles of Economic Theory,* Oxford: Clarendon Press.

Inquiry into the Value of Pensions (1981), *Report,* Cmnd 8147, London: HMSO.

Johnson, H. G. (ed.) (1972), *Readings in British Monetary Economics,* Oxford: Clarendon Press.

Kessel, R. A. (1965), *The Cyclical Behavior of the Term Structure of Interest Rates,* New York: National Bureau of Economic Research.

Life Offices' Association, Associated Scottish Life Offices, Industrial Life Offices Association and the Linked Life Assurance Group (1978, 1983), *Life Insurance in the United Kingdom 1973–77 and 1978–82.*

Malkiel, B. G. (1966), *The Term Structure of Interest Rates: Expectations and Behavior Patterns,* Princeton, NJ: Princeton University Press.

Mercantile and General Reinsurance (Guaschi, F. E.) (1983), *Recent Developments in Long-Tail Reinsurance Business,* privately published.

Nash, R. L. (1883), *Fenn on the English & Foreign Funds etc,* London; Effingham Wilson.

National Accounts Statistics: Sources and Methods (1968), London: HMSO.

Pember & Boyle (1945–), *British Government Securities in the Twentieth Century,* various editions, privately published.

Pember & Boyle (1975–), *A Guide to the Gilt-Edged Market,* various editions, privately published.

Pézier, J. (ed.) (1983a), *The Twenty Year Gilt Interest Rate Contract,* London: LIFFE Ltd.

Pézier. J. (1983b), *Arbitrage Techniques,* London: LIFFE Ltd.

Phillips, P. (1984), *Inside the Gilt-Edged Market,* Cambridge: Woodhead-Faulkner.

Redington, F. M. (1952), 'Review of the principles of life office valuations', *Journal of the Institute of Actuaries,* vol. 78.

Report by the Government Actuary on the Draft of the Social Security Benefits Uprating Order 1983 (1983), Cmnd 8969, London: HMSO.

Richardson, G. (1983), 'The provision of pensions', *Bank of England Quarterly Bulletin,* December.

Robinson, J. (1951), 'The rate of interest', *Econometrica,* April.

Rose, H. and Kay J. A. (1983), 'The economics of pension arrangements', *Bank of England Panel of Academic Consultants, Paper* No. 20, March.

Sayers, R. S. (1956), *Financial Policy 1939–45,* London: HMSO and Longmans.

Sayers, R. S. (1976), *The Bank of England 1891–1944,* 3 vols, Cambridge: Cambridge University Press.

Shiller, R. J., Campbell, J. Y. and Schoenholtz, K. L. (1983), 'Forward rates and future policy: interpreting the term structure of interest rates', *Brookings Papers on Economic Activity,* No. 1.

Stigum, M. (1978, 1983), *The Money Market,* Homewood Ill.; DowJones-Irwin.

Taylor, C. T. and Threadgold, A. R. (1979), ' "Real" national saving and its sectoral composition', *Bank of England Discussion Paper,* No. 6, October.

Serial publications

Annual Abstract of Statistics, London: HMSO.
Bank of England, *Report and Accounts*, annual.
Bank of England Quarterly Bulletin (BEQB).
Consolidated Fund and National Loans Fund Accounts: supplementary statements,
London: HMSO, annual.
Economic Trends, London: HMSO, monthly.
Financial Statistics, London: HMSO, monthly; *Explanatory Handbook*, London:
HMSO, annual.
Financial Times, London, daily.
Journal of the Institute of Actuaries, London, quarterly.
MQ5 Business Monitor: Insurance companies' and pension funds' investment,
London: HMSO, quarterly.
The Investment Analyst, London, quarterly.
The Stock Exchange Fact Book, The Stock Exchange, annual.
TSB Group, *Group Reports*, annual.

Press releases, prospectuses

Bank of England, (1977), Prospectus: 'Particulars of an issue of £400,000,000
Variable Rate Treasury Stock 1981', 27 May.
Bank of England (1981a), 'Issue of Government Stock' [2% Index-Linked 1996],
10 March.
Bank of England (1981b), 'Issue of Non-Marketable Government Stock to the
National Debt Commissioners', 16 April.
Bank of England (1981c), No title, Policy on maturing issues, 19 August.
Bank of England (1982), 'Issues of Government Stock', 12 March.
HM Treasury (1982), 'Arrangements Governing Borrowing by the Corporate and
Public Sectors', 25 June.
Inland Revenue (1985), No title, Introduction of new bond-washing rules, 28
February.

Statutes, statutory rules and orders, statutory instruments

Banking Act, 1979.
The Building Societies Act, 1962.
The Building Societies (Authorised Investments) (No. 2) Order, 1977.
Building Societies (Designation for Trustee Investment) Regulations, 1972.
Capital Gains Tax Act, 1979.
Currency and Bank Notes Act, 1928.
Finance Acts, 1932, 1937, 1971–84.
The Government Stock Regulations, 1965.
Income and Corporation Taxes Act, 1970.
Insurance Companies (Valuation of Assets) Regulations, 1981.
Insurance Companies Act, 1982.

The Local Government Superannuation (Amendment) (No. 2) Regulations, 1983.
The National Loans Act, 1968.
Pensions (Increase) Act, 1971.
The Social Security Acts, 1973 and 1975.
The Trustee Investments Act, 1961.
Trustee Savings Banks Acts, 1969, 1976 and 1981.

Annual reports of funds under management with the National Debt Commissioners
(all published in London by HMSO)

Crown Estate Abstract Accounts.
Employment Protection (Consolidation) Act 1978:
  Maternity Pay Fund Account.
  Redundancy Fund Account.
Funds in Court in England and Wales, Accounts.
Insolvency Services (Accounting and Investment) Act 1970, Accounts.
Irish Land Purchase Fund, Account.
Mineral Workings Acts 1951 and 1971, Ironstone Restoration Fund, Account.
National Heritage Memorial Fund, Account.
National Insurance Fund, Account.
National Savings Bank, Investment Account Fund Residual Investments, Accounts.
National Savings Bank, Investment Deposits, Accounts.
National Savings Bank, Ordinary Deposits, Accounts.
Tithe Act 1936, Accounts.
Trustee Savings Bank Act 1981, Fund for the Banks for Savings, Accounts.

The remaining accounts appear annually in the *Consolidated Fund and National Loans Fund Accounts: supplementary statements.*

Index